THE GENRE OF
Troilus and Criseyde

THE GENRE OF
Troilus and Criseyde

Monica E. McAlpine

Cornell University Press

ITHACA AND LONDON

Cornell University Press gratefully acknowledges a grant from the Andrew W. Mellon Foundation that aided in bringing this book to publication.

First published in 1978 by Cornell University Press.
Published in the United Kingdom by Cornell University Press Ltd.,
2-4 Brook Street, London W1Y 1AA.

Excerpts from Geoffrey Chaucer, *The Book of Troilus and Criseyde*, ed. Robert Kilburn Root (copyright 1926, 1954 by Princeton University Press), pp. 3–405, some material adapted, are reprinted by permission of Princeton University Press.

International Standard Book Number 0-8014-0962-4
Library of Congress Catalog Card Number 77-12511
Printed in the United States of America by York Composition Co., Inc.
Librarians: Library of Congress cataloging information appears on the last page of the book.

To the memory of
    MARY DOYLE McALPINE (1900–1966)
    and
    WILLIAM J. McALPINE (1898–1966)

Contents

Preface

Many readers of Chaucer's *Troilus and Criseyde* have felt uneasy with the generic label—"tragedye"—that the narrator of the poem gives his "litel book." Some have dealt with that unease by trying to enter sympathetically into the world view of a story that recounts the rise and fall of a hero of high degree, making no pejorative comparisons to modern perceptions of the tragic. Such sympathy is valuable, but not if it implies a silencing of our critical faculties, a form of condescension to things medieval that Chaucer's work does not need or justify. Other readers seem to have chosen to ignore what they thought they could not challenge in order to create room for many sensitive readings of the text that a consistent focus on "tragedye" might have obstructed. As a result, a too deferential and insufficiently critical attitude toward the narrator's generic concept has made it an albatross around the necks of Chaucer's readers.

This book aims to use "tragedye" as I believe both Boethius and Chaucer used it: not as an organizing concept to shape their representations of human experience but as a foil or "contrarie" helping to reveal their alternative, richer depictions of that reality. The narrator of *Troilus and Criseyde* is seen as dramatizing a creative struggle to integrate tragedy with love—a struggle that Chaucer himself may have experienced and one in which he certainly invites his reader to participate. From the narrator's and the reader's joint efforts, I believe, Chaucer intended new conceptions of tragedy and comedy to emerge, and with them, partly by virtue of those efforts, an awareness of all such constructs as fallible human instruments. In the prevailing critical view, tragedy is taken to embody the characteristically human vision of man's experience and comedy to embody the divine vision; here, in contrast, both are interpreted as human inventions that the divine vision subsumes and transcends.

For me, Chaucer's critique of "tragedye" helps to illuminate what has often been hinted at but just as often obscured in modern commentaries: the extent to which Troilus' career represented a new kind of comedy and Criseyde's a new kind of tragedy. In its details this interpretation supports and extends the many attempts to rehabilitate Troilus as a moral hero. It opposes, however, what has become the conventional approach to Criseyde as a symbol of the mutable world and insists on her status as one who experiences the imperfection of the world in which her tragedy takes place. What is novel and perhaps controversial in my interpretation nevertheless reflects some common concerns of Chaucer criticism—the uses of a persona, the concept of fictions—and supports some of its common themes—the continuity of human and divine love, the discontinuity of human and divine knowledge. My notes cannot fully document the debts I owe to other readers of Chaucer, particularly for the pleasure I have had in joining them in such intimate dialogue.

It is a special pleasure to be able to thank publicly those who fostered this work: Robert Hinman and Russell Peck, my graduate teachers of Chaucer at the University of Rochester; Louise Dunlap, Mary Anne Ferguson, and Mary Shaner, my colleagues at the University of Massachusetts at Boston who read and commented on the manuscript at various stages; Taylor Stoehr, who encouraged me to offer it for publication; the staff of Cornell University Press; Eileen and Marguerite Hepp, who typed the manuscript; and Rebecca Saunders, who proofread it. To my husband, Bob Crossley, I am indebted for much inspired editorial advice, much practical help, and unflagging enthusiasm; in the making of this book, his friendship has been "founde at preve."

Grateful acknowledgment is made to the following publishers for permission to reprint copyright material: Houghton Mifflin Company and Oxford University Press, Oxford, for excerpts from *The Canterbury Tales* and *Boece* from *The Works of Geoffrey Chaucer,* edited by F. N. Robinson, © F. N. Robinson 1957; Harvard University Press and William Heinemann Ltd. for material from the Latin text of Boethius' *Consolation of Philosophy,* edited by E. K. Rand, translated by H. F. Stewart and E. K. Rand (1918), and newly translated by S. J. Tester (Loeb Classical Library, 1973); and Frederick Ungar Publishing Co. for excerpts from Boccaccio's *The Fates of Illustrious Men,* translated by Louis Brewer Hall (1965).

MONICA E. MCALPINE

Boston, Massachusetts

THE GENRE OF
Troilus and Criseyde

1

The Hypothetical Genre
of *Troilus and Criseyde*

"Go, litel book, go, litel myn tragedye." The narrator's fare-
well to his book at the end of *Troilus and Criseyde* (5.1786)[1] is
so familiar to readers of Chaucer that it is little wonder if we are
no longer capable of responding to it as an event in the reading
of the poem. Familiarity tends to dim the perception of the narrator's action here as a significant moment in the drama of his
story telling, and to dim the memory of what may once have
been a complex response on our part in favor of a simplified,
conditioned response. I would like to try to recover a fresh experience of the passage by suggesting that the narrator's generic
labeling of his book may be both expected and unexpected, both
welcome and unwelcome to the reader.

The very act of labeling produces some gratification in its own
right. We naturally like to be able to put names to our experiences, and so to sum them up and compare them with other
experiences. Because of the narrator's extraordinary tardiness in
characterizing his work, the gratification associated with naming
is enhanced in the *Troilus* by the gratification of achieving
closure. As we approach an ending, we welcome all those narrative strategies that contribute to a quality of definitiveness at

1. All quotations from *Troilus and Criseyde* are from *The Book of
Troilus and Criseyde by Geoffrey Chaucer*, ed. Robert Kilburn Root
(Princeton: Princeton University Press, 1926). I assume here a distinction
between the narrator and the poet that I argue for later in this chapter.
Chaps. 4 and 7 analyze the narrator's performance in detail.

the close. Moreover, because it appears in an address by the narrator, this naming draws to itself the authority we are instinctively disposed to grant to the artist contemplating his own work. The term "tragedye" itself also tends to have an honorific value for many of us and thus to occupy a certain solemn and unchallengeable status. We notice, however, that all of these gratifications except the last could be achieved by the narrator's applying any generic label to the work at the same point.

But Chaucer has prepared us for the designation "tragedye." The very opening lines of the poem adumbrate a structure in Troilus' adventures that is reminiscent of the familiar rise-and-fall sort of tragedy, and Book 4 opens with a description of Fortune's wheel—the traditional emblem of medieval tragedy—and with a prediction that Troilus will be cast down from that wheel. For some readers, then, or perhaps for all readers to some degree, the generic labeling fulfills an expectation that the narrator had earlier created. This pattern of expectation and fulfillment is curiously weak, though, principally because the early allusions to tragedy are ambivalent. The controlling term in the initial description of Troilus' adventures seems to be "lovynge," and love is not the usual subject of medieval tragedy. A reader might chiefly attend either to the suggested structure of the adventures, which is conventionally tragic, or to the substance of those adventures, which is not. The material that opens Book 4 might understandably be regarded as a patch of commentary referring only to certain imminent actions, and not to the work as a whole, since the narrator habitually strives for such local effects.[2] In any case, the work is not *explicitly* labeled a tragedy on either of what seem, on reflection, these very appropriate occasions.

2. E.g., cf. the narrator's remarks on "blynde entencioun" (1.211–217) and on Fortune (3.617–623), and Robert Jordan's discussion in *Chaucer and the Shape of Creation* (Cambridge, Mass.: Harvard University Press, 1967), pp. 79 and 83, of the narrator's "will to elaborate" and his "spasmodic mode of statement and development."

Thus the narrator's late, explicit reference to his work as a tragedy forces us to confront this generic definition of the work in a way that neither of the earlier passages had. By the time we have reached this point, however, we have acquired our own experience with the story. The allusion to tragedy in the poem's opening lines has supplied us with a working hypothesis, one of which we are reminded in Book 4 and one which we are challenged to integrate with our still evolving experience of the story. When we come to the narrator's envoy, we are in a position to ask whether this tragic hypothesis has actually been verified and to answer that question for ourselves.

To the limited degree, then, that the narrator's labeling of his work completes an interpretive pattern suggested earlier, and insofar as it supplies certain gratifications in its own right, the labeling may be experienced as both expected and welcome. It adds something to our experience of the poem. Yet just as the ambivalences in the earlier allusions to tragedy may also cause it to be experienced as unexpected, so other considerations may make it actually unwelcome. The generic label may seem to subtract something from the poem by suddenly narrowing a richly diverse experience that has included the impending doom of Troy, the excesses of Troilus' infatuation, the complex portrayal of Criseyde, the exaltation of the lovers' consummation, the abrupt turning of the plot in Book 4, the lovers' decisions not to flee Troy, and Troilus' meditation on fate and free will. But it is probably our painfully fresh experience of Book 5 that makes us most uneasy with the constrictions of a "tragedye" that apparently claims only to trace the rise and fall of its hero. Empathy with the lovers' profound and *mutual* loss, disgust with Troilus' inertia, admiration for his constancy, pity for Criseyde's plight, and revulsion against her inconstancy—a flood of such responses may set us in conflict even with ourselves. Finally, an experience that has been richly diverse may threaten to become unmanageably problematical when the narrator struggles against the authority of his sources to avoid condemning Criseyde and at the same time seems to lose hold on all his characters as they fade back into the old books (5.799–840).

Although the narrator's late and solemn designation of his book as a tragedy is presumably crucial information, its provision does not immediately clarify our experience of the poem. Troilus is the declared hero of the story (1.260–266), and yet we have just left him (5.1744–1747) in a strangely indeterminate state. He sorrows over his loss, seeks revenge against Diomede, and continues to love Criseyde. His death, of course, has not yet been mentioned; instead the narrator has just assured us (1763–1764) that Troilus will not die in his feud with Diomede. Indeed the narrator's latest reference to Troilus (1765–1771) emphasizes his worthy success as a warrior. But if the narrator's tragedy is not Troilus', neither apparently is it Troy's, for Hector's death, the crucial loss that presages Troy's defeat, has earlier been squeezed in between Cassandra's interpretation of Troilus' dream and Troilus' finding of the brooch on Diomede's coat. Curiously, the most immediate context for the narrator's sudden reference to his book as a tragedy is his disgressive apology for representing Criseyde as unfaithful and his warning to women generally to beware of men. Clearly, the narrator's belated generic characterization of his work does not immediately solve any problems, but rather raises a number of urgent questions. What is the narrator's concept of tragedy? If his story is a tragedy, whose tragedy is it? Does his concept of tragedy embrace all the materials of his story and all our experiences as readers? As the narrator is dismissing his book, the reader is being required to begin again— to submit the narrative, the narrator's tragic theory, and his own experience as reader to critical examination. My analysis of the poem is the record of one such attempt to test the hypothesis that we have been reading a tragedy.

The Tragedy

One purpose of Chaucer's strategy in withholding until the end the narrator's explicit identification of his work as a tragedy must surely be to cause us to *interpret* the term "tragedye" in the light of our fresh knowledge of this particular story. Accordingly, we should expect the tragedy to reside not in a prefabricated structure that the experience portrayed must fit, and could have been predicted to fit, but in a potentiality within that experience that may or may not have been realized. Criticism of the poem, however, has generally depended explicitly or implicitly upon a prescriptive definition of tragedy. The usual prescription is the conventional medieval definition, a version of which Chaucer found and translated in Boethius' *Consolation of Philosophy*:

What other thyng bywaylen the cryinges of tragedyes but oonly the dedes of Fortune, that with unwar strook overturneth the realmes of greet nobleye? [*Boece*. 2. pr. ii. 67–70][3]

This apparently simple, and in some respects actually simplistic, definition has several parts that are worth isolating.

The "overturning" of the victims was commonly referred to as a "fall" and acquired connotations of absolute totality and finality.[4] The definition assigns causality by identifying Fortune as the agent of the change. The only motive, such as it is, lies in the very arbitrariness of Fortune as expressed by its "unwar strook." The specification of the "realmes of greet nobleye" as the victims seems to arise from a desire to display Fortune's power in the most emphatic, not to say sensational, way possible. This specification (and the larger context of Boethius' argument) makes clear that Fortune effects an external change in the victim's material prosperity and not an internal change in his or her

---

3. All quotations from Chaucer's *Boece* are from *The Works of Geoffrey Chaucer*, ed. F. N. Robinson, 2d. ed. (Boston: Houghton Mifflin, 1957). Here and in Chap. 2 I use the conventional abbreviations for the prose and verse parts of the work: "pr." for *prosa* and "met." for *metrum*.

4. For a survey of medieval uses of the themes of the fall and of the proud man (mentioned below), see Howard R. Patch, *The Goddess Fortuna in Mediaeval Literature* (Cambridge, Mass.: Harvard University Press, 1927), pp. 67–72.

character or spiritual condition. In this definition there is no hint
that the human victims are responsible for the tragedy, and thus
I refer to this version of the genre as the "tragedy of fortune."
But from very early times, an alternative plot, what I call the
"tragedy of the proud man," evolved in which the victim's ethos
somehow provokes Fortune's attack. A distinctive feature of late
medieval tragedy is the vacillation between these two plots.
Boccaccio's *De Casibus Virorum Illustrium* (*Concerning the
Falls of Famous Men* [1355–1374?]) was the great original of
this bivalent type and gave us the modern critical term "*de casibus*
tragedy." Chaucer's *Monk's Tale* (1374–1386?), Lydgate's *Fall
of Princes* (1430–1440?), and the *Mirror for Magistrates* (1559–
1610) all exhibit this characteristic vacillation.[5] Chaucer was
surely aware of the existence of the two plots, of writers' ten-
dencies to vacillate between them, and of a fundamental similarity
of concept underlying their obvious difference. When I speak of
Chaucer's uses of the conventional medieval concept of tragedy,
then, I mean the bivalent type and I use the term "*de casibus*
tragedy."[6]

It is at least slightly inaccurate, though, to refer to this famous
passage from the *Consolation* as providing a "definition" of
tragedy, because Boethius' purpose here—as he speaks through
Philosophy who is in turn impersonating Fortune—is not to
define a literary genre but to call emphatic attention, by means
of a rhetorical question, to the thematic contents of some classical

5. See Willard Farnham's discussions of these works and authors in
The Medieval Heritage of Elizabethan Tragedy (Oxford: Blackwell,
1936) and Madeleine Doran's excellent brief discussion of *de casibus*
tragedy in *Endeavors of Art: A Study of Form in Elizabethan Drama*
(Madison, Wis.: University of Wisconsin Press, 1964), pp. 116–128.
6. I have settled on this threefold distinction of terms as best serving
to clarify my argument. There is no uniform usage, but J. W. H. Atkins,
in *English Literary Criticism: The Medieval Phase* (Cambridge: Cambridge University Press, 1934), pp. 159–161, and William Matthews, in
The Tragedy of Arthur (Berkeley: University of California Press, 1960),
pp. 105–107 and 117–119, use the phrase "tragedy of fortune" to refer to
what I call "*de casibus* tragedy."

tragedies. The rhetorical question is followed by allusions to two such tragedies, and the question and the allusions together constitute merely an ornament of the larger argument. But this innocent passage has since become the center of a set of interlocking, and mistaken, assumptions and interpretations that for decades have seriously impaired our reading of *Troilus and Criseyde*. The tragedy of fortune has been wrongly characterized as "Boethian" as if it genuinely embodied or were reconcilable with Boethius' philosophy.[7] Second, the *Consolation* itself has sometimes been regarded as a tragedy of fortune or even as a tragedy of the proud man, although the latter type is not explicitly mentioned in the work.[8] Third, Chaucer's glossing of the passage has been taken as evidence that he fully accepted this definition of the tragic genre.[9] Fourth, his use of the definition in his *Monk's Tale,* now expanded to include the alternative plot of the proud man (VII.2761–2766), as well as the *Tale's* in-

7. Bernard L. Jefferson, *Chaucer and the Consolation of Philosophy of Boethius* (Princeton: Princeton University Press, 1917), p. 86; D. W. Robertson, *A Preface to Chaucer* (Princeton: Princeton University Press, 1962), pp. 472–473, and his earlier article, "Chaucerian Tragedy," *ELH*, 19 (1952), rpt. in *Chaucer Criticism II: Troilus and Criseyde & The Minor Poems,* eds. Richard J. Schoeck and Jerome Taylor (Notre Dame: University of Notre Dame Press, 1961), pp. 86–121 (hereafter cited as *Chau. Crit. II*). Also see Helen Corsa, *Chaucer: Poet of Mirth and Morality* (Notre Dame: University of Notre Dame Press, 1964), p. 41; Donald R. Howard, *The Three Temptations: Medieval Man in Search of the World* (Princeton: Princeton University Press, 1966), pp. 138 and 149–153; and Nevill Coghill, *The Poet Chaucer,* 2d ed. (London: Oxford University Press, 1967), pp. 49–51. In notes 7 through 11, I have limited my citations almost exclusively to book-length studies and to the explicit statements of critics. But agreement with all or most of the propositions I list is implied or assumed in many other commentaries on the poem.

8. Cf. Farnham, *Heritage,* pp. 80 and 111; John Lawlor, *Chaucer* (New York: Harper & Row, 1969), p. 71; Robertson, "Chaucerian Tragedy," *Chau. Crit. II,* pp. 88–89.

9. Root, *The Book of Troilus,* p. 409; Corsa, p. 210; Coghill, p. 50; Patricia Kean, *Chaucer and the Making of English Poetry* (London: Routledge & Kegan Paul, 1972), 1, 119.

debtedness to Boccaccio's *De Casibus,* has been adduced as
further evidence of this acceptance on Chaucer's part.[10] Finally,
in *Troilus and Criseyde* the narrator's late characterization of his
work as a tragedy, with its implications that the tragedy is
Troilus' and that it somehow fits the conventional type alluded
to in the prologues to Books 1 and 4, has been treated as if it were
an unambiguous, authoritative characterization of the poem
offered by Chaucer himself.[11] While individual critics sometimes
reject one or more of these assumptions or interpretations,[12] and
while it is unfashionable to say that *Troilus and Criseyde* is a
de casibus tragedy, there is, I believe, no modern reading of the
poem that wholly escapes the shaping influence of this set of
assumptions.

One result is that we readers of Chaucer have been keeping a
guilty secret: if the critical consensus accurately reflects its generic
nature, *Troilus and Criseyde* is in some respects a poor poem.
The *de casibus* conception of tragedy requires us to accept several
propositions that are integral to it but that violate, I submit, not
only Boethian philosophy and Christian theology, but also some

10. Jefferson, p. 86; Root, p. 409; Atkins, *Literary Criticism,* p. 159;
Farnham, pp. 138–139; Kemp Malone, *Chapters on Chaucer* (Baltimore:
Johns Hopkins Press, 1951), pp. 104–105; Robertson, "Chaucerian Tragedy," *Chau. Crit. II,* pp. 86 and 93; Corsa, p. 210; Howard, *Three
Temptations,* p. 149; Coghill, p. 50; Kean, p. 119.

11. Jefferson, p. 125; Root, pp. xlix, 409; Atkins, p. 160; Farnham, pp.
138 and 154–155; Theodore A. Stroud, "Boethius' Influence on Chaucer's
Troilus," *Modern Philology,* 49 (1951–1952), rpt. in *Chau. Crit. II,* p.
125; Malone, p. 105; Howard, *Three Temptations,* p. 149, and "Chaucer
the Man," *PMLA,* 80 (1965), 341; Coghill, p. 49; and Jordan, *Shape of
Creation,* pp. 102–105.

12. John Norton-Smith, in *Geoffrey Chaucer* (London: Routledge &
Kegan Paul, 1974), p. 162, recognizes that the old definition is at odds
with Boethian philosophy. John Steadman, in *Disembodied Laughter:
Troilus and the Apotheosis Tradition* (Berkeley: University of California
Press, 1972), pp. 94–98, points out that Boethian philosophy is antitragic;
Paul Ruggiers, in *The Art of the Canterbury Tales* (Madison: University
of Wisconsin Press, 1965), p. 185, and Ian Robinson, in *Chaucer and the
English Tradition* (Cambridge: Cambridge University Press, 1972), pp.
144–145, deny that the Monk's definition of tragedy is also Chaucer's.

still common notions of "truth to human nature."[13] Always we must agree that loss per se is tragic. In that version of the old tragedy emphasizing the hero's responsibility, we are required to grant that human beings can avoid loss, and that Troilus could have done so by avoiding human love altogether, or by choosing to love someone other than Criseyde, or by learning to love women in a different way. Although this approach attempts to internalize, and thus to deepen, the tragedy by identifying some mistake by, or flaw in, the hero, the tragedy nonetheless depends on some blow from without to provide its catastrophe. Fortune, stripped of that randomness which is the true source of its terror, is transformed into a machine for dispensing rewards and punishments. As a tragedy of the proud man, *Troilus and Criseyde* would present Troilus' loss as deserved but avoidable. The alternative plot that emphasizes fate would have us believe Troilus' loss was undeserved yet nevertheless inevitable. The catastrophe still inheres in an event external to the character, though, and in addition we must accept the proposition that all human careers are inescapably tragic, at least on this side of death. All wordly goods, in fact, are rejected as worthless simply because they are mutable. A "divine comedy" governs the next world, perhaps, but in this life, apparently, man knows nothing of genuine comic experience.

In both interpretations of Troilus' experience, it is assumed that in each human life there is a single catastrophe and that such a catastrophe, when it occurs, must be total and final. There can be no recovery, and the nature of the hero's response to the catastrophe is not a significant element of the tragedy. Furthermore, when loss of some kind provides the catastrophe, everything and everyone but the hero must be perceived as a possession. As a result Criseyde must be, in relation to Troilus, a "worldly good," and not a character of the same status as Troilus himself. This built-in definition of her is so powerful that even though she too

13. Cf. Raymond Williams, *Modern Tragedy* (Stanford, Calif.: Stanford University Press, 1966), pp. 19–23, and Ruggiers, p. 185.

suffers loss in love, and is sometimes said to suffer a fall, it has been almost impossible to consider seriously the possibility that she might be a tragic figure. These two views of Troilus, then— as either Fortune's chastised penitent or its innocent victim—have, despite their difference, several presuppositions in common. Even the difference is wholly predictable, for it duplicates the two possible plots for the old tragedy as they had evolved by the fourteenth century: the deserved overthrow of the proud man by a just Fortune and the senseless destruction of innocent and guilty alike by an arbitrary Fortune. One of the basic disagreements in modern criticism of the poem simply reflects the ambiguities inherent in the narrator's chosen genre.

In the past twenty-five years, the typical approach of several major critics has been to admit tacitly the shallowness of the *de casibus* concept while attempting to prove that Chaucer manipulated it to somehow deepen, complicate, or modify it. One motive of D. W. Robertson's early essay on "Chaucerian Tragedy" (1952) was to show that "the *de casibus* theme may imply more than the somewhat mechanical fall of men of high estate," and that there is in Chaucer's tragedy "an intellectual coherence that is rooted firmly in Christian doctrine and Boethian philosophy."[14] Robertson attempts to reconcile Boethian philosophy with the old definition of tragedy by substituting for the arbitrary Fortune of the tragic definition the providential Fortune subsequently described by Philosophy. Actually, the hero of Robertson's tragedy, blinded by passionate and blameworthy attachment to worldly goods, continues to interpret Fortune as arbitrary, while the audience is invited to see Fortune not only as representing a larger providential design but also as dispensing a kind of divine but humanly comprehensible justice. Robertson also imports into the tragedy of fortune Boethius' own emphasis on freedom and responsibility. He interprets "the realmes of greet nobleye" metaphorically as signifying a "spiritual elevation"—that is,

14. *Chau. Crit. II,* pp. 118–119.

pride—that somehow brings down adverse fortune on the hero. Thus the hero can be said to be responsible for his own "plight," although it is unclear whether Robertson means this "plight" to refer to the hero's spiritual condition alone, his material adversity alone, or both. At the same time, Robertson wishes to preserve the sense of fatedness characteristic of the old tragedy, and so he postulates a moment at which the hero, sunk in cupidity, effectively loses his free will "so that when adversity . . . strikes, his doom has a certain inevitability" (p. 91).

But Robertson's theory shows the strain of attempting to reconcile the irreconcilable. It attempts to preserve the tragic catastrophe while introducing Boethian concepts that implicitly deny the reality of such catastrophe. If Fortune is providential, if all fortune is really good fortune, there can be no catastrophic fall in the old tragic sense, and without such a catastrophe there can be no tragedy. Nor can this flat contradiction be finessed by distinguishing the hero's point of view from the audience's. In fact, Boethius' emphasis on a man's responsibility for the state of mind in which he endures adversity, although it does not deny suffering, does deny catastrophe, since it reserves to the inner man the unlimited power to determine the meaning of his own experience. Misinterpreting Boethius, however, to mean that a man is responsible for a *prior* state of mind that somehow makes him vulnerable to adversity, Robertson is thus able to preserve for his definition the outer catastrophe. Robertson's theory actually reverses Boethius' by eliminating the suffering while it retains the catastrophe; the moralistic emphasis on a man's responsibility leads to the extreme position that Fortune is only "a form of behavior." Even in Robertson's version, though, Boethian freedom finally poses such a threat to tragic catastrophe that it must be eliminated altogether. The claim that the hero loses his freedom through cupidity would make sense if freedom were defined as the full ability to be authentically oneself, one's best self; but if freedom means, as it seems to in Robertson's argument, the ability to make significant choices, it is neither logical nor orthodox to speak of the hero's losing his freedom. Actually, there is no evidence that as Boethius redefined such concepts as Fortune, he also intended to redefine tragedy. On the contrary, from the point of view of Boethian philosophy, the old tragic definition cannot be salvaged.

Although Robertson and those critics most influenced by him stress the flaw in the heart of the hero, perhaps the predominant number of critics stress the flaw at the heart of the world. But these critics, too, are committed to saving the old definition. In his article, "The Ending of Chaucer's *Troilus*" (1963), E. T. Donaldson argues that Chaucer avoids the mere imposition of an a priori, *de casibus* "moral" on his story by dramatizing the narrator's struggle with that moral in such a way as to arrive a posteriori at a "meaning" that is "a complex qualification of the moral."[15] The "moral," according to Donaldson, is that "human love, and by a sorry corollary everything human, is unstable and illusory" (p. 35). After exploring the narrator's attraction to and repulsion from this moral, Donaldson arrives at this formulation of the "meaning": "The poem states, what much of Chaucer's poetry states, the necessity under which men lie of living in, making the best of, enjoying, and loving a world from which they must remain detached and which they must ultimately hate" (p. 44). That is, the narrator would prefer to adopt a single attitude: either to love the world as his plot and his characters initially tempt him to do, or to hate the world as he thinks the moral of the story requires him to do. Donaldson's view is that if the narrator would be "mature" and "complex" (p. 42), he must do both.

The "meaning" Donaldson finds in the poem is essentially a reconciliation of two contrary world views. But Donaldson's attempted reconciliation does not represent an intellectual or spiritual transcendence of sentimentality, on the one hand, and piety, on the other, but a state of mind approaching schizophre-

15. "The Ending of Chaucer's *Troilus*," in *Early English and Norse Studies: Presented to Hugh Smith in Honour of His Sixtieth Birthday,* eds. Arthur Brown and Peter Foote (London: Methuen, 1963), pp. 35–36.

nia. In effect, the God of Donaldson's interpretation creates men whose nature requires them to love a world that the good of their souls requires them to hate. Finally, though, the world-hating *de casibus* moral swamps its competition, for Donaldson's argument provides no grounds for loving the world—a world whose one remaining value seems to lie in its providing the subject matter for poetry (p. 43). Donaldson's emphasis on the rejection of simple morals in Chaucer's poem is just and valid, but the attempt to state the alternative is doomed by an unnecessary allegiance to the old concept of tragedy. The narrator's problem stems as much from the deficiencies of his working concept of tragedy as from his longing for simplicity. There is no way to reconcile love of the world and hatred of the world. The *de casibus* moral cannot be rendered more true or more profound by being made more tortuously complicated.

More recently (1972), John Steadman's *Disembodied Laughter* has made a fresh contribution to the study of the poem's genre. Although Steadman does not specifically challenge the authority of the old definition, he does see that the general drift of Boethian philosophy is antitragic (p. 94). It is difficult to plot a rise and a fall in terms of gaining and losing goods that are, as Steadman puts it, transitory and worthless (or as I would put it, extrinsic to the self and imperfect). Steadman believes that Chaucer perceived the contradiction between his Boethian principles and literary convention, and that he resolved it in *Troilus and Criseyde* by working out a compromise. The main action of the poem is presented according to the tragic concept, although tragic experience itself is ultimately revealed to be a kind of illusion, both by the Boethian allusions throughout and by Troilus' divinely comic vision from the eighth sphere. In other words, the tragedy assumes that worldly goods are innately valuable and that their loss can be catastrophic, whereas the comic vision shows that wordly goods are worthless because transitory and that their loss is meaningless since man's true felicity lies in eternity (pp. 95–98). This distinction between two visions is very close to Robertson's, but Steadman's version also attempts to address the issue of the superiority of divine knowledge to human knowledge. Specifically, a literary convention is accurately perceived as a human construct and thus (though Steadman does not draw this conclusion) as inevitably flawed.

Steadman does not succeed, however, in preserving a consistent distinction between his two visions. For example, he correctly argues at one point that "for Stoics, Platonists, and Christian theologians alike, death was a good, not an evil; separation from the body was a prerequisite for the full felicity of the soul" (p. 82). And yet, in his later analysis (pp. 125–127) of the "fyn" or end of Troilus' career (5.1828–1834), he invokes without qualification the *de casibus* characterization of death as a catastrophe in order to enforce the proposition that wordly goods are worthless because they are transitory, because they "end in death." Ultimately he attributes to Chaucer the very position Donaldson saw even the narrator as, in some confused way, transcending: "a condemnation that applies not only to the transitory pleasures of the flesh but to all 'thise wrecched worldes appetites,' and indeed to the world itself."

The problem is that Steadman's two visions are really one vision, the *de casibus* vision. This particular way of embracing eternity requires a total rejection of the temporal that is in turn based on bitter disappointment in wordly goods, and that disappointment is in fact a continuing symptom of worldliness. We never really escape the *de casibus* assumptions and experience. What is presented here as a divine vision is only one human style of compensating for wordly disillusionment; Chaucer's Monk's near-despair is another style. Steadman's treatment of the divine vision is unsatisfactory on two counts. In one respect, the divine vision is made too human, for it becomes, paradoxically, something that human beings can both articulate and comprehend. But in another respect, the split between the human and the divine is made too absolute. Steadman seems to suggest that the *de casibus* vision would, from a human point of view, serve people well enough as an interpretation of their experience; it is only when the divine perspective is consulted that the *de casibus* vision is found to be wanting—indeed to be totally wrong. But unless there is no continuity at all between the material and the spiritual aspects of man's nature, a vision that misrepresents man's eternal destiny must also misrepresent his earthly experience. Thus, if Chaucer did attempt to impose on his story the compromise Steadman has outlined, he must have written a bad poem, for he allegedly developed his plot and his characters according to an interpretive theory that other aspects of the work show to be quite worthless. One consequence of this approach is that despite Steadman's emphasis on anticipations of the epilogue throughout the work, the old and troublesome sense of a divorce between the body of the work and the epilogue is not satisfactorily resolved. Instead it is revived in a new way. The issue now is not only the meaning and value of the world and of human love, but also the meaning and value of the very genre it is claimed Chaucer used in selecting, shaping, and focusing the material of his story.

Despite my quarrels with the details of these critical arguments, I am in full agreement with their main theses. Robertson, Donaldson, and Steadman make the right claims: that Chaucer's tragedy is intellectually coherent and philosophically and theologically orthodox; that his work has not an a priori moral but an a posteriori meaning; that the poem confronts human judgment and vision with divine judgment and vision. Nevertheless, the ways in which all these things are true cannot be fully demonstrated as long as we continue to try to see Chaucer's poem as a *de casibus* tragedy, however much improved by genius. Although Chaucer did recognize the usefulness of the *de casibus* genre as a kind of "literature of disaster,"[16] it is clear, I believe, that he rejected it as an adequate conception of tragedy. In order to follow Chaucer here, we need to revise our sense of the tradition behind the late medieval concept. Such a revision

16. Robert Heilman's term in *Tragedy and Melodrama: Versions of Experience* (Seattle: University of Washington Press, 1968), p. 21 and *passim*.

needs to be argued in detail, because the influence of long familiar assumptions and the power of the *de casibus* concept itself are such that even critics who openly scorn the concept sometimes end up simply refurbishing it in new terms.[17] In my analysis of the *Consolation of Philosophy*, I try to show that Boethius does not lend his authority to the old definition of tragedy; that the plot of the *Consolation* does not constitute a tragedy of fortune but is in fact antitragic; that Chaucer found in the *Consolation* the basis for alternative definitions of tragedy and comedy centered not on the "dedes of Fortune" but on the deeds of human beings; and finally, that Chaucer also found there the suggestion of the fallibility of all literary constructs as of all human knowledge.

Just as Boethius' work provided the theory for rejecting *de casibus* tragedy, and the inspiration for constructing an alternative definition, Boccaccio's *De Casibus* provided the practical, negative example and not an authoritative literary precedent compelling assent and imitation.[18] From Chaucer's orthodox perspec-

17. Walter Clyde Curry vehemently rejects the Monk's definition of tragedy in "Destiny in *Troilus and Criseyde*," *Chaucer and the Mediaeval Sciences,* 2d ed. (1960), rpt. in *Chau. Crit. II,* p. 64 and p. 70, n29. Still, and in spite of his emphasis on destiny, Curry ends up with a definition of Troilus' tragedy close to Robertson's tragedy of the proud man: Troilus "is brought into conflict with circumstances and with destinal powers . . . and . . . because his passions overshadow and becloud his reason and judgment, is brought into subjection to adverse destiny and finally to his destruction" (Curry, p. 65). Another critic of *de casibus* tragedy, John Norton-Smith, in *Geoffrey Chaucer,* pp. 193–198, offers a Senecan version of Chaucerian tragedy that locates the tragic flaw in the imperfection of life, "in the nature of how life must cause us to experience it," a definition allied to the alternative *de casibus* plot, the tragedy of fortune.

18. I follow the general opinion that Chaucer was familiar with the *De Casibus,* and that he drew the general plan for the *Monk's Tale* and details for a half dozen of its stories from Boccaccio's work. The evidence is summarized by Robert Kilburn Root in *Sources and Analogues of Chaucer's Canterbury Tales,* eds. W. F. Bryan and Germain Dempster (1941; rpt. New York: Humanities Press, 1958), pp. 615–616. Herbert G. Wright, in *Boccaccio in England, from Chaucer to Tennyson* (London: Athlone Press, 1957), p. 5, takes a more skeptical view of the evidence.

tive, Boccaccio's work demonstrated what the brief reference to tragedy in the *Consolation* only implied: that *de casibus* tragedy is a genre that remains innately and radically committed to worldliness even as it laments the frustrations of man's power in this world. Chaucer's *Monk's Tale,* matching the spiritual condition of its teller to the moral orientation of his chosen genre, dramatizes this critique of *de casibus* tragedy, and at the same time clarifies the real though limited value of the genre as a nontragic representation of man's vulnerability to disasters inflicted by external forces. More important for our purposes, the *Monk's Tale* suggests by inversion what the nature of authentic Chaucerian tragedy and comedy might be. Thus when the narrator of *Troilus and Criseyde* attempts to use the *de casibus* concept to expound the tragedy he intuits in his story, his project is from the start doomed to an ambiguous success at best.[19]

This approach to the tradition (Chapters 2 and 3) and to the role of the narrator's tragic theory within the poem (Chapter 4) leads to a reading of *Troilus and Criseyde* (Chapters 5 and 6) that departs significantly from the current critical consensus. Yet there has always existed, side by side with the common acceptance of the poem as an "improved" *de casibus* tragedy, a pattern of other, antithetical responses to the work. Admittedly, only one critic has challenged the consensus to the extent of questioning Troilus' tragic stature;[20] usually even those who find his performance as lover wanting do not allow this supposed shortcoming to undermine his tragic preeminence. C. S. Lewis, however, did suspect that Troilus' pain in Book 5 might be only a parody of tragic suffering, and more recently, Alfred David has wondered aloud whether Troilus' "error" in attempting to love a human being with an ideal spiritual love can be considered a

19. My argument does not assume any particular chronological relationship between the composition and revision of the *Monk's Tale* and of *Troilus.* See Chap. 3.

20. Gordon Hall Gerould, *Chaucerian Essays* (Princeton: Princeton University Press, 1952), p. 91.

tragic error.[21] More numerous are those readers, mainly earlier critics, who have proposed that the tragedy is not only Troilus' but also Criseyde's.[22] With the possible exception of Lewis, though, these critics have not been led by their perception of Criseyde as a tragic figure to reconsider seriously the conventional concept of tragedy or the classification of Troilus' career as tragic. Finally, many readers see the work as not just tragic but as somehow combining comedy and tragedy. Pointing to the plot's double change of fortune, Robert Kilburn Root calls the poem "first a comedy and then a tragedy." Nevill Coghill calls the poem a tragicomedy, "a work in which a hidden philosophical seriousness [defined by the *de casibus* concept] underlies the smiling account of human behaviour, the tears and the buffoonery, and gives them a secret direction." Charles Muscatine seems to define the comedy as being a matter of mood and tone; Helen Corsa sees in the figure of Pandarus and in Troilus' final vision

21. *The Allegory of Love* (1936; rpt. New York: Oxford University Press, 1960), pp. 195–196; "The Hero of the *Troilus*," *Speculum,* 37 (1962), 578. In a new book that came to my attention late, *O Love, O Charite!: Contraries Harmonized in Chaucer's Troilus* (Carbondale, Ill.: Southern Illinois University Press, 1976), esp. pp. 140–141, Donald W. Rowe describes Troilus' career as a comic cycle that includes a descent into an experience of the world's tragedy with Criseyde and a final ascent into a divine comedy.

22. George Lyman Kittredge, *Chaucer and His Poetry* (1915; rpt. Cambridge, Mass.: Harvard University Press, 1970), p. 135; Jefferson, *Chaucer and the Consolation,* pp. 128–129; Nathaniel Edward Griffin, introduction to *The Filostrato of Giovanni Boccaccio,* ed. Griffin and Arthur Beckwith Myrick (1929; rpt. New York: Biblo and Tannen, 1967), p. 103; Lewis, *Allegory,* p. 189; Coghill, *Poet Chaucer,* pp. 59–60. John Lawlor, in his *Chaucer,* pp. 76–77 and 86, specifically denies that Criseyde achieves tragic stature, while Paull Baum, in *Chaucer: A Critical Appreciation* (Durham: Duke University Press, 1958), pp. 155–159, charges Chaucer with an inability to perceive or develop the "latent" tragedy of Criseyde. Donald Rowe, *O Love, O Charite!,* says that "the human tragedy of this world is figured primarily in Criseyde, not Troilus" (p. 136). Rowe's tragedy of Criseyde seems to fit the traditional *de casibus* mold, however; discord and mutability are seen as tragic (at least to human understanding), and Criseyde, a symbol of cupidity (pp. 79–85), is a variation on the hero of the tragedy of the proud man.

kinds of comedy whose ultimate consequence is to heighten the tragic effect of the work. Robert Jordan, like Steadman, proposes that while the action in the human sphere is tragic, a final divine action or vision is implied in which mundane tragedy is transcended by divine comedy.[23] Obviously there exists a fairly widespread, if confused, sense that the concept of "tragedye," especially if it is understood to center on Troilus alone, does not adequately account for all the important elements of the poem.

Ironically, these scattered, minority views of the poem, sometimes at odds with their authors' own general approaches to the work, add up after a fashion to the most accurate reading of *Troilus and Criseyde*. Although they may occasionally be expressed in ways that seem impressionistic, idiosyncratic, or inappropriately modernistic, they point in a direction wholly consistent with Chaucer's philosophical and theological orthodoxy. Once the un-Boethian and anti-Boethian nature of the old definition of tragedy is recognized, and once the alternative possibilities for tragedy and comedy in Boethius' philosophy are perceived, it becomes clear that the story is not, by any of these definitions, Troilus' tragedy, although the belief that it is his tragedy is the premise of all readings with which I am familiar. Rather Troilus' career is a Boethian comedy, while Criseyde's career is the authentic Boethian and Chaucerian tragedy. At the critical moments Troilus makes morally enhancing choices, but Criseyde, in one instance, makes a morally degrading choice. The new maturity Troilus achieves through love is reflected in his refusal to oppose Criseyde's exchange—a refusal, in effect, to be another Paris—and in his continuing to love the unfaithful Criseyde, even beyond death. Criseyde, too, uses her freedom well by refusing

23. Root, *The Book of Troilus,* p. 409; Coghill, *Poet Chaucer,* p. 49; Charles Muscatine, *Chaucer and the French Tradition* (Berkeley: University of California Press, 1957), p. 129; Corsa, *Mirth and Morality,* pp. 48–68; Jordan, *Shape of Creation,* p. 107; Steadman, *Disembodied Laughter,* pp. 93–98. Rowe's thesis in *O Love, O Charite!* is essentially a development of Jordan's and Steadman's: "Life's tragic cycle is only a part of a larger divine comedy" (p. 133).

to be another Helen and by trying to preserve some fidelity toward
Troilus in the midst of infidelity. Yet she is finally overwhelmed
by the peculiar coincidence in her exchange of the three forms of
fate to which all human beings are subject: the inheritance of
original sin, one's own fundamental character, and the impingement of others' free choices. Her infidelity with Diomede, although it is a lesser treason than those she avoids, changes
Criseyde in a disfiguring way, and this negative change constitutes her tragedy just as the positive changes in Troilus constitute his comedy.[24] Nevertheless, Criseyde does not suffer the
total change predicted in a *de casibus* "fall" but continues to live,
fated and free, among the ambivalences and the integrity of her
widowhood. By creating for his characters a world in which
tragedy does not exclude comedy, and in which fate does not
exclude freedom nor freedom fate, Chaucer arrives at that truth
of human nature no *de casibus* tragedy, however deepened, complicated, or modified, can achieve.

Such a reading of *Troilus and Criseyde* requires us to reconsider the critical commonplace that *de casibus* tragedy represents
the sole medieval conception of tragedy. It is true that the Middle
Ages produced no other critical or quasi-critical theory of tragedy.
But it is not true that *de casibus* tragedy was the only type that
could be derived from orthodox medieval philosophy and theology. On the contrary, *de casibus* tragedy, like the *memento mori*
tradition, had its roots in a common though aberrant aspect of
orthodox mentality and cannot be reconciled with the heart of
Boethian philosophy or with the central mysteries of the Christian
faith.[25] In rejecting *de casibus* tragedy, then, and in working out

24. Cf. Ruggiers, *Art of the Canterbury Tales,* p. 46: "Governance,
self-possession, self-control become for [Chaucer] central considerations in
both the serious and the non-serious tales. For Chaucer the distinction
between a happy or a sad ending becomes a matter of the retention or
loss of these." Cf. Ruggiers' recent "Notes towards a Theory of Tragedy
in Chaucer," *Chaucer Review,* 8 (1973), 89–99.

25. For this analysis of the *memento mori* tradition, see Johan
Huizinga, *The Waning of the Middle Ages* (1924; rpt. New York:
Doubleday Anchor, 1954), pp. 138–151.

his own different conceptions of tragedy and comedy centered on character, Chaucer did not have to reject medieval orthodoxy but only plumb it more deeply. I offer no claim here that Chaucer was "ahead of his time," that he anticipated Renaissance insights. What I do assert is that Chaucer—and this is one measure of his greatness—was attuned to the profoundest insights of his own age and able to distinguish and reject its characteristic aberrations.

The Tragedian

"Go, litel book, go, litel *myn* tragedye": the personal pronoun is as significant as the generic designation and has proved to be equally controversial. Who is it that designates *Troilus and Criseyde* a tragedy? Is it Chaucer the poet, speaking from his full command of the poetic vision of the whole work?[26] Or is it a narrator, a fictionalized figure of some sort who is presumably differentiated from Chaucer, in part, by some limitation of understanding? The answer is important because it determines the amount and kind of authority we attribute to the generic characterization. If the speaker is construed to be the poet, then it follows that the term "tragedye" is meant to be a fully adequate description of the work, that the tragedy is of the type alluded to in Books 1 and 4, and that the declared hero of the story, Troilus, is also the hero of the tragedy. But if the poet has interposed a fictionalized narrator, one whose responses to the story consistently mediate between the poet's vision and the audience's interpretation, then the narrator's generic description of the story may serve only to introduce the genre of the work as a problem. We would have no more reason to trust his statement that the

26. Chaucer the poet is not to be equated, of course, with Chaucer the man but is rather to be understood as "the author as revealed in the totality of the work." See Robert Durling, *The Figure of the Poet in Renaissance Epics* (Cambridge, Mass.: Harvard University Press, 1965), pp. 1–10. In making such formalistic distinctions, I am not seeking to evade the task of describing the vision of Chaucer the artist and the man; rather I understand such distinctions to be initial steps toward the accurate description of that vision. Cf. Howard, "Chaucer the Man."

story is a tragedy than we would to accept his assertion that one night of bliss in love is worth his immortal soul (3.1317–1320). In general such a narrator would be no more reliable as a tragedian than he is as a poet of love.

The prevailing critical opinion, which I share, is Donaldson's view that the speaker is not the poet but a fictionalized projection of the poet, that typical Chaucerian persona who deals in supposedly solid facts and comparatively simplistic interpretations.[27] Meanwhile, the poet, working from behind the narrator, engineers amplifications, qualifications and even denials of the narrator's statements. The poem is in effect an extended speech by the narrator that is discrepant from, even as it points to, the poet's controlling vision. Strangely enough, this approach to the poem has been widely applied to the theme of love but not to the problem of genre. The narrator's treatment of love has been widely criticized while his treatment of tragedy has passed largely

27. "The Ending of Chaucer's *Troilus*," p. 28. Bertrand H. Bronson's objection, in *In Search of Chaucer* (Toronto: University of Toronto Press, 1960), pp. 25–32, that the conception of a persona would be foreign to Chaucer's oral tradition has been answered by Howard, "Chaucer the Man," pp. 338–340, and by Jordan, *Shape of Creation*, pp. 67–76. Geoffrey T. Shepherd, in "Troilus and Criseyde" in *Chaucer and Chaucerians: Critical Studies in Middle English Literature*, ed. Derek S. Brewer (London: Nelson, 1966), pp. 71–72, usefully compares Chaucer's situation to that of the established comedian, the well-recognized features of whose mask will modify and be modified by his material. See also Henry Lüdeke, *Die Funktionem des Erzahlers in Chaucers Epischer Dichtung* (Halle: Max Niemeyer Verlag, 1928); Leo Spitzer, "Note on the Poetic and the Empirical 'I' in Medieval Authors," *Traditio*, 4 (1946), 414–422; Morton W. Bloomfield, "Distance and Predestination in *Troilus and Criseyde*," *PMLA*, 72 (1957), rpt. in *Chau. Crit. II*, pp. 196–210; Dorothy Bethurum, "Chaucer's Point of View in the Love Poems," *PMLA*, 74 (1959), rpt. in *Chau. Crit. II*, pp. 211–231; Robert O. Payne, *The Key of Remembrance: A Study of Chaucer's Poetics* (New Haven: Yale University Press, 1963), esp. pp. 227–232; Lawlor, *Chaucer*, pp. 47–89; and Ida Gordon, *The Double Sorrow of Troilus: A Study of Ambiguities in Troilus and Criseyde* (Oxford: Clarendon, 1970), esp. pp. 61–92. Many recent studies of narrators are indebted to Wayne Booth's *The Rhetoric of Fiction* (Chicago: University of Chicago Press, 1961).

unchallenged. Both the character of the poem's persona and the nature of its genre can be clarified, though, by being considered together. As for those readers who are skeptical of the very concept of a persona, I hope that the cumulative evidence of my full interpretation of the poem will convince them. But here I would like to explain more briefly why I adopt Donaldson's concept of the narrator and how I would modify it.

Perhaps the chief challenge to Donaldson's position comes from those critics who believe all of the poem's multiplicities and ambiguities of meaning can be adequately accounted for by regarding the speaker as the poet who simply speaks ironically at times.[28] In that case, the discrepancy between apparent meanings and the poet's vision would be only sporadic, not continuous; the poem's felt doubleness of vision would be a local effect rather than a structural feature; and the speaking voice would be heard as always in control of the many meanings of its speech.

It is certainly true that there are passages in which the speaker clearly implies and intends a meaning other than, or more than, the literal meaning his statements carry. For example, consider the speaker's comment on Diomede's speech to Criseyde on the tenth day of her exile in the Greek camp: "What sholde I telle his wordes that he seyde? / He spak inough, for o day at the meeste" (5.946–947). The speaker's distaste for Diomede's glibness is perfectly clear, though not explicitly stated. A more complicated case is presented by the speaker's remark after he has described the lovers' consummation: "Reson wol nat that I speke of slepe, / For it acordeth nought to my matere;— / God woot, they took of that ful litel kepe" (3.1394–1396). Initially, the first two lines should be read "straight"—that is, as the speaker's wordy and pompous way of saying his sources do not authorize him to speak of sleep. But the third line, with its interjection and its directness and economy of expression, shows that the speaker

28. E.g., Bronson, *In Search of Chaucer*, pp. 29–30, and Gordon, who does not wholly reject a fictional narrator but clearly prefers an ironic poet: *The Double Sorrow*, pp. 9–13 and 62–63.

is not as impervious to the humor of the situation as first appeared. Instead he is making a deliberate joke that embraces both the characters' behavior and his own relationship to his sources. In these passages and similar ones, I would agree that there are multiple meanings clearly intended and controlled by the narrative voice.

As so many readers have observed, however, the speaker, while capable of both sarcasm and humor, as the foregoing instances show, often does not comment on, and apparently does not notice, ironies in human behavior. His summary of Troilus' first letter to Criseyde, written under Pandarus' tutelage, is an instructive example. At this point Troilus is only infatuated with Criseyde and not genuinely in love; nevertheless, his hope and dread as he attempts the letter are real enough: he sincerely wants to say the right thing, but his experience does not yet live up to the conventional rhetoric of a love letter (and in some respects it never will). The speaker shows himself aware of the letter's conventionality by lumping together some of Troilus' addresses to Criseyde as "thise other termes alle, / That in swich cas thise loveres alle seche" (2.1067–1068). Twice he comments on the length of Troilus' arguments, and he conveys a vague sense of impatience with the whole project by stringing together the items in his table of contents with "and's." He does not comment at all, however, on perhaps the most startling fact: Troilus' laughing out loud as he writes that "Hym self was litel worth" (1078). The speaker does not relate this behavior to the courtly ideal of the lover's servanthood or to Troilus' own dedication of himself as Criseyde's man—a dedication the speaker earlier reported with due seriousness (1.421–434). Nor does the speaker comment on the general questions concerning sincerity that the letter-writing itself raises. Instead he closes his account by describing Troilus' bathing his seal in tears without alluding to the fact that Pandarus advised him to do something like this (2.1086–1087 and 1027). To sum up, the speaker does not merely record the event, but through direct comments and through the tone and rhythm of his speech, shows himself aware of and somewhat impatient with the letter's conventionality; at the same time the gaps in his response show that he has little understanding of the problematical nature of that conventionality.

A narrative situation of yet another kind is represented by the speaker's response to the lovers' second night of love. The speaker claims that the lovers' joy surpassed the power of human wit to understand or describe. Indeed "Felicite, which that thise clerkes wise / Comenden so, ne may nat here suffise" (3.1691–1692). Here "felicite" is, of course, a philosophical concept, the true happiness that Boethius equates with the Good, the End, the One, Godhead. The narrator's claim that this concept is inadequate to render the reality of Troilus and Criseyde's love may well be granted if we consider that all such large concepts lose in immediacy what they gain in generality, and that the experiential values of Troilus and Criseyde's love may not seem to be fully reflected in the abstract definition. If the narrator's statement implies, on the other hand, that human love is greater than the actuality, rather than the mere human description, of divine love, then it is false.[29] But the narrative voice betrays no reservation or hesitation. In fact, this is one of the speaker's most fully committed, most solemn tributes to the lovers' bliss. There is no anticipation of the final admonition to youth to love Christ. Any doubts we feel about this formula of praise we must supply in spite of the speaker's unreserved commitment, at this narrative moment, to the excellence of human love.[30]

The failures to address problems fully, the silences, are part of the meaning of these passages, and the purposiveness of the silences cannot be assigned to the speaker. We cannot say that

29. For another perspective on this passage, see Chap. 4.

30. Similarly, in his pioneering article on "Chaucer the Pilgrim," *PMLA*, 69 (1954), rpt. in *Chaucer Criticism I: The Canterbury Tales*, eds. Richard J. Schoeck and Jerome Taylor (Notre Dame: University of Notre Dame Press, 1960), pp. 1–13, Donaldson noted in the narrator of the *Tales* among other things a penchant for small jokes, an inability (often betrayed by significant silences) to see through ambiguous characters and situations, and an admiration (often expressed in hyperbole) for "all kinds of superlatives."

the speaker intentionally maintains a silence on some points to create an ironic effect. To make such a statement about the passage on Troilus' letter would be to obliterate the speaker's mild impatience, and in the passage on felicity, such a reading would contradict the speaker's committed solemnity—and that impatience and that solemnity are parts of the meaning of the text. The fuller meaning can be achieved only by an analysis that recognizes and preserves the incompleteness of the speaker's responses while seeking to transcend them by comparing his various acts of interpretation with each other and with the substance of the story as he reports it. The ambiguity, the complexity of meaning, is not merely textual, that is, local, but contextual, that is, structural.[31] The only way, it seems to me, to take into account the explicit statements, implicit statements, expressive silences, and contradictions in the story is to posit an ever-present narrating voice that is manipulated by the poet. In the criticism of *Troilus and Criseyde,* the concept of a narrator-persona does not render the simple inappropriately complex, but offers the only adequate account of the complexity with which the poem confronts us.

Such a persona probably should not be thought of as having the same status as the other characters, however. Although certain biographical details, as his unlikeliness for love, are supplied, they are only those relevant to his role as teller of this particular story. He does not occupy a time and a space in the same way the other characters do, and he is known to us only through this one act of story telling. On the other hand, neither is he simply a mechanical device made to serve any purpose at any moment; such an interpretation tends to collapse the distinction between poet and persona and present us again with a poet who speaks ironically. Rather the narrator has certain consistent

31. Borrowing a formula from Gordon's discussion of Christian love and courtly love, *The Double Sorrow,* p. 19, we may say that the poem consists of a pattern of incongruities that add up to a congruity. As Robert Jordan puts it, *Shape of Creation,* p. 73, to see the narrator is to see beyond him.

traits: a deep empathy with his characters, a marked deference to authorities, a great fertility of responsiveness to his "matere" (a virtue often overlooked in criticisms of the quality of his responses), and a tendency wholly to commit himself, for the moment, to each variety of response. It is these last two traits that interest me most here, for they point to the most significant deficiency in the narrator: the absence of a unifying vision. As Robert Jordan says, the narrator is "dissociated from a poetic sensibility." Or to put it in Robert Durling's terms, what Chaucer has done is to exaggerate the "tension between local moment and totality," assigning the vision appropriate to each to the narrator and himself, respectively.[32]

The narrator reacts to separate aspects of the story out of a fund of responses, some given by the literary traditions, some emanating from his own dispositions and emotions. He does not ask whether a response is sufficient or whether or how it might be reconciled with responses to other aspects of his "matere." Chaucer commits himself to none of these local interpretations (a detachment that it is exceedingly difficult for the reader to emulate), but instead provides an ultimate perspective of perspectives. Thus, even though the narrator may occasionally express an opinion that we believe closely resembles Chaucer's, the narrator does not thereby move closer to the poet in identity, because the context of all the narrator's opinions is the flow, the succession of local responses he makes to each narrative moment. The same opinion set in the context of the poet's synthesizing perspective has a different significance. The relationship between the narrator and the poet does not fluctuate, as some have suggested;[33] it is a constant. For instance, the narrator's final char-

32. Jordan, p. 67; Durling, *The Figure of the Poet*, p. 3.
33. This is the thesis of Ann Chalmers Watts in "Chaucerian Selves—Especially Two Serious Ones," *Chaucer Review*, 4 (1970), 229–241. Although Bronson rightly complained of a theory that presents us with the *alternating* presences of the narrator and Chaucer, it has become fashionable to "moderate" Donaldson's position in this way. But almost the whole virtue of Donaldson's theory was his insistence that the irony of Chaucer's narratives is pervasive, not sporadic.

acterization of his work as a tragedy represents a confused mix of continuing reliance on mere convention and of profound insight into his material; it is not informed by the poet's clarity about the nature of the authentic tragedy or about the relationship of comedy and tragedy in the poem.

Significantly, it is on this very line of the poem—"Go, litel book, go, litel myn tragedye"—that the concept of a persona has recently foundered. Some of the most fervent advocates of the concept renege when they come to this famous passage.[34] Here, they claim, the poet doffs his mask and speaks directly to us. The evidence advanced for this shift in speakers is principally of two kinds. Robert Jordan points out (p. 103) that through his references to the classical poets, to the problems of linguistic change and textual integrity, and to the historical personages of John Gower and Ralph Strode, the speaker of the last eighty-three lines of the poem identifies himself as an English man of letters of the fourteenth century. But Jordan does not explain why we should equate this man of letters with Chaucer rather than see him as a dramatized version or mask of Chaucer. Second, Jordan and others claim the tone of these last lines is so markedly different from the rest of the poem that it compels us to recognize a shift in speakers. The new tone is said to be "straight, free of ironic humor and of ironic seriousness as well" (Jordan, p. 103), and even "holy and mysterious" (Shepherd, p. 83). Tone, of course, is notoriously difficult to argue, yet it is hard to see how the much admired address to "yonge fresshe folkes" (5.1835–1848), for example, is incomparably superior to the speaker's earlier celebration of Venus as representative of a cosmic principle of love (3.1–49). One of the distinctive characteristics of this speaker is the variety and range of his responses to his material, and the last twelve stanzas of the work seem to me to represent a climactic

34. Jordan, *Shape of Creation,* pp. 102–107; Shepherd, "Troilus and Criseyde," pp. 84–85. Watts, p. 238, says that the narrator "comes rather close to the author himself." Howard, "Chaucer the Man," p. 341, claims rather that here we discover that it has been Chaucer speaking all along.

and not improbable flurry of such responses, rather than a total redefinition of the speaker.[35] There is also at least one positive piece of textual evidence for the continuity of the speaker's identity. As Donald Howard has pointed out, in lines 1799–1801 the speaker of the envoy to his tragedy explicitly identifies himself as the same storyteller who had shortly before (5.1751–1757) described Troilus' vengeful wrath against the Greeks—as the same teller, that is, who has been speaking since the opening line of the poem.[36]

In citing the ending of the poem as evidence either that Chaucer the poet has all along been the speaker or that he steps forward here to replace a narrator, readers have been seduced, I suspect, by the many explicit references in these last stanzas to literary matters. Perhaps because we know so little about Chaucer the man, we cannot resist the temptation to hear the poet speaking directly to us here about his hopes for fame and his relationships to contemporary artists. Then, too, an author's (supposed) interpretive statements about his work always have a special fascination, and the word "tragedy" still makes a forceful appeal to readers. In a more general way, we tend to take seriously, or "straight," any statements about those literary matters that are our own serious concerns as critics. The argument becomes circular. We say that the work is a tragedy because it is so described in this authoritative passage; but the passage is regarded as authoritative partly because it talks about tragedy, about the poem's genre, a subject on which we think the poet ought to deal straightforwardly with us. It is this kind of thinking that has long exempted the narrator's performance as tragedian from the kind of criticism his performance as poet of love has often received.

It may seem that my approach to the genre of *Troilus and Criseyde* will only heap up new reasons for regarding the narrator as a dupe and new reasons for readers to congratulate themselves on their superiority to the narrator. Skeptics may

35. Muscatine's view, *The French Tradition,* p. 161.
36. Howard, "Chaucer the Man," p. 341.

suspect, too, that once again the faults of an actual author are about to be sloughed off on a fictional persona. Actually, this is the one respect in which I would like to modify or clarify Donaldson's description of the narrator, for it has been understood or misunderstood both to suggest that the narrator does not change significantly in the course of his story telling, and to place too great an emphasis on the narrator's being the victim or butt of the poet's irony. It is true that as tragedian the narrator does not transcend his usual, rather chaotic habits as storyteller. He alludes to tragic ideas and formulas only when specific narrative situations prompt him, instead of being guided at all points by a unifying concept of the tragic. He begins, at least, with very conventional ideas about tragedy, as about love, and he does not systematically test these ideas against the facts of his narrative. Nonetheless, his chief difficulties as tragedian arise not from his general weaknesses as storyteller, but from his very strengths in his competing role as love poet and from the innate deficiencies of the *de casibus* concept itself.

Through the activity of rendering the lovers' joy, the narrator simultaneously earns genuine credentials as a priestly poet of love and so shapes the action and the characters that they become uncongenial to the requirements of *de casibus* tragedy. At the same time, the vicarious experience of the lovers' joy causes him to feel all the more deeply the sense of tragedy in his tale, the vague intuition of which was, from the beginning, a sign of his sensitive insight. Consequently, although the narrator never rejects the *de casibus* theory of tragedy, the only theory available to him, he frequently deviates from it in practice. It is his narrative decisions that help to reveal the contradictions between Troilus' experience and the *de casibus* pattern and that ultimately point to the comedy of Troilus' career. It is his detailed portrayal of Criseyde in Book 2 that rescues her from being the mere "wordly good" *de casibus* theory requires, and it is his deep empathy with her and his struggle with the old books on her behalf in Book 5 that help to expose to us the true tragedy he never clearly perceives. Thus there is a triple sense in which the narrator may rightly refer to the work as "*myn* tragedye": he has perceived that the story is somehow tragic; insofar as the work is an attempted (and failed) *de casibus* tragedy whose hero is Troilus, it is the narrator's tragic poem and not Chaucer's; and, finally, it is this same narrator's heroic struggle with his material that helps point us toward the true Chaucerian tragedy of Criseyde.

I have laid a great deal of stress in this introduction on Chaucer's rejection of the *de casibus* concept. Moreover, because of the powerful hold the idea still has on readers of Chaucer, I have chosen to stress this point repeatedly throughout my arguments later in this book. I would not want to appear to be suggesting, however, that *Troilus and Criseyde* is a poem devoted essentially to the negative analysis of a concept that I myself claim is rather trivial to begin with. I hope my full analysis will not justify any fears of such a reductionist approach to an almost inexhaustibly rich poem. Therefore I would like to clarify here the two positive uses that I believe Chaucer made of *de casibus* tragedy and that I have tried to imitate in my interpretation.

In the first place, Chaucer uses *de casibus* tragedy as a foil or "contrarie" as a means of presenting his own alternative Boethian genres more effectively. Although Chaucer found the germ of his new genres in the *Consolation,* it was *de casibus* tragedy that helped him to flesh out their definitions. He answers, point by point, the world view *de casibus* tragedy implies in order to construct an alternative world compatible with Boethian philosophy in which both genuine tragedy and genuine comedy can occur. As a result, Chaucer manipulates the expectations readers bring to the conventional tragedy in order to lead them to the deeper insights of his own generic visions.[37] Furthermore, Chaucer uses

37. In its role as foil in Chaucer's poem, *de casibus* tragedy may well be a more fully developed concept, a more "perfect" example of its kind, than we are likely to find in any straightforward *de casibus* tragedy of

de casibus tragedy as a paradigm of types of literature that he believes "falsen" their "matere": not only by distorting the human experience they portray but, more fundamentally, by misrepresenting the relationship between art and actuality, and by claiming for the work of art and for the artist an undeserved authority. In my seventh and last chapter, I examine some of the ways in which Chaucer tries to make us aware of the story as a made thing, shaped by cultural and literary traditions and by the countless decisions of many "auctours." Chaucer's own story ultimately shuns the pretensions to omniscience and the related presumption to render final judgments that *de casibus* tragedy typifies, and embraces instead the limited vision and persistent fallibility that flow inescapably from art's human origins. The making of an ending is the last and the quintessentially revealing act that distinguishes the two types of art. Thus Chaucer's narrator-tragedian becomes the representative of every artist confronting his vocation, and *de casibus* tragedy the provocation for a profound exploration of the epistemological and moral status of the work of art.

---

the period. This is likely to be the case whenever a genre is itself one of the subjects explored by a work of art. Cf. W. T. H. Jackson's analysis of Chrétien de Troyes' relationship to the romance genre in "The Nature of Romance" in *Approaches to Medieval Romance,* Yale French Studies, No. 51 (New Haven: Yale University Press, 1974), 12–25.

2

The Tragedy of Fortune and the *Consolation of Philosophy*

The structure of Boethius' *Consolation of Philosophy* is built in part on the pedagogical principle that false ideas must be analyzed and rejected before the truth can be perceived and embraced. As Philosophy explains it (1. pr. vi and 3. met. i), the mind will not tolerate a vacuum. When men abandon the truth, false ideas rush in to fill the void, and these in turn must be recognized for what they are and expelled before the truth can regain its rightful place. Philosophy consistently acts on this principle. She does not attempt to assist the prisoner[1] until, urging him to uncover his wound (1. pr. iv), she draws out of him his own mistaken interpretation of his experience, an exercise that requires the whole of Book 1. Nor does Philosophy then hasten to advance her own different interpretation; rather, in Book 2, she conducts a patient critique of the answers the prisoner has given to two questions: How is the world governed? and, What is man? She analyzes both the rule of Fortune, which appears to be the fundamental law in man's world, and the material goods that are often confused with the essence of the self. Only after

1. Throughout my discussion, I shall refer to the persona of the *Consolation* according to his generic roles as exile, prisoner, poet, scholar. I shall refer to Boethius the historical personage and artist by name. Both Edmund T. Silk, in "Boethius' *Consolatio Philosophiae* as a Sequel to Augustine's Dialogues and Soliloquia," *Harvard Theological Review,* 32 (1939), 32, n51, and D. W. Robertson, in *A Preface to Chaucer* (Princeton: Princeton University Press, 1962), p. 359, cite glosses by medieval commentators that distinguish between Boethius and his persona.

this negative preparation does she reveal in Book 3 the nature of the true law of the universe and the nature of true selfhood—and even here she repeats her pedagogical procedure once again as she first demonstrates why fortune's gifts cannot constitute man's true happiness (pr. iii–pr. ix) before she attempts to describe directly that ultimate good and goal (met. ix–met. xii). Similarly, once the prisoner has regained his status as Philosophy's scholar, the two examine the hydra-headed problems of good and evil, of human free will and divine foreknowledge, in a manner that they are fully aware runs contrary to common opinion. Each of the problems in Book 4 is deliberately framed according to popular understanding and deliberately rejected in that form (prosae iv, v, vi). Finally, the rejection of popular judgments in Book 4 is prelude to the acceptance in Book 5 of that divine judgment which supersedes all human judgments. At every step in Philosophy's exposition, then, an accurate comprehension of what is being recommended depends on a detailed understanding of what is being rejected and why.

The Rejection of the "Cryinges of Tragedyes"

The structure of Philosophy's argument mirrors the structure of the work as a whole, for the *Consolation* begins with the dramatization, through the wounded Muses and the poem they inspire, of a vision of life that it is Boethius' purpose to discredit. The prisoner's opening lament may seem to be only that—a simple though powerful *cri du coeur* stating the main facts about his predicament—but as Philosophy later implies (1. pr. v and 2. pr. i), the prisoner has in fact already embraced an *interpretation* of his experience. Only a detailed understanding of how his song specifies that interpretation can help us appreciate the righteous anger with which Philosophy drives away the Muses.

Perhaps the central feature of the prisoner's interpretation is his belief that his life has been shaped by a force external to himself, Fortune; indeed, he attributes not only his present catastrophe but also his former prosperity to her agency. As a

result, he renounces any claim to the power to endow his own
life with meaning, believing instead that the meaning of a life
is definitively revealed in just those experiences in which Fortune's
will is most opposed to man's. His former prosperity, then, must
now be judged worthless. He denies that he has ever been happy
and sees all his life as mere prelude to this catastrophe:

> Quid me felicem totiens iactastis amici?
> Qui cecidit, stabili non erat ille gradu. [1. met. i. 21–22]

> O ye, my freendes, what, or wherto avaunted ye me to be
> weleful? For he that hath fallen stood noght in stedefast
> degre. [Chaucer, *Boece*. 1. met. i. 30–32][2]

The prisoner interprets the change in his circumstances as an
irreversible fall, the fall as an end, and the end as the deter-
minant of the meaning of his experience. So total and hopeless
does the catastrophe appear to him that he longs for death as
the only event that can place an adequately expressive seal on
the entirety of his losses.[3] If such a position were to be fully
occupied, such a victim would reserve to himself no resources
with which to make an inner and personal response to an outer

2. All quotations from Boethius' *Consolatio* are from the Loeb Classical
Library edition (Cambridge, Mass.: Harvard University Press, 1918; rpt.
1973), ed. and trans. Hugh Fraser Stewart and Edward K. Rand and
newly rev. S. J. Tester. Throughout this chapter Chaucer's translation of
Boethius in F. N. Robinson's edition is provided for the assistance of the
general reader and the scrutiny of Chaucer scholars. When brief quotations appear in my text, the line numbers in Boethius' Latin text are
given first and those in Chaucer's translation, second, after the semi-colon.
3. While the prisoner says that he has been condemned by the Senate
"morti proscriptionique" (1. pr. iv. 132), the circumstances surrounding
Boethius' actual condemnation are very obscure. The *Consolation* may
have been written after the passage of a nonbinding Senate decree but
before a later trial presided over by the Prefect Eusebius at which
Boethius, still unheard, was officially convicted and sentenced. See
Charles Coster, *The Iudicium Quinquevirale* (Cambridge, Mass.:
Mediaeval Academy of America, 1935) and Coster's later article, "The
Fall of Boethius: His Character," *Annuaire de l'Institut de Philologie et
d'Histoire orientales et slaves*, 12 (1952), 45–81.

event. But this prisoner is saved, in part, by the fact that he is also a poet. He has expressed his vision in a form in which it can be contemplated and assessed, and so his creative act calls up the countervision represented by Philosophy. Although Philosophy drives the wounded Muses from the sick poet's bed, however, she has not yet succeeded, after fourteen centuries, in dislodging their interpretation of experience from the minds of Boethius' readers.

The *Consolation* is commonly understood to teach that the instability of this world represented by Fortune is both a tragedy in reality and, in literature, a proper tragic subject. Boethius, it is believed, offers consolations for such tragedy but does not challenge the judgment that the world's mutability is tragic.[4] In effect the whole of the *Consolation* is taken to be in harmony with the Muses' song in suggesting that the essential meaning of man's experience is predetermined by the nature of the world he lives in. Readers of this persuasion, it is true, do not cite the opening song as authority for their interpretation, perhaps because the Muses are so clearly—if from this point of view, inexplicably—rejected. Yet the text invariably cited in support of this reading is nothing but the call of the sirens, as Philosophy characterizes the Muses (1. pr. i), in another guise. That text is, of course, the familiar formula for tragedy in Book 2:

Quid tragoediarum clamor aliud deflet nisi indiscreto ictu fortunam felicia regna vertentem? [pr. ii. 38–40]

What other thyng bywaylen the cryinges of tragedyes but oonly the dedes of Fortune, that with unwar strook overturneth the realmes of greet nobleye? [67–70]

It is easy to understand why medieval readers, mining the *Consolation* for scraps of knowledge backed by classical authority, and modern readers, seeking keys to medieval thought, have seized on this passage as especially significant. Yet in context this definition, together with the preceding references to Croesus and

4. For references to critics, see Chap. 1, n7.

Perses, serves merely as an illustration or amplification of the idea that the prisoner cannot claim to have been ignorant of Fortune's ways. It is principally through the opening song, and not through this illustration, that Boethius dramatizes the prisoner's vision of life as ruled by Fortune. That vision, its assumptions and structure, is the same in both passages, however; the center of the tragedy is what Chaucer calls the "dedes of Fortune" and not the deeds of men, and the purpose of the tragic "clamor," as of the song, is only to lament and not to resist such a conception of reality. Thus the rejection of the Muses and their song in Book 1 ought to keep the reader, when he comes to Book 2, from falling into the modern error of thinking that whatever is called "tragic" is also recommended as "true," and should help him to identify the "cryinges of tragedyes" as one expression of the very interpretation of experience that Boethius is attempting to discredit.

But even if the reader does not connect this passage with the rejected song, the argumentative context in Book 2 ought to alert him to the correct status of the definition, because Philosophy does not recite the tragic definition in her own person nor lend her authority to its vision. Rather she places the definition in the mouth of a putative Fortune while staging a mock trial in which Fortune is the accused and the prisoner is the plaintiff.[5] The mock trial is Philosophy's tactic for exposing the illogic of the prisoner's neurotic projection, derived from his own (misunderstood) situation, of a model of the universe that he both appeals to and complains of as the cause of his plight. All things act according to laws of their own, says Philosophy, taking up Fortune's defense. Why should Fortune alone be denied this right? Fortune's law, her very nature, is change. Those who believe in Fortune's power cannot rightly regard any good as truly their own and must expect the random succession of arbitrary gains and losses

5. The provenance of the definition is correctly described by John Norton-Smith in *Geoffrey Chaucer* (London: Routledge & Kegan Paul, 1974), p. 192, n66.

that Fortune distributes. In a specific instance Fortune's stroke cannot, of course, be foreseen; on the other hand, it cannot but be expected. The person who fully embraces this vision would escape despair, it would seem, only by embracing a numbing stoicism or a precarious cynicism.

The purpose of Philosophy's mock trial is not to bring the prisoner to such a plight but precisely to save him from it by drawing out the implications of his position. In fact, Philosophy is counting on the residual belief in order, which the prisoner's outcry against Fortune's stroke in one sense implies, even as the last lines of his lament admit of a more hopeful reading than he intended. Even Philosophy can agree that whoever falls has never stood secure: that is, that the person who mistakenly interprets loss as an irremediable fall has never achieved that self-possession which is Philosophy's main bulwark against the world's instability. The whole of the *Consolation* can be understood as the working out of this alternative interpretation of the Muses' song. Boethius does not passively accept the characterization of experience implied alike by the Muses and by the "tragedyes," and then offer consolation for such a life; instead an essential part of his genuine consolation consists of exposing the errors implicit in such a characterization. An examination of the plot of the first three Books, in which the cure of the prisoner is largely completed, will show how intricately the analysis of these errors is interwoven with the exposition of Philosophy's teachings.

The Antitragic Plot

In a sense Boethius' prisoner begins where the hero of the tragedy of fortune ends;[6] the *Consolation* takes place after what would ordinarily be the last act and portrays what Philosophy would say to such a hero. As she takes the place of the Muses, Philosophy's first purpose is to offer an alternative analysis of the prisoner's sorrow, one that will lead him to express, and ultimately to criticize, his own view of his experience. She begins with a

6. Cf. Chap. 1, n6 for an explanation of my terminology.

complaint (met. ii), though one very different from the Muses';
she does not lament his material losses but the perturbation of
his thought, and her lament is not an end in itself but only a
natural and necessary prelude to more positive, curative action.
The cure begins with a question concerning identity: "Tune
ille es" ["Art nat thou he?"] (pr. ii. 3; 4). Philosophy reminds
the scholar that he is one of her disciples and places her hand on
his breast, signifying that his illness is of the soul. At this early
stage, she diagnoses that illness by its symptoms rather than its
causes: he is suffering from a lethargy, a defensive stance of the
soul against both "terror" (met. i) and self-criticism. Philosophy
then dries his eyes with the hem of her garment, a gesture indicating the restoration of his philosophical insight, at which the
prisoner experiences an ecstatic sense of release from claustro-
phobic confinement (met. iii) and finally recognizes Philosophy.[7]
Like the hero of the tragedy of fortune, however, he is still reading all reality in terms of his own sense of loss, and he asks
Philosophy whether she too is accused of crime, exiled and imprisoned. In response Philosophy urges him not to repress his
grief but to give full expression to it, knowing that his cure involves the uncovering of his wound (pr. iv). And the sick man
must actually be urged to do this, for the attempt to confront
grief in some objective fashion requires more courage than his
earlier recital of complaints. By the end of this passage, however,
the prisoner is ready to take the risk of expressing, and thus exposing, his personal vision.

The account of his political career that follows has often been
regarded as an incompletely dramatized portion of the work, as
simply a direct expression of Boethius' desire to give posterity a
true record of his actions.[8] But the prisoner's account reflects

7. The symptoms of the prisoner's lethargy were already conventional.
See Silk, "*Consolatio* as Sequel," p. 26, and W. Schmid, "Boethius and
the Claims of Philosophy," *Studia Patristica*, 2 (1957), 368–375.
8. Some important estimates of Boethius as a political figure are:
William Bark, "Theodoric vs. Boethius: Vindication and Apology,"
American Historical Review, 49 (1944), 410–426, and "The Legend of

the profound insight that a reconstruction of one's autobiography is frequently, if not inevitably, a stage in personal crisis. Like many such autobiographies, the prisoner's is partly true and partly false. Philosophy recognizes this when she says that without his own story, she could not know how desperate his exile is. His initial demand for pity, his belief that he is no longer the man who encountered Philosophy in his library, and his final insistence on the totality of his losses are its falsest elements. On the other hand, in recalling the actions and motives of a career that has brought him into exile, the prisoner realizes anew the deep conviction out of which he acted and recognizes that he would not change any of his actions. He wished the safety of the Senate and will never cease wishing it (pr. iv. 71–78; 140–151). The will persists in the full knowledge, in the very experience, of its consequences. Over and over again, he distinguishes the merits of things, "rerum merita," from their mere results, "fortunae . . . eventum," which provide the standard of vulgar estimations (154–158; 281–288). The loss of reputation is his final misery because it rests on the gross assumption (the germ of the alternative *de casibus* plot of the proud man) that the man who suffers ill fortune deserves it. The prisoner has already come a long way from the passivity of his opening elegy; in his own valuations he is beginning to discover human means of victory over time and change.

Through this exercise of memory, the exile regains a firm sense of the inner meaning of his own history. Still he is horrified by its apparent contextual meaning, its relation to whatever scheme governs the universe. It is a monstrous thing that there should exist both a good God and evil, that men should have not only the will but the power to do evil. In one of the most celebrated poems of the *Consolation* (met. v), the prisoner elaborates his sense of outrage. The order the prisoner observes in nature

Boethius' Martyrdom," *Speculum,* 21 (1946), 312–317; Helen Barrett, *Boethius: Some Aspects of His Times and Work* (1940; rpt. New York: Russell & Russell, 1965); and the two studies by Coster cited in n3.

testifies that God is seated in his "perpetuo . . . solio" ["perdurable chayer"] (2; 2–3), but on earth "perversi resident celso / Mores solio" ["folk of wikkide maneres sitten in heie chayeres"] (31–32; 37–38). The distinctive metaphysical pain of the prisoner's experience is precisely expressed through the poem's complex tone of reverent belief mixed with tortured questioning. Though still believing that man and God are related, the exile has lost all sense of the practical content of that relationship. Specifically, he is asking for a law (46–48; 54–58)—a desire shared by the prisoner and Fortune's tragic hero. But while the self-defeating response of Fortune's hero is to conceptualize change itself as law, and thus create an alien and tyrannical universe where man must always be an exile, the prisoner instead clings to the hope that there is a higher law.

Philosophy reacts to the prisoner's biography and his song not with the pity he demands, however, but with cogent criticism. She distinguishes his political exile, which can be observed in his outward circumstances, from his spiritual exile, which is the product of his own understanding of his experience. If in his self-pity he prefers to think of himself as driven out of his fatherland, then he must admit that he has driven himself away, since his inner kingdom is governed by one king, his radical self.[9] Yet in this same condition Philosophy finds the most promising hope for his recovery, for this one king "frequentia civium non depulsione laetetur" ["rejoisseth hym of the duellynge of his citezeens, and nat for to putten hem in exil"] (pr. v. 13; 21–23). This inner kingdom is the Rome from which he can never be forcibly banished, Philosophy says, alluding to a citizen's rights under ancient civil law. It is also the true seat of the truths of philoso-

9. Chaucer glosses the one king in these phrases: "that is God, is lord of thi cuntre" (20–21). Robinson's edition fails to identify these phrases as a gloss, but they are correctly italicized in W. W. Skeat's edition, *The Complete Works of Geoffrey Chaucer* (Oxford: Clarendon, 1894), 1, 18, and in V. L. Dedeck-Hèry's edition of Jean de Meun's French translation, *Medieval Studies*, 14 (1952), 183. Chaucer may have derived his gloss from Jean.

phy, his library being only the storehouse of his books. Although
Theodoric's Rome has disappointed him and his library is now
inaccessible, the prisoner is no less the man he was.

Philosophy is now concerned with making a more fundamental
diagnosis (pr. vi). She finds that the prisoner believes the universe is governed not by chance but by God according to reason.
Further questioning reveals, however, that this belief contains a
conviction only about the beginning of things. Ironically, the
exile who earlier sang of Fortune and a fall has no true sense of
the nature of the law by which the universe is governed or of the
end toward which the universe is moving. Philosophy marvels
that beginnings and endings could become disjoined, and it will
be her task to help the prisoner reestablish the connection, to
complete the circle again. Within what may seem the rather
abstract terms of this diagnosis, there is in fact a paradigm of
one of the central human dilemmas. As a modern critic has
phrased it, man experiences only the successiveness of time but
demands "fictions of relation."[10] Indeed, the need for a sense of
meaningful relations between beginnings and endings is, like the
need for law, a concern shared by the prisoner and Fortune's
tragic hero. As Philosophy observes, the loss of a sense of an ending has created a weakness in the prisoner's soul like a breach in
the wall of a fort, through which anxiety has entered (21–24;
33–37). But while the tragedy of fortune imposes meaning on
human experience by insisting on a diametrical opposition of beginnings and endings, Philosophy finds meaning by revealing the
essential identity of man's beginning and end. The end Philosophy
promises to reveal is both a cosmic purpose inherent in the
nature of all things and a goal that offers the only complete
satisfaction of all human desire.

Philosophy pursues her diagnosis still further, expanding her
earlier query "Tune ille es" with the question "Quid igitur homo
sit" ["what thyng is a man?"] (pr. vi. 35; 59). The prisoner's

10. Frank Kermode, *The Sense of An Ending* (New York: Oxford
University Press, 1967).

reply, that he is "rationale animal atque mortale" ["a resonable mortel beste"] (36–37; 61), is merely a rote catechism definition, and Philosophy expresses dissatisfaction with it because, as we learn later (3. pr. x), man is not only an animal but a being destined for divinity, for participation in godhead. As Philosophy observes, the exile has forgotten not only who he is as an individual, but also what he is as a creature. Questions about the end of things and about the nature of man may seem very different, but they will have one answer; Boethius' approach to godhead is through an exploration of manhood.

Philosophy's closing song (met. vii) appropriately describes a kinetic situation. First she describes the prisoner's illness in imagery of frustration and disturbance—still the most pressing realities for the exile—but then offers hope in the prescription of a rigid self-discipline. It is temporary advice for an early stage in the process of the prisoner's reclaiming his freedom, that freedom which Philosophy defined as the rule of the inner king. In Book 1 we have seen the prisoner acting under self-deceiving compulsions, we have witnessed the initial sense of release that restored insight can confer, and we have heard his own full account of his losses. Most significant of all, however, is the simple fact that the prisoner has opened his closed universe to criticism and comment, for the hero of the tragedy of fortune is able to believe that his experience is tragic only by stubbornly maintaining the prison of his own solipsism. The simple kinesis with which Book 1 ends represents a radical transformation of an initial situation that has seemed irredeemable.

In Book 2 Philosophy says to the prisoner what she might say to all the heroes of tragedies of fortune: his predicament is due to a misjudgment or false opinion about what he has lost (pr. i. 9–11; 20–24). The first four prosae and metra set up the relationships between law and change, change and loss, loss and possession, possession and essential natures. Using these terms of reference, Philosophy then analyzes individually Fortune's gifts of riches, honors, power, and fame, and the possibilities of either possessing or losing them. She concludes, first of all, that change is not necessarily loss, that good things suffering change do not thereby become unreal or despicable; second, that loss is not new, unique, or extraordinary but common and in fact unavoidable; and third, that loss, even when it is real and substantial, need never be total and fatal.

In attempting to change the prisoner's notions of loss, Philosophy takes the sick man's starting point as her own: the terror of change expressed in his initial elegy. She notes that in prosperity he was not a devotee of Fortune but one who, drawing on the teachings of philosophy, scorned Fortune's power (pr. i. 13–15; 26–31). He had not yet felt the full force and reality of change, however; now he understandably reverses his view and sees Fortune as an omnipotent force and himself as a wholly impotent victim. This is the sense, and the only sense, in which he has come under Fortune's power (15–18; 31–35); terrified by change, he has surrendered his own autonomy.[11] But while Philosophy attacks the very reality of Fortune's power by revealing it to be a fantasy inspired by terror, the tragedy of fortune implicitly confirms a belief in that power by its failure to provide any alternative interpretation of the hero's career. Philosophy, on the other hand, through the mock trial already discussed, now tries to expose the illogic of the "tragoediarum clamor" even as she reminds the prisoner of its existence: it is illogical to alienate oneself from all the sources of power within oneself, to project all power onto an external and arbitrary law, and then to lament one's impotence.

Through the prisoner's behavior Boethius dramatizes the traumatic impact of change while specifically denying that change is itself tragic. The trauma arises partly from misinterpretations such as the belief that change must equal loss. Thus Philosophy next attacks the notion that past happiness is utterly lost merely

11. Cf. D. W. Robertson's view in "Chaucerian Tragedy," *ELH,* 19 (1952), rpt. in *Chau. Crit. II,* pp. 88–89, that to be subject to Fortune means to submit both to false doctrines and to vices.

because it is past (pr. iii). In Book 1 the characteristic exercise of memory was autobiography (pr. iv); now Philosophy supplements and corrects that autobiography with biography. She recalls that the prisoner received as a youth and a private man honors that few mature and public men attain. She asks whether any misfortune *can* dim the memory of his sons' elevation to the consulship. Contrary to the expectations of the modern reader, perhaps, she does not point to the transience of past joys as a proof of their worthlessness, but argues instead for their value despite their transience. Within a world of mortality (pr. iii. 44–51; 79–92), transience in itself does not prove that any human happiness has been immoral, and only to those possessed by a dream of power will it seem to prove that that happiness has been contemptible. The prisoner does not need to reinterpret and reject his prosperity; he needs to reinterpret and transcend his "tragic" wretchedness.

Although in Book 1 the prisoner's recital of his losses produced an unexpected sense of self-possession, here Philosophy's recital of his possessions produces an unexpected sense of loss:

"Vera," inquam, "commemoras, o virtutum omnium nutrix, . . . Sed hoc est quod recolentem vehementius coquit. Nam in omni adversitate fortunae infelicissimum est genus infortunii fuisse felicem."
[pr. iv. 1–6]

"O norice of alle vertues, thou seist ful sooth . . . but this is a thyng that greetly smerteth me whan it remembreth me. For in alle adversites of fortune the moost unseely kynde of contrarious fortune is to han been weleful." [1–9]

That this passage has resonated through the centuries for so many readers of the *Consolation* is one indication of how deeply the old tragic idea appeals.[12] Still, Philosophy's detection of a consuming self-pity in the prisoner's reply is correct because the

12. Cf. its uses by Dante in his story of Francesca and Paolo (*Inferno,* Canto 5), by Boccaccio in his story of Theseus (*De Casibus Virorum Illustrium,* Book 1), and, of course, by Chaucer (*Troilus,* 3.1625–1628).

prisoner exhibits the common tendency to discount all possessions in grief and rage over any particular loss. As Philosophy noted earlier (pr. iii. 37–41; 69–75), he is inclined to call Fortune to a strict account for each loss. Philosophy insists, though, not only that all is not lost, but also that loss is not new:

Anxia enim res est humanorum condicio bonorum et quae vel numquam tota proveniat vel numquam perpetua subsistat.

[pr. iv. 43–46]

Forwhy ful anguysschous thing is the condicioun of mannes goodes; for eyther it cometh nat altogidre to a wyght, or elles it ne last nat perpetuel. [75–78]

By contrast, the belief in the power of Fortune's stroke, while gratifying to the desire to see one's life as having form and drama, runs the risk of making loss intolerable and unassimilable to the rest of one's experience. In the Boethian universe change and loss are very real, but they are causes not of spectacular tragedy but only of a pervasive anxiety natural to man's condition.

Just as the prisoner's response to change depends on his understanding of loss, so his sense of loss depends on his understanding of possession. Putting aside the matter of Fortune's changeableness, Philosophy now poses a further question: Is there anything in Fortune's gifts that *can* really belong to the exile? The question of possession has been the central legal consideration in Philosophy's mock trial, but the demarcation of the proper realms of Fortune and of the individual will also constitute a definition of the radical self. Proceeding here by her usual strategy, Philosophy begins negatively by first defining what the self is not: it is not the gifts of Fortune. The proper understanding of any relationship of possession, she explains, requires a knowledge of the natures of the things possessed and of the possessor. Are the natures of the things most men call riches, power, honors, and fame such that a man, given his nature, can truly be said to possess them? Philosophy's answer is no, and her argument is perhaps clearest in her analysis of riches (pr. v). Gold, gems, household goods, rich clothing and ornaments are all beautiful, but their beauty is their own, as the beauty of the flowering field is its own, and cannot be assimilated to something of a different nature. The man cannot be changed or enriched by things that must always remain merely extrinsic ornaments (for example, 75–84; 132–148).

Indeed the attempt to possess what cannot be possessed always leads man into perversion. Riches will make the impoverished spirit avaricious and power will make the enslaved spirit cruel. Perhaps Boethius' description of Nero's murder of his mother provides the best example of this phenomenon:

> Corpus et visu gelidum pererrans
> Ora non tinxit lacrimis, sed esse
> Censor extincti potuit decoris. [met. vi. 5–7]

> He lookede on every halve uppon hir colde deede body, ne no teer ne wette his face, but he was so hardherted that he myghte ben domesman or juge of hir dede beaute. [8–12]

"Sed esse . . . potuit": Nero discovered and actualized a terrible possibility in himself and thus revealed the realities that may lie behind received notions of Fortune's gifts. Taking care to distinguish kinds of power, as the tragedy of fortune often does not, Philosophy concludes that such "power" is not an enhancement of human nature but virtually a denial of it. Every man, though he is not guilty of spectacular crimes like Nero's, denies his nature when he tries to assimilate inferior goods to it. Each nature finds its true good in that which is above it and which possesses the Good more abundantly. Man's destiny is not to "possess" inferior goods, which is not even possible, but to *participate* in a higher Good.

The emphasis on bounds and order in Philosophy's closing song (met. viii) is deliberately reminiscent of the prisoner's great appeal for law (1. met. v). Now Philosophy reveals that the true

law of the universe is not change or loss but love. Love is also
the ultimate principle of order in the individual soul, and
finally the content both of true self-possession and of participation in the divine. "O felix hominum genus, / Si vestros animos
amor / Quo caelum regitur regat" ["O weleful were mankynde,
yif thilke love that governeth hevene governede yowr corages"]
(28–31; 24–26). At the end of Book 1, Philosophy could speak
of law only as self-discipline preparatory to insight; now she can
speak, at least tentatively and hopefully, of the full understanding of law as the final resolution of the prisoner's dilemma and
the ultimate content of his happiness.

Philosophy's song of love arouses the prisoner at last from his
lethargy and makes him eager to hear more. Now that she has
an attentive and willing pupil, Philosophy announces explicitly
the purpose of her argument: to change the prisoner's images of
reality (3. pr. i. 17–20; 35–39). In contrast to Philosophy's
argument, the tragedy of fortune offers only a pandering echo of
man's sense of victimization, representing all those "whorish"
(1. pr. i) types of literature that confirm man's belief in false
images, while claiming for themselves a definitive and undeserved authority as mirrors of truth. One mark of this bogus
authority is an infatuation with endings—to the exclusion of
beginnings—as the determinants and manifestations of meaning.
Thus it is significant that the specific images of the prisoner's
that Philosophy hopes to change are precisely his images of endings—and of beginnings (pr. iii and xi). By reconnecting the
two, Philosophy points to an ending that is not arbitrarily imposed from without by Fortune or some other power, and that
human beings are left only to stage-manage, but an ending that
is the natural goal of all human desires. Whereas the tragedy of
fortune rejects the hero's prosperity as deceptive sham and claims
to reveal the true meaning of his experience in his fall, Philosophy confirms the significance and value of present, this-worldly
experience (Book 2) and offers (Book 3) a transcendent ending
beyond the power of any individual or art to make immanent.

Philosophy's humble tool in working this transformation of images is words. The power of Book 3 is sometimes missed because it appears to some readers merely a repetition of Book 2's analysis of Fortune's gifts. But such a reading fails to pay sufficient attention to Boethius' very deliberate and very detailed manipulation of his words and their contexts. We might profitably recall here part of Alcibiades' description of Socrates' conversation:

> He is always repeating the same things in the same words, so that any ignorant or inexperienced person might feel disposed to laugh at him; but he who opens the bust and sees what is within will find that they are the only words which have a meaning in them, and also the most divine, abounding in fair images of virtue, and of the widest comprehension, or rather extending to the whole duty of a good and honourable man.[13]

Boethius is perhaps nowhere more Socratic than in his relentless attempt to analyze the "substantiam" lying behind the "nomina" of riches, honor, glory and power (3. pr. ix. 41–44; 78–84). Although the names are the same, the implications of the arguments are significantly different in Books 2 and 3. In the former he is concerned to show that Fortune's gifts are not part of the self, part of the proper definition of man. In the latter, he shows that they do not constitute the way to the end or goal of human life.

Happiness was defined as self-possession in Book 2; here it is defined more broadly as possession of the good: "esse beatitudinem statum bonorum omnium congregatione perfectum" ["blisfulnesse is a parfyt estat by the congregacioun of alle goodes"] (pr. ii. 10–12; 18–19). The good is defined as that which once attained leaves nothing further to be desired. Philosophy then briefly reviews the chief forms of human happiness to show that even a superficial view of things reveals that all men

13. *Symposium*, 222, trans. Benjamin Jowett in *The Dialogues of Plato*, Vol. 1 (1892; rpt. New York: Random House, 1937), p. 344.

pursue the good. Moreover, the desire for the good is naturally implanted in men, even as it is in the caged lion and bird, and that desire is directly linked to the search for an ending (met. ii. 34–38; 39–46). Surprisingly, Philosophy asserts that sufficiency, honor, power, fame and joy are all indeed goods and that men are not mistaken to seek them. But in an elaborate analysis (pr. iii–viii), she shows that the *means* available to human beings in this world are not sufficient to achieve these *ends*, for in wealth there is much poverty, in power much servitude, in pleasures much suffering, and so forth. The prisoner summarizes her conclusions:

"Atqui video," inquam, "nec opibus sufficientiam nec regnis potentiam nec reverentiam dignitatibus nec celebritatem gloria nec laetitiam voluptatibus posse contingere." [pr. ix. 3–6]

"For sothe," quod I, "I se wel now that suffisaunce may nat comen by rychesse, ne power by remes, ne reverence by dignites, ne gentilesse by glorie, ne joie be delices." [6–9]

Again, as in Book 2, Philosophy's criticism of Fortune's gifts does not focus on their mutability, a fact already dealt with in the vision of the Muses and the "tragedyes." Rather Philosophy details an experience the modern reader may still recognize as basic: the discovery that no good or combination of goods, even while possessed, can utterly satisfy all the desires of the human heart.

Philosophy does not leave the subject of human frustration until she has explained why this is so. Her explanation reveals that the conventions of human language help to distort reality. Sufficiency, power, fame, reverence, and joy are good, she claims, because they are aspects of, or ways of understanding, the one perfect Good. Nevertheless, men believe that each name represents a separate reality, while in fact all are "nomina" for one "substantiam." There is no way to possess one without possessing all the others—without possessing the Good itself. As a result, riches, for example, can neither produce the sufficiency men seek through them, nor the perfect Good that men do not think to seek, having been misled even by their language. Man's very nature, then, will not allow him to rest in any, necessarily partial, ending that his own efforts can make immanent here. The prisoner concludes that no mortal thing can produce perfect happiness and thus obtains his first glimpse of what true happiness, in contrast with Fortune's gifts, must be.

As he sees, Philosophy has in fact been proceeding by negation to define the highest good. For this work of definition, she drew on her own resources, withdrawing briefly into the chamber of her mind to consult the mind of God within man (pr. ii). But as she and the prisoner now agree (pr. ix), the subject of how to *attain* true happiness requires a more direct communication with the divine, a prayer (met. ix). The address of the famous prayer[14] defines the dimensions of the self in positive relation to the godhead, rather than in negative relation to Fortune, and climactically completes the argument of Book 2. The celebration of the godhead itself expresses with poetic intensity the central theme of Book 3. In Philosophy's prayer the divine nature is revealed to be the original and ultimate image (6–9 and 16–17; 11–14 and 29–32) after the pattern of which all other natures are formed. Philosophy's project, then, of changing the prisoner's images is revealed to be an integral part of the larger process of restoring his true identity and of revealing his true end. He is himself, the prisoner is told, a being created in the image of God who, though a creature, may yet become a god by "participation" in that divine nature from which he proceeds (pr. x. 88–90). Consequently, the transformation of man's images becomes not only the way to his end but the end itself. The closing petition of the prayer asks that man's vision, purged of earthly

14. *Metrum* ix is Boethius' epitome of the first part of Plato's *Timaeus*. For a discussion of Boethius' neo-Platonism, see Pierre Courcelle, *Late Latin Writers and Their Greek Sources,* trans. Harry E. Wedeck (Cambridge, Mass.: Harvard University Press, 1969), pp. 295–318.

clouds, may be conformed to God's vision, and concludes by asserting that this sight or knowledge of God is both man's true beginning and his end.

The approach to the end that the distraught exile could no longer articulate is, we learn at last, *through beginnings*. Philosophy's prayer was addressed to the Father without whom "nullum rite fundatur exordium" ["is ther no thyng founded aryght"] (pr. ix. 104; 199), and all of her subsequent arguments to prove God is happiness are about beginnings (pr. x): the existence of imperfect goods points to the existence of a perfect good; since nothing can be better by nature than its source, God must not merely possess the highest good, but He must be, in His nature, the highest good; since there cannot exist two highest goods that differ one from another, God alone is the perfect and highest Good; and finally, the highest Good is itself both the cause of all man's desires and the sum of all that man seeks. Having explored the good as a beginning, Philosophy now approaches the good as an end and thus completes the circle (pr. xi). Starting from her earlier proof that the good is one, she goes on to say that in fact things *become* good by acquiring unity. Furthermore, the desire for unity is the basic desire of all created things, for unity is life and the loss of unity is death. Thus rooting the desire for the good in the natural desire for life, Philosophy is ready to answer the prisoner's critical question about the end of things: the good, which is also the one, is not only the beginning but also the end toward which all things move.

All that is left is for Philosophy to apply these insights to the last of the prisoner's original questions: How is the world governed? With this answer, she says, returning to one of the work's central metaphors, she will have brought him back safely to his own country (pr. xii. 28–29; 48–52). Philosophy reminds the prisoner of his earlier affirmation that God rules the world. He reaffirms this belief here in a way that reveals his new philosophic appreciation of the nature of God. He describes and accounts for the order in the universe, repeating several times the formula "nisi unus esset" ["but yif ther ne were oon"] (17, 19, 23; 33, 37, 42). Philosophy then returns to that aspect of oneness that was most important in defining and reconstituting the well-ordered self: sufficiency. Since God is completely self-sufficient and absolutely good, he must rule the world by his goodness. Yet if the good is the end toward which all things naturally move, all things accept God's rule willingly and freely. The prisoner himself draws the conclusion: God's rule, unlike Fortune's, is not the bondage of slaves but a government designed for the welfare of willing citizens. The exile has now discovered himself to be truly a citizen and a citizen of two kingdoms: his own inner kingdom of well-ordered selfhood and that eternal kingdom in which he participates in the absolute Good.

The closing metrum of Book 3, Boethius' reinterpretation of the myth of Orpheus and Eurydice, marks the achievement of the prisoner's reintegration in a particularly complex way. Orpheus is a poet not unlike the poet whose tears inspired the opening elegy. His music is strangely powerful and yet ineffectual; its effects on the woodlands, the rivers and the animals are a measure of its inability to alleviate or cure the grief in the poet's own heart. As the coda of the poem makes clear, Eurydice is the poet's lost self or lost integrity. Just as Orpheus attempts to bring Eurydice back from hell, so the disordered man tries "in superum diem / Mentem ducere" ["to lede his thought into the sovereign day"] (53–54; 61–62). Eurydice-in-hell and Eurydice-in-the-light represent two different states of mind. Looking back on Eurydice-in-hell means making a fatal pause to contemplate with perverse attraction the mind in its self-indulgent disorder. Orpheus looks back on the very threshold of hell, signifying that the attraction to disorder, the resistance to health, may be strongest in the final moments when liberation has at last become possible.[15] The old image of man as Fortune's slave exerts a

15. For different interpretations of this metrum, see Robertson, *Preface,* pp. 383–384, and John Block Friedman, *Orpheus in the Middle Ages* (Cambridge, Mass.: Harvard University Press, 1970), pp. 90–96. Chau-

powerful attraction, one that is lessened but not ended by the availability of the new image of man as a free citizen of both an inner and an external kingdom. The extraordinary power of the tragedy of fortune has been well documented by its appeal for many subsequent generations of artists and readers. For Philosophy's client, the exchange of images ultimately requires a choice.

Tragedy and Comedy in a Boethian Universe

To readers accustomed to a rather different reading of the *Consolation*, I may seem to have exaggerated the opposition between Philosophy's argument and the tragedy of fortune. I believe and hope that this is not the case. Indeed, so insistent is Philosophy on the concepts of the inner kingdom and the eternal kingdom that it may well seem that she has rejected not only the tragedy of fortune but all conceivable tragedies as truthful representations of man's nature and experience. John Steadman has recently made this very suggestion:

The cornerstone of [Boethius'] system—pursuit of an otherwordly felicity based on an unchangeable good, together with contempt of the world and condemnation of earthly felicity as false—would seem to undermine the traditional foundations of tragedy, shifting its emphasis from temporal to eternal values. If the goods of fortune are valueless, their loss is hardly an occasion for tragic grief. If earthly adversity and prosperity are ultimately meaningless, the fall from high degree is scarcely a breathtaking fall.[16]

---

cer's glosses on the final lines of the metrum seem to adopt a traditional interpretation passed on through Trivet that identifies the issue as a choice between earthly and celestial things.

16. *Disembodied Laughter: Troilus and the Apotheosis Tradition* (Berkeley: University of California Press, 1972), p. 94. Cf. John Norton-Smith's less sympathetic version in *Geoffrey Chaucer*, p. 192: "Boethius' blend of the Stoic and the neo-Platonic leaves no room for a genuine tragic paradox. The lamenting Muses are quickly sent packing and Boethius' tears are hardly tolerated. By book IV we know that wickedness is a form of mental illness. The mistaken and sad are justly rewarded with punishment and they take proper pleasure in that measure of justice whether they are aware of it or not."

As I have already argued, I think it is somewhat inaccurate to say that Boethius teaches contempt of the world or asserts the meaninglessness of secular experience. Rather he claims that worldly goods, though they have their own limited value, cannot truly be possessed: that is, they cannot become part of the self. Consequently, they cannot, strictly speaking, be lost either. Also, though the goods man desires are indeed goods, and though it is natural and inevitable that man should seek the Good, the means available to him in this world cannot bring him to that end. Thus having or not having these means has no bearing on a man's ultimate possession of the Good. What men commonly think of as loss is indeed painful, but it is not, in any philosophically meaningful sense of the term, tragic. Making such fine distinctions may seem like hair-splitting, but it is out of just such distinctions that the entire argument of the *Consolation* is constructed.

While different in detail from Steadman's, my reading leads me to the same conclusion. Boethius seems to have agreed with Plato (*The Republic*, 10) that tragedies must inevitably express and encourage only the weakest side of man's nature. Like Plato, too, Boethius might be accused of setting up a straw man—of addressing himself only to a trivial definition of tragedy that can be rather easily exposed and ridiculed. On the other hand, the vision at the heart of the tragedy of fortune is basic and must be considered, however briefly, by anyone who confronts the problem of evil. Moreover, this tragic definition has always enjoyed a strong hold on the popular imagination. Its influence may have moved Boethius to construct a counterargument so inimical to tragic possibilities that it rejects all other tragic definitions, too, through guilt by association.[17] And yet, although Boethius disvalued the tragic vision in general and was certainly not con-

---

17. Boethius sometimes cites particular passages from the tragic poets approvingly, however; for example, in 3. pr. vi, Euripides on fame. In Ludwig Bieler's edition of the *Consolatio* in *Corpus Christianorum*, Ser. Lat., 94 (Turnhout, 1957), the list of sources and analogues includes thirty-one references to tragedies.

cerned to define literary genres, I think it is possible both to reconcile a certain concept of tragedy with his system and to draw that very concept from his own teachings.

Again Steadman has made a pregnant suggestion: "The potentialities for tragedy [in Boethius' system] would appear to lie less in action than in character, in the hero's ignorance of his human condition, and his bondage to passion" (p. 94). However, a further distinction is also required here, lest the prisoner-persona of the *Consolation* be taken as an example of such a tragic or potentially tragic character.[18] The prisoner is a good man who is temporarily overwhelmed by grief; his memory is dulled, he is confused about his true identity, but he is not in any sense corrupt. Indeed, Philosophy describes explicitly the limited power of that anxiety which the prisoner suffers:

Verum hi perturbationum mores, ea valentia est, ut movere quidem loco hominem possint, convellere autem sibique totum exstirpare non possint. [1. pr. vi. 30–32]

But swiche ben the customes of perturbaciouns, and this power they han, that they mai moeve a man from his place (*that is to seyn, fro the stabelnesse and perfeccion of his knowynge*); but certes, thei mai nat al arrace hym, ne aliene hym in al. [49–54]

Such a view is, in fact, the only one that could accord with Philosophy's teaching that the inner kingdom is by its nature essentially invulnerable to Fortune's blows: neither the blows themselves nor the grief they cause can wholly "uproot" ("exstirpare") the good man.

According to Boethius' system the overthrow of man's inner kingdom can only be accomplished by the self, a possibility represented not by the prisoner but by the evil men discussed in Book 4. In their degradation lies what might genuinely be called a tragedy of character, and that degradation is a matter of tragic magnitude since such men forsake both the common goal of all existence and their own human nature. While good men become

18. Cf. Chap. 1, n8.

like gods, evil men become like beasts, more truly corrupted than Circe's captives (4. pr. iii. and met. iii), because the change is spiritual and not merely physical. Philosophy presents a surprisingly detailed analysis, identifying three aspects of the evil act each of which contributes to the inner transformation of the person: the will to do evil, the power to do it, and the performance itself (pr. iv. 6–16). It is impossible to embrace evil in any of these ways without being changed by the contact, and that dehumanizing change is, Philosophy claims, the essential—and the worst—punishment the evil person can suffer. The most important change that any act works is not one that it effects in the external world, but always and primarily the change it effects in the inner world of the actor himself. The tragedy of the world's evil, then, lies not in the abuse of the good man who may be its victim, but in the degradation of the evil man who is its perpetrator.

Such a tragedy of character differs significantly from the tragedy of fortune (and the related tragedy of the proud man). The crucial action is initiated by the hero himself, not by an external force, and the change that action effects concerns not the hero's worldly prosperity but his moral being. Moreover, while the fall of the traditional hero is interpreted as rendering a judgment on his entire career, each act of Philosophy's evil men is appraised separately, and has its own qualities that do not necessarily reveal or affect the qualities of other acts. It is for this reason that the change Philosophy describes is not, like the traditional fall, represented as either total or irreversible. Indeed Philosophy declares wickedness is not a crime but a disease, a disease that is curable and that should call forth our sympathy, not our hatred (pr. iv). It is possible, of course, for the evil man, by repeated acts, to deepen and confirm his own disfigurement. Still, Philosophy seems specifically to reject the infliction of death as the suitable response to wickedness (met. iv), while it is death that always waits in the wings to punish the hero of the tragedy of pride.

It cannot be stressed too much that in the Boethian universe evil acts are not necessarily punished by any external event, neither loss of worldly goods nor death. The whole discussion of good and evil arises, after all, from the prisoner's accurate observation that to all outward appearances the good are seldom rewarded and the evil seldom punished (pr. i). Furthermore, Philosophy argues that externally imposed punishments have no power to add anything essential to the real punishment of the wicked: the diminution of their human nature that is inherent in their own acts (pr. iii and iv). Philosophy even claims that the wicked would be happier, not more miserable, if they were brought to justice. But she does not make this suggestion for reasons "quod cuivis veniat in mentem" ["that any man myghte thinke"] (pr. iv. 44–45; 83), that is, because the evil person might himself be reformed, or (as the rationalization for the tragedy of the proud man so often claims) because others might be warned by his example. Rather, since happiness is the Good, and since punishment inasmuch as it is just is also good, the evil man acquires some good and thus becomes happier when he endures just punishment.

The modern reader may well echo at least the latter half of the prisoner's response to this argument:

"Cum tuas," inquam, "rationes considero, nihil dici verius puto. At si ad hominum iudicia revertar, quis ille est cui haec non credenda modo sed saltem audienda videantur?" [4. pr. iv. 91–94]

"Whan I considere thi resouns," quod I, "I ne trowe nat that men seyn any thing more verrayly. And yif I turne ayein to the studies of men, who is he to whom it sholde seme, that he ne scholde nat oonly leven thise thinges, but ek gladly herkne hem?" [176–181]

Indeed the common judgment of men does not seem to be very different today from what it was in Boethius' day, judging by the neglect of this portion of Philosophy's argument. Even those readers who have qualified the wholly fatalistic tragedy lamented by the wounded Muses have only grafted Philosophy's emphasis on personal responsibility onto the old structure of a rise and a fall punctuated by Fortune's "unwar strook."[19] The hero is seen as having in some sense brought adversity on himself, and the adversity is in turn interpreted as the revelation, judgment, and punishment of the hero's guilt. Although this formulation may accurately reflect some later medieval literary practice, it represents a misreading of the *Consolation*. Such a formulation rests on an assumption nowhere advanced in the *Consolation* and everywhere rejected by it: that worldly adversity is an accurate index of moral worth.

The initial situation of the prisoner—a good man suffering extreme adversity through loss of family, fatherland, freedom, and fame—itself contradicts such an assumption. It is true that Philosophy teaches that the good are always rewarded and the evil always punished (pr. iii), but these rewards and punishments are inward, not outward, and arise from the very nature of man's being. Good acts take a man closer to that Good which is his natural end and goal, and evil acts take him farther away from it. It is also true that Philosophy teaches that what appear to be the erratic movements of Fortune are ultimately to be understood as the good governance of Providence (pr. vi and vii). Yet this good governance cannot be observed by the outward eye of man; it must be believed in, despite appearances, on grounds furnished by reason. The order of the universe Philosophy celebrates is acted out in the souls of men and beheld by the eye of God. Any work of art depicting that order as expressed in the vicissitudes of worldly prosperity and adversity and as visible to the eye of man cannot appeal to Boethius' *Consolation* as authority for its vision.

A Boethian tragedy, then—that is, a tragedy that, while not explicitly defined by Boethius, can be extrapolated from his system—has these characteristics: it consists essentially of the

19. Robertson, "Chaucerian Tragedy," *passim,* and William Matthews, *The Tragedy of Arthur* (Berkeley: University of California Press, 1960), pp. 116 ff.

inner degradation of a person caused by the free commission of an evil act; the punishment for that act is inherent in the act itself and is not likely to be echoed or expressed in external events; and the change that the performance of such an act effects in the actor, though real and grave, is neither total nor irreversible. The background of an imperfect and mutable world is assumed in this definition, for only in such a world, according to Boethius, could a person so gravely subvert his own greatest happiness by choosing a partial good in preference to that perfect Good which is his natural end and goal. But this mutable world does not, like the world of the tragedy of fortune, predetermine a tragic career for men. It is still possible freely to choose good acts.

So far, because of the contexts provided by the Muses' lament, the tragic definition, and modern critical controversies, I have concentrated on the tragic possibilities in the acts of evil men. But Philosophy gives equal attention, in Book 4, to the acts of good men, thereby also implying the possibilities for comedy. Philosophy first argues that, contrary to appearances and popular opinion, the good are powerful and the evil are impotent (pr. iv). All men naturally desire the good, but the wise attain the goal by means of the virtues, while the evil fail to attain it by a variety of concupiscences. Second, the good are always rewarded while, as we have seen, the evil are always punished by the dehumanizing effect of their own acts; the good become like gods by the very fact of being good (pr. iv). Finally, Philosophy claims that the good, by being good, are always happy, so that their fortune, however it may appear, can always be said to be good (pr. vii). From Philosophy's parallel discussion of good men, then, we may extrapolate a second and parallel generic definition. A Boethian comedy consists in the inner moral enhancement—Boethius would say divinization (3. pr. x. 88–90; 146–150)—of a person caused by the free commission of a good act. That enhancement arises from the act itself and, as the prisoner's own plight demonstrates, may not be mirrored in the unstable world of men and affairs. In addition, while this increase in virtue is important and significant, it is neither total nor irreversible for, as Philosophy observes, a man can lose his reward by ceasing to be virtuous (4. pr. iii. 19–21; 33–36). Therefore the comic hero dwells in the same imperfect world as the tragic hero. Nothing in Philosophy's description of the good man exempts him from the universal anxiety of living amid mutability: he must endure the same losses as other men, suffer the same frustrating discrepancies between outward fortune and inner worth, and deal with the fact of his own persistent capacity for both good and evil. This mutable world is the necessary backdrop for both Boethian comedy and Boethian tragedy, although it does not define the essence of either nor help us to distinguish one from the other. At the heart of both Boethian genres lies not an "unwar strook" but a complex reality, whose right depiction might engage the highest powers of any narrative or dramatic artist: a human choice.

Boethius' Philosophical Aesthetics

The extrapolation of these generic definitions seems to me faithful to the import of Boethius' work in two ways. In the first place, despite Boethius' seeming hostility to tragedy, these definitions are, I believe, consistent with his teachings. But beyond that, they may be seen as advancing a cause that Boethius himself embraces: the reconciliation of poetry and philosophy. Contrary to the initial impression that the expulsion of the wounded Muses may create, the *Consolation* does not reject poetry per se.[20] Structurally, the opening poem is prologue not just to Book 1

20. A conflict between two muses and eventual rejection of one had by the sixth century become a topos for dramatizing the problem of authentic inspiration: Ernst Curtius, *European Literature and the Latin Middle Ages,* trans. Willard R. Trask (1953; rpt. New York: Harper & Row, 1963), pp. 228–246. Cf. Boccacio's treatment of Boethius' Muses in his *Genealogia Deorum Gentilium,* 14.20, in *Boccaccio on Poetry,* trans. Charles G. Osgood (1930; rpt. New York: Bobbs-Merrill, 1956), pp. 94–96.

but to the whole work, since only Book 1 begins with a metrum. Indeed the very first word of this philosophical work is "carmina" ["vers"]. Dramatically, the prisoner is, like Boethius himself, both a philosopher and a poet, so that his reintegration suggests the reunification of the two disciplines as well. Using the language of Boethius' own *De Musica,* the poems of the *Consolation* provide "instrumental music" that gives language and form to the silent rhythms of "world music" (the order of the physical world); and the two together, through their rational proportions, offer exemplars for the "human music" (the harmony of rational and irrational appetites) that the prisoner seeks to reestablish in his own soul. But philosophy and poetry together fulfill their highest mission when they cooperate to imitate "divine music," that music which exists in God and by which He first creates and thereafter maintains world music.[21]

The highest aspiration of Boethius' art is to construct an image of that divine nature which Philosophy proposes as the ultimate object of both man's knowledge and his existence. That is, through philosophic arguments and songs, with their interdependent definitions, inferences, and proofs, Philosophy attempts to "weave"[22] a whole which is an image of the Platonic sphere or circle which is, in its turn, a traditional image of the divine nature.[23] The symbolical structure of the work itself becomes a mode for imitating divine music. This project can never be more than partially successful, however, because the *Consolation* exposes the representational limits as well as the aspirations of its

21. I am indebted to David S. Chamberlain's fine study, "Philosophy of Music in the *Consolatio* of Boethius," *Speculum,* 45 (1970), 80–97.

22. The metaphor is both Boethian (3. pr. xii. 83) and Chaucerian (156).

23. See Georges Poulet, "The Metamorphoses of the Circle," originally entitled "Introduction" in his *Les Metamorphoses du cercle* (Paris: Plon, 1961) and translated by Carley Dawson and Elliott Coleman for *Dante: A Collection of Critical Essays,* ed. John Freccero (Englewood Cliffs, N.J.: Prentice-Hall, 1965), pp. 151–169. Poulet cites certain chiastic passages of Augustine's as attempting to offer verbal equivalents of the divine circle (p. 156).

own aesthetics. In the end, even Philosophy must recognize an impassable barrier: no human work can perfectly imitate the divine nature in its whole, perfect, and simultaneous possession of endless life (5. pr. vi. 9–11). The *Consolation* implies, then, that every product of man's imagination should embody both the aspiration to represent this ultimate reality and a confession of its own inevitable failure fully to realize that aspiration.

It is the prisoner who first calls attention to Philosophy's claims for philosophical argument by commenting late in Book 3 on the "inextricabilem labyrinthum" ["hous of Dedalus"] (pr. xii. 82–83; 156) formed by Philosophy's discourse. When Philosophy presses the terms of her earlier discourse into still new uses, the prisoner asks whether she is playing with him:

". . . quae nunc quidem qua egrediaris introeas, nunc vero quo introieris egrediare, an mirabilem quendam divinae simplicitatis orbem complicas?" [3. pr. xii. 83–86]

". . . thow that otherwhile entrist ther thow issist, and other while issist ther thow entrest? Ne fooldist thou nat togidre (*by replicacioun of wordes*) a manere wondirful cercle or environynge of the simplicite devyne?" [158–162]

After briefly reviewing Philosophy's argument up to this point, the prisoner describes her achievement in more pointedly admiring terms:

"Atque haec nullis extrinsecus sumptis sed ex altero altero fidem trahente insitis domesticisque probationibus explicabas." [97–99]

"And thise thinges ne schewedest thou naught with noone resouns ytaken fro withouten, but by proeves in cercles and homliche knowen, the whiche proeves drawen to hemself heer feyth and here accord everich of hem of othir." [179–184][24]

24. The reuse of the circle image here in the phrase "proeves in cercles" is Chaucerian, not being found in the Latin text or in Jean de Meun's French translation, and may suggest Chaucer's sensitivity to the importance of the image throughout this passage and throughout the work.

Philosophy then defends her practice in a most solemn manner:

"Ea est enim divinae forma substantiae ut neque in externa dilabatur
nec in se externum aliquid ipsa suscipiat . . . rerum orbem mobilem
rotat, dum se immobilem ipsa conservat. Quod si rationes quoque
non extra petitas sed intra rei quam tractabamus ambitum col-
locatas agitavimus, nihil est quod admirere, cum Platone sanciente
didiceris cognatos de quibus loquuntur rebus oportere esse ser-
mones." [102–112]

"For this is the forme of the devyne substaunce, that is swich that
it ne slideth nat into uttreste foreyne thinges, ne ne resceyveth
noone straunge thinges in hym; . . . that thilke devyne substaunce tornith the world and the moevable cercle of thinges, while
thilke devyne substaunce kepith itself withouten moevynge. (*That
is to seyn, that it ne moeveth nevere mo, and yet it moeveth alle
othere thinges.*) But natheles, yif I have styred resouns that ne ben
nat taken from withouten the compas of the thing of which we
treten, but resouns that ben bystowyd withinne that compas, ther
nys nat why that thou schuldest merveillen, sith thow hast lernyd
by the sentence of Plato that nedes the wordis moot be cosynes to
the thinges of whiche thei speken." [189–207]

The model for the design of Philosophy's argument is nothing
less than the nature of the divine essence itself. Her argument
constitutes not merely a statement about the order of the universe; it is itself an imitation, a symbol, of that ultimate order.

Indeed Book 3 outlines a set of correspondences between the
divine nature and man's soul, and between both of these and
man's works of art. Philosophy's characterization of her argument clearly echoes the description of the divine nature in the
famous ninth metrum of this book (1–17) and the description
of man's search for true knowledge in metrum xi (1–6). Just as
God is moved to create not by any external necessity but by the
form of the Good within him, so man in seeking truth ought not
to look outward but rather turn an inner light on himself, and
likewise Philosophy's propositions ought to draw their power of

conviction from one another and not from extraneous considerations. And just as God who is immovable creates things that move and yet reflect, albeit imperfectly, his stable nature, so man should bend the "movings" of his thought into a "circle" of unified vision, and so Philosophy's argument, through its dialectical to and fro, ought to achieve a circular structure that is an emblem of the divine nature it treats. The relationships of man's works to the divine nature can be only analogous ones, however, and there are necessarily differences as well as likenesses.

One set of differences in the *Consolation* arises from the need to accommodate pedagogically the nature of human knowing. The Truth may be one but man understands it only in fragments; the Truth may be immutable but it is always being learned anew by individuals. The necessity of process in human knowing is opposed to the simplicity of divine knowing (5. pr. iv and v). The narrative element, the plot, of the *Consolation* answers this need for process. Although the diagnosis of the prisoner's illness in Book 1 is the work's most elaborately structured sequence of incidents,[25] every statement and gesture derives its significance in part from its position in the narrative sequence. Even the philosophic vision of the last two books is from one point of view a cosmic projection of the hard-won personal integration of the prisoner, and thereby part of the resolution of the initial dramatic situation. It is also true, though, that the very degree to which Philosophy successfully works out her circular design dictates a difference in procedure in the later books. The proportion of argument to narrative expands as the prisoner recovers that part of himself that Philosophy represents. Emphasis shifts from the deficiencies of Philosophy's scholar to the particulars of their increasingly shared vision. The imitation of the unmoving sphere necessitates a progress from the contingency of narrative toward the "nexas . . . ordine . . . rationes" ["resouns yknyt by

25. Edward K. Rand, in *Founders of the Middle Ages* (1928; rpt. New York: Dover, 1957), p. 168, remarked on the dramatic qualities of Book 1 that he felt surpassed anything to be found in Cicero.

ordre"] (4. pr. vi. 19–20; 38–39), from the time-bound seeker toward the timeless reality itself. Still the most the work can do is move toward stability; process can neither be omitted from the start nor at any point be wholly dispensed with.

Because of the nature of human knowing, all of man's instruments, and most especially his language, share in these same strict limitations on their representational powers. Perhaps one of the best examples of how the *Consolation* points toward unity as it remains committed to multiplicity is provided, appropriately enough, by Philosophy's treatment of the word "One." The word and the concept are first introduced in terms of the one king, the symbol of psychological integrity (1. pr. v). In Book 2 the goods of Fortune are rejected because they are alien to this oneness of the self, and in Book 3 they are rejected for the additional reason that they are only parts of the ultimate One (pr. ix). The fulfillment of all desires is defined as the Good, the Good is God, God is the One, and the One is the End that all things seek (pr. ix, x, xi). The word and the concept "One" embrace and transcend the specialized significances of many other philosophical words and concepts: "the good," "happiness," "the end." All words, Philosophy intimates, are but names for fragmentary aspects of the reality expressed in the word "One." In its simplicity "One" contains the perfect and whole truth that ethics, psychology, theology, and aesthetics each grasp imperfectly and partially in the characteristic verbal and conceptual constructs of their disciplines.[26] Ironically, it requires what the prisoner calls Philosophy's "inextricabilem labyrinthum" to demonstrate that ultimately all words are "nomina" for one "substantiam." The tension between divine simplicity and human multiplicity appears in the paradox that it takes many words to pare away all the nonessential words. Thus the work of art, even as it attempts

26. Silk, "*Consolatio* as Sequel," 25, n21, quotes Augustine, *De Ordine*, 2, 44, to the effect that Philosophy's disciple has full right to the title of philosopher "when once he has reduced all the truths of all the disciplines to one single truth."

to imitate divine reality, confesses by its very existence how distant it remains from a unitary experience of the Truth.

What Philosophy says, then, of created nature can be applied to man's artistic productions as well. Art is a moving imitation of that unmoving life it cannot attain to. It binds itself to "qualemcumque praesentiam huius exigui volucrisque momenti" ["som maner presence of this litle and swifte moment"], it takes the "infinitum temporis iter" ["infynit wey of tyme (*that is to seyn, by successioun*)"] so that "continuaret eundo vitam cuius plenitudinem complecti non valuit permanendo" ["it sholde contynue the lif in goinge, of the whiche lif it myght nat enbrace the plente in duellinge"] (5. pr. vi. 50–56; 82–95). Similarly, while Philosophy's analogy between the human craftsman and God (4. pr. vi. 44–51; 82–92) suggests a likeness between divine and human makers, it also clearly places all the products of human creativity in that time-bound sphere far from the center of the circle of divine simplicity. Even Philosophy's crucial description of her aesthetics of the circle immediately follows a passage where the prisoner is requested to set their earlier arguments in opposition to each other (3. pr. xii. 71–74). Provoked by contraries, man's mind moves lineally. His ultimate purpose is to make a circle, to achieve that vision of unification in which all opposites are reconciled, but the lineal movement of the dialectical process (cf. 3. pr. i. 22–26 and pr. ix. 74–77) reminds us of the abiding gulf between man's instruments and his goal.[27] Finally words can be *only* "cognatos" ["cosynes"] to reality.

The *Consolation* includes other recognitions, explicit and implicit, of its own limitations. In the early books Philosophy discourses confidently on the issues central to the treatment of the sick man: the nature of man, his true beginning and end, and

27. In pr. xii (137–140) Chaucer apparently follows Jean de Meun (66) in describing the relationship of ideas as a "conjunccioun" rather than an opposition. In the two earlier passages, however, he preserves the linear quality by speaking of turning one's eyes in the opposite direction (pr. i. 47–51 and pr. ix. 138–143).

the means by which the universe is governed. But in Book 4, after these lengthy preliminaries, the newly strengthened scholar finally raises directly the issue that his own suffering has so dramatically focused: the apparent injustice in a divinely governed universe. Now Philosophy's approach is openly tentative and modest:

"Ad rem me," inquit, "omnium quaesitu maximam vocas, cui vix exhausti quicquam satis sit. Talis namque materia est ut una dubitatione succisa innumerabiles aliae velut hydrae capita succrescant. . . ." [4. pr. vi. 5–9]

"Thou clepist me," quod sche, "to telle thing that is gretteste of alle thingis that mowen ben axed, and to the whiche questioun unnethes is ther aught inowgh to laven it. (*As who seith, unnethes is ther suffisauntly any thing to answeren parfitly to thy questioun.*) For the matere of it is swich, that whan o doute is determined and kut awey, ther waxen othere doutes withoute nombre, ryght as the hevedes wexen of Idre (*the serpent that Hercules slowh*)." [10–20]

The questions that Philosophy lists as parts of the hydra are the very subjects of the rest of the *Consolation:* the simplicity of Providence, the course of Fate, unforeseeable chance, divine foreknowledge and predestination, and free will. These problems are not symptoms of personal disintegration but universal expressions of the mystery of man's existence in this universe. Moreover, the figure of the hydra constitutes a recognition of the permanent tentativeness and fallibility of philosophical formulations, no less than of poetical constructs. In spite of formulations, all these questions remain inexhaustibly mysterious.

Philosophy's scholar later speaks more explicitly of this situation in one of his own songs: "Quis tanta deus / Veris statuit bella duobus" ["Which God hath establisschid so gret bataile bytwixen these two sothfast or verrei thinges"] (5. met. iii. 2–3; 4–6). The scholar has only three songs in the *Consolation:* his opening elegy, his lamenting prayer (1. met. v), and this lyric questioning. Each frames his sense of mystery in terms progressively less self-pitying, more objective, more universal, and at the same time less capable of a fully satisfying resolution. The argument of the *Consolation* does not, and cannot, dispel all mystery; rather, by helping the prisoner to recover a richer definition of self, Philosophy helps to make mystery more tolerable. The revelation of Philosophy's limitations is timed to coincide with the scholar's ability to accept a tentative solution to the very dilemma of injustice at the heart of his own earlier agony. The patient and student who earlier required a figure of imperial authority now joins with his physician and teacher in common recognition of their human fallibility. At the end of her discussion of the problem of evil, Philosophy quotes Homer to the effect that she cannot treat these matters as if she were a god: "Neque enim fas est homini cunctas divinae operae machinas vel ingenio comprehendere vel explicare sermone" ["it nis nat leveful to man to comprehenden by wit, ne unfolden by word, alle the subtil ordenaunces and disposiciounis of the devyne entente"] (4. pr. vi. 197–199; 333–336). Because neither the philosopher nor the poet are gods, their noblest constructs must fail in some degree to imitate perfectly the sphere of the divine nature.

The ending of the *Consolation* testifies implicitly to this noble failure. It is a rather abrupt, even anticlimactic ending and, I believe, deliberately so. The fifth book differs from the other books in lacking the poem with which all the others close, and thus the whole work ends, not with the powerful lyric statement the reader might well expect, but merely with a lengthy argument reconciling providence and free will. Philosophy's contest with the hydra of mysteries and doubts is suspended but not ended, and the former exile is exhorted to accept the burden of his own freedom and responsibility in a mutable world as he awaits the divine judgment. No more complete contrast with the spurious sense of finality characteristic of the opening elegy could be imagined. There is no last act here, no definitive coda. Philosophy's ending, unlike the one proposed by the wounded Muses, has the openness of life itself. The former prisoner still has options and must still accept risks; the meaning of his life is still evolving. Even the death by execution that awaits both the prisoner-persona and the author himself is judged to be irrelevant here and is not mentioned. Reflecting to the last both the aspirations and the limitations of art, Boethius avoids the sort of conclusive ending that implicitly defines the fictive world as real; instead, he gives us an ending that is a beginning and consequently reminds us—while completing a human, mundane circle—that the circle of divine reality can be completed only in an extraterrestrial realm.[28]

The tension between the virtues of art, poetical or philosophical, and its inevitable failure is much like that between earthly goods and the Good. Art may be counted as one of those earthly goods that man may use and enjoy but must also finally transcend. Boethius cares enough about man and his art in their earthly condition to construct a detailed and psychologically acute drama of the testing and repossession of wisdom in the midst of a very earthly crisis. Indeed, a proper respect for this dimension of his work would require a much more minute analysis of the separate elements of the work than I have attempted here.[29] But, ultimately, Boethius' work is diverse in order to be single, dynamic in order to be static, linear in order to be circular. As the *Consolation* tries to transcend itself and only partially succeeds, the work's final virtue is that it points its readers beyond its own limits. In Boethius' system symbols are valuable only as they take men back to reality. Thus, while the *Consolation* provides the materials of potential, and philosoph-

28. See Barbara Herrnstein Smith's *Poetic Closure: A Study of How Poems End* (Chicago: University of Chicago Press, 1968), esp. pp. 210–259 on failures of closure and on anticlosure.
29. See Paul Piehler's subtle analysis in *The Visionary Landscape: A Study of Medieval Allegory* (London: Edward Arnold, 1971), pp. 31–45.

ically sound, tragedy and comedy, it also clearly demarcates the limited authority of all human constructs and images. A work of literature faithful to its Boethian inspiration would, like the *Consolation* itself, contain within its very structure what Plato (*The Republic*, 10) called the antidote to the dangers of poetry: the knowledge of what such things really are.

3

De Casibus Tragedy:
Boccaccio and Chaucer

There is ample evidence that Boethius' *Consolation of Philosophy* may, in some respects at least, have been misread in the Middle Ages. The mock trial of Fortune proved especially seductive to medieval readers. Although Boethius attempted to discredit the very concept of Fortune, his description of her wheel became the major source and inspiration for the countless uses of this image in medieval literature and graphic arts.[1] Fortune's definition of tragedy, too, provided a ready vehicle for the expression of that contempt of the world by which, as Willard Farnham has brilliantly argued, the Middle Ages from the twelfth century onward balanced and to a degree absolved the "sin" of its increasing espousal of the world.[2] This misreading of Boethius was, then, from one point of view both creative and necessary. An author who attempts to change his readers' images—and who must therefore represent what he would ultimately reject—runs a singular risk of being misunderstood, especially when the urgencies of a later age differ substantially from those of his own.

The relevant question for this study, of course, is: How did Chaucer interpret the *Consolation*, particularly with respect to the old definition of tragedy? The indispensable, and by far the

1. See the *Consolation of Philosophy*, 2. pr. ii. 28–31 and Howard R. Patch, *The Goddess Fortuna in Mediaeval Literature* (Cambridge, Mass.: Harvard University Press, 1927), pp. 154–177.
2. *The Medieval Heritage of Elizabethan Tragedy* (Oxford: Blackwell, 1936), pp. 36–41.

most significant, piece of evidence is the *Consolation* itself. Therefore we ought first to strive for an accurate reading of Boethius'
work in its own terms, so that we can be relatively sure that
misunderstandings of ours do not distort the study of Chaucer's
response. In addition, there are several sources of information
varying in their degrees of remoteness and relevance. To take
the most remote evidence first, we may briefly note the well-
known fact that Chaucer could have drawn very little assistance
from medieval literary scholarship as he approached the problem
of defining tragedy.[3]

Like the rest of his contemporaries, Chaucer would have had
practically no knowledge of the Greek dramatists, a limited knowledge of Roman drama, and only a vague idea of the form of
classical drama. One result was that medieval writers, like
Nicholas Trivet in his fourteenth-century commentary on the
tragedies of Seneca, made no clear-cut distinction between narrative and acted forms of tragedy and comedy. One common
theory of classical stage performance imagined the author de-
claiming his work from a kind of pulpit as the actors performed
a silent mime. Moreover, the designations "tragedy" and
"comedy" were loosely applied to narrative works of very different sorts, and Chaucer himself drew on a great diversity of
narrative sources for the materials of his Monk's tragedies. When

3. General sources include: J. W. H. Atkins, *English Literary Criticism:
The Medieval Phase* (Cambridge: Cambridge University Press, 1934),
pp. 31–33, 86–87, 159–161, and 176; Joel E. Spingarn, *A History of
Literary Criticism in the Renaissance,* 2d ed. (New York: Columbia
University Press, 1908), pp. 64–67; Edmund K. Chambers, *The Medieval
Stage* (London: Oxford University Press, 1903), 1, 206–211; and
Madeleine Doran, *Endeavors of Art: A Study of Form in Elizabethan
Drama* (Madison, Wis.: University of Wisconsin Press, 1964), pp. 116–
128. More specialized studies include: M. H. Marshall, "Boethius' Defini-
tion of Persona and Medieval Understanding of the Roman Theater,"
Speculum, 25 (1950), 471–482, and "Theater in the Middle Ages: Evi-
dence from Dictionaries and Glosses," *Symposium,* 4 (1950), 1–39;
Marvin T. Herrick, *Comic Theory in the Sixteenth Century* (Urbana, Ill.:
University of Illinois Press, 1964), pp. 57–70; and John Norton-Smith,
Geoffrey Chaucer (London: Routledge & Kegan Paul, 1974), pp. 162–171.

Boethius spoke of tragedy, then, he would have had in mind the minor works of the Roman theater of his own day and the greater Roman and Greek dramatists of earlier days. In the fourteenth century, Chaucer would have understood the term in the context of a broad body of literature that was primarily if not exclusively narrative or, in the case of Seneca's tragedies, understood to be so.

This slight acquaintance with classical plays, and with the conditions of their performance, was matched by an extremely thin inheritance in the realm of critical theory about tragedy and comedy. Misinterpretations of Aristotle's treatment of these genres were transmitted through grammarians like Donatus in the fourth century and through encyclopedists like Cassiodorus and Isidore of Seville in the sixth and seventh centuries. From these latter sources medieval readers learned to distinguish tragedy and comedy primarily in terms of their outcomes. Tragedy was commonly said to begin in tranquillity and end in misery and terror, and comedy to begin in turbulence and end in happiness. Through a misunderstanding of Aristotle's emphasis on nobility of character that seems to have reached back almost to his own time, the personages of the two genres were sharply differentiated according to social rank; the characters of tragedy were kings and leaders, those of comedy, ordinary men and private citizens. The serious actions of tragedy, such as exile and bloodshed, were to be drawn from history, while the more familiar situations of comedy, such as love affairs and seductions, might be drawn from the poet's invention. Finally, tragedy was to be composed in an elevated and sublime style, comedy in a low and unstudied style. But, even though these commonly cited characteristics can be codified into a neat list, it would be a mistake to think of these early commentators as offering systematic theories of the genres. Rather their remarks on tragedy and comedy were almost always incidental and tangential to their main purposes. Furthermore, these fragmentary remarks share the general characteristics of much of the learning transmitted through these sources: they

are commonplaces which by Chaucer's time had been petrified
by restatement and were devoid of vivifying inspiration.

Given Chaucer's complex, often playful, and sometimes ir-
reverent attitudes toward "auctoritees" and "glosers," it is
difficult to assess the weight these mere scraps of classical learning
would have carried for him. An echo of this tradition of commentary does appear in his own gloss on the tragic definition in
the *Consolation:* "Tragedye is to seyn a dite of a prosperite for
a tyme, that endeth in wrecchidnesse" (2. pr. ii. 70–72). Chaucer's gloss may have been partially inspired by the gloss of
Nicholas of Trivet, whose commentary on Boethius Chaucer almost certainly consulted. According to Trivet, tragedy is a
"carmen de magnis iniquitatibus a prosperitate incipiens &
in adversitatem terminans": a song of great iniquities beginning in prosperity and ending in adversity. A similar gloss appears
in the commentary of Pseudo-Aquinas, a work Chaucer may or
may not have known: "tragedia est carmen reprehensivum
viciorum incipiens a prosperitate desinens in adversitatem":
tragedy is a song in reproof of vices beginning in prosperity and
ending in adversity.[4] We notice, however, that Chaucer's gloss,
unlike the others, lacks any reference to iniquity or vice as a
cause of tragedy. In this respect, Chaucer's is the most faithful
of the three glosses to Boethius' text, for the tragedy described
there by Fortune imputes no responsibility to the tragic hero for
his own fall. From another point of view, though, Chaucer's

4. For Trivet's gloss, see D. W. Robertson, *A Preface to Chaucer*
(Princeton: Princeton University Press, 1962), p. 473; for Pseudo-
Aquinas', John Steadman, *Disembodied Laughter: Troilus and the
Apotheosis Tradition* (Berkeley: University of California Press, 1972),
pp. 99–100. There is no gloss for this passage in Jean de Meun's transla-
tion, but for other medieval glosses, see Wilhelm Cloetta, *Beiträge zur
Literaturgeschichte des Mittelalters und der Renaissance* (Halle, 1890),
1, 44 ff. Also see W. W. Skeat, *The Complete Works of Geoffrey Chaucer*
(Oxford: Clarendon, 1894), 2, xxxviii–xli; Bernard L. Jefferson, *Chaucer
and the Consolation of Philosophy of Boethius* (Princeton: Princeton
University Press, 1917), pp. 9–15; and Kate O. Petersen, "Chaucer and
Trivet," *PMLA,* 18 (1903), 173–193.

gloss is very inadequate. It is much simpler in concept than the text upon which it comments. As we saw in Chapter 1, Fortune's definition includes several distinct ideas whereas Chaucer's formula only prescribes a change from prosperity to wretchedness, the lowest common denominator of all the medieval textbook definitions of tragedy. It would certainly be unwise, then, to depend in any way on this gloss as a key either to Chaucer's interpretation of the *Consolation* as a whole or to his mature thought about the genre of tragedy.[5] Here Chaucer the translator merely provides a service of an undistinguished sort.

Obviously it is in Chaucer's work as a poet that we should expect to find the most relevant and crucial evidence concerning both his interpretation of the *Consolation* and his conception of tragedy. Fortunately for us, Chaucer took tragedy as his subject in a work other than *Troilus and Criseyde*. His *Monk's Tale* brings the old definition of tragedy from the *Consolation* (524) to bear on materials from both Jean de Meun's *Roman de la Rose* (1277?) and Boccaccio's *De Casibus Virorum Illustrium* (1355–1374?). Both these authors, in turn, knew and borrowed from the *Consolation*. While Chaucer's indebtedness in the *Monk's Tale* to Jean and Boccaccio is well known,[6] it has not been observed that they treat tragical story in ways radically divergent from each other. While Jean de Meun faithfully preserves the traditional context of Boethian philosophy, Boccaccio sets his stories against the background of a tentative secularism.

In the works of other poets, then—almost certainly more compelling than the commentaries of grammarians and encyclopedists—Chaucer would have found a choice of interpretations. His *Monk's Tale* offers us the opportunity to see how he integrated the late classical definition of tragedy reported by Boethius with the two different medieval understandings of tragedy reflected

5. Cf. Chap. 1, n9.
6. R. K. Root, *Sources and Analogues of Chaucer's Canterbury Tales,* eds. W. F. Bryan and Germain Dempster (1941; rpt. New York: Humanities Press, 1958), pp. 616–617; Robinson's Explanatory Note, p. 746.

in the works of Jean and Boccaccio. In this chapter I shall first discuss the *Roman* briefly and then in more detail the *De Casibus* as preparation for analyzing Chaucer's version of *de casibus* tragedy in his *Monk's Tale*.

Jean de Meun's treatment of conventional tragical materials in the *Roman de la Rose* displays an accurate grasp of Boethian philosophy. His stories of Fortune's power are placed in the mouth of Reason who attempts to convert the Lover from his devotion to Fortune and her gifts. But, both more cautious and less subtle than Boethius, Jean de Meun does not introduce his stories of falls from high place until he has first set forth in an explicit manner several positive Boethian ideas that are intended to guide our responses to these stories. Reason's account of Fortune's wheel, for example, is developed in such a way as to challenge the common understandings of good and bad fortune. "Bad" fortune is really good, she argues, because it produces wisdom, while "good" fortune is really bad because it fosters ignorance. Moreover, the gifts of Fortune are inherently imperfect; riches cannot produce true wealth; power cannot produce true strength. By contrast true happiness is defined as Boethian "soufisance seulement": a self-sufficiency equivalent to the Boethian inner king. Such sufficiency is the one possession of man that is not subject to Fortune; it cannot be lost.[7] Because this is so, no one need ever be inwardly defeated by Fortune however much she abuses him. It follows from this, too, that there is no necessary correlation between a man's fortune and his worth; the goddess is a blindfolded tyrant who tends to debase the worthy and honor the evil. Prepared by such Boethian instruction, we are able to read the stories of Seneca, Nero, Croesus, Manfred, and Conradin and Henry without falling into the usual errors. We do not assume that Fortune's gifts are true goods whose loss can be catastrophic, that the operation of Fortune is

7. References are to lines 4977 and 5331–5336 in *Le Roman de la Rose par Guillaume de Lorris et Jean de Meun*, Vol. 2, ed. Ernest Langlois (Paris: Société des anciens textes français, 1920).

an expression of justice, or that the fall from high place need entail the spiritual defeat of the individual.

Instead the emphasis in the stories themselves falls on the aloofness of Fortune's operations from all human values and powers. In the case of Nero (6183–6488), Reason insistently makes the point that Fortune's gifts cannot turn his viciousness to virtue. The same series of events that plots the rise of his worldly power also plots the deepening degradation of his humanity. The story of Croesus (6489–6630), who was forewarned of his fall by dream and prophecy, shows that no human knowledge or foresight can limit or restrain Fortune's wholly arbitrary power. Reason does suggest that the arrogance of these two protagonists challenges in a special way the very arbitrariness of Fortune and thus motivates her to cast them down in particularly spectacular ways. Yet she nowhere implies that Fortune is any more just than her victims are virtuous. The elaboration of the chess metaphor (6654–6698) in the account of the three modern figures seems to suggest that their political and military defeat, though deserved, need not have been interpreted as a final spiritual defeat; they might have made an inward response to adversity, profited by it, and preserved their inner, spiritual "kings." Finally, at the conclusion of these stories of catastrophe, Reason extends her critique of Fortune's power by briefly considering the opposite case of those who enjoy prosperity: we learn that even they can never know such complete happiness that in the very midst of pleasure they will not experience some woe. Ultimately Reason's argument establishes both the absolute power of Fortune over worldly goods and the irrelevance of the loss *or possession* of such goods to the true happiness of the inner man.

The extraordinary accomplishment of this part of Jean de Meun's *Roman* lies in its adaptation of Boethian materials to medieval taste without sacrificing genuine Boethian philosophy. In his treatment of Fortune's wheel and in his lengthy accounts of the falls of the mighty, Jean expands upon some of the most popular elements of the *Consolation*. At the same time he does not insensibly slip into the vision that properly belongs to Fortune but preserves the larger perspective of Philosophy. His chief strategy for maintaining that perspective is the use of the figure of Reason, who both criticizes the Lover's devotion to Fortune and offers him an alternative: the love of Reason herself. She can nourish that inner life which alone provides self-sufficiency and true happiness. Thus the *Roman* does not lament Fortune's power to determine man's happiness and unhappiness; instead the work shows that reputed power to be an illusion and offers a different description of man's life governed by reason.

Jean de Meun's method of joining philosophy and tragedy is somewhat crude and mechanical, though. The Boethian commentary surrounds the tragical narratives but is not fully integrated with them. Indeed precisely because of Jean's care to be philosophically accurate, the basic antagonism between a narrative centered on the vicissitudes of material prosperity and a philosophy premised on an unchangeable interior good cannot be wholly obliterated. The French poet works scrupulously with the traditions he has received, but he does not address the problem of how to construct a tragedy that would fully represent the conditions and circumstances of human action while simultaneously remaining faithful to Boethian philosophy. Nevertheless, the explicitness of his versified philosophy leaves no doubt that it was possible for a medieval reader to follow the subtler distinctions of Boethius' argument, and it is especially significant that we find evidence of such understanding in one of Chaucer's chief sources. This section of the *Roman* may have guided, corrected, or corroborated Chaucer's own reading of the *Consolation*. Coming, then, from the *Consolation* reinforced by the *Roman*, Chaucer would have recognized in Boccaccio's *De Casibus* a remarkably different kind of tragical narrative.

Although we usually think of Boccaccio's work as constituting a collection of tragedies, Boccaccio reveals in his last story—an account of his contemporary, Philippa of Catania—that he regards his entire collection as a single tragedy of the conventional type:

Vt scilicet opus totu[m] suis partibus in aliquo videretur esse conforme: in quibus quu[m] exordiatur a laetis & in miseriis finiatur: visum est vti a nobilissimo homine operi initium datum est sic in plaebeiam degeneremque foeminam finis imponeretur.

I wish to point out that all this work, by its parts, seems to be arranged in some form: it started in happiness and will end in misery. It seems that the work began with the most noble of men [Adam], so it should end with a common and degenerate woman.[8]

The ambition revealed in this passage is matched, however, by the superficiality of thought it suggests. The note of misogyny, not uncommon in the *De Casibus,* is only the most minor indication of this quality. More important is the implication that Boccaccio chose to open his work with the story of Adam, not because he hoped to trace a universal human tragedy having its origins in the first Fall, but merely because Adam's story offered a uniquely impressive height from which to measure a conventional tragic fall. As Willard Farnham has shown, Boccaccio improves upon the old tragedy of fortune which tended to concentrate exclusively on the hero's end by developing in some of his tales a "pyramidal" structure in which both the hero's rise and his fall are fully elaborated and bound together by causal links.[9] But the best Boccaccio could do for the structure of his work as a whole was to emphasize the old and simple opposition between beginning and ending. If Boccaccio's practice was occasionally strong, his tragic theory seems to have been pronouncedly weak, and this may be the underlying reason for what

8. The Latin text is that of the Paris edition of 1520, from a facsimile reproduction, introd. Louis Brewer Hall (Gainesville, Florida: Scholars Facsimiles & Reprints, 1962), Fol. cxv^r, ll. 4–7. I have silently replaced the old style "s" with the modern character. The English translation is Hall's in *The Fates of Illustrious Men* (New York: Frederick Ungar, 1965), p. 234.

9. *Medieval Heritage,* p. 99.

Farnham recognizes as Boccaccio's puzzling failure to achieve complexity more consistently.

To a reader of Chaucer's theological, philosophical, and literary interests, Boccaccio's embracing of the old tragic definition, especially in such a superficial version, might raise suspicions that he will repeat the errors Boethius and Jean de Meun had already taught Chaucer to reject. These suspicions might also be aroused or confirmed by other references to and echoes of the *Consolation* in the *De Casibus*. Especially revealing is the fact that Boccaccio regards the experience of Boethius' prisoner-persona as a tragedy and a fit subject for his collection (Fol. xcviii^v; Hall, p. 214).[10] Boccaccio also uses uncritically, as a conclusion to his tale of Theseus (Fol. vii^r. 39–42; Hall, p. 23), a variation of the prisoner's famous self-pitying declaration that the greatest misfortune is once to have been happy. Moreover, the chief reward Boccaccio offers the virtuous man, fame, is in Boethius' scheme one of the gifts of Fortune to be discredited. Boccaccio, on the other hand, has the revered Petrarch come forward to celebrate fame in terms Boethius reserves for the Good: while it is sought in different ways, it is acquired only through virtue (Fol. xc^v. 28; Hall, p. 204).

Furthermore, a survey of Boccaccio's tales would confirm the fear that he has not been able to escape some of the worst consequences of his chosen definition of tragedy. The crucial experiences that his characters undergo consist of outward changes in worldly circumstances such as power, wealth, and reputation, and not of inward moral or spiritual changes. Over and over again, Boccaccio emphasizes the contrast between the hero's beginning and his end, often working out elaborate, almost mathematical, equations of pleasure and pain to illustrate his general principle that falls must be proportional to ascents (Fol. xxvii^v. 34–36; Hall, p. 88). The meaning of the experience, no matter how complex, is found in the fall, always a calamity from

10. The folio page (p. 204 of the facsimile) is incorrectly marked xciii, but the correct number is given in the index to the work.

which no recovery is possible. Death is, of course, the preferred ending, and many of the characters appear in Boccaccio's framing vision bearing the bloody wounds of their death scenes, a bit of melodrama later much favored by Boccaccio's English imitators in the *Mirror for Magistrates*. We are led to the conclusion that what may seem to the modern reader to be virtues in the more complexly structured tales, would have seemed to Chaucer, from his Boethian perspective, to be faults.

But while Boccaccio may well have appeared to Chaucer to be repeating old errors in modern dress, he was in fact aspiring to a new tragic conception. It is this double perspective on the *De Casibus* that we must try to maintain as we examine its achievement in greater detail. Although the old tragedy of fortune self-assuredly assigns the cause of tragic suffering to the arbitrary vagaries of unstable Fortune, Boccaccio's tragedy shows a new concern with the causes of tragedy and a new uncertainty about what those causes are. Not content merely lamenting the disasters to which man is liable, Boccaccio attempts to understand and expound their sources. The return to and exploration of beginnings within the pyramidal structure is part of this search for causes. Boccaccio's concern with beginnings differs radically from Philosophy's, however, since he seeks to explain or justify the traditional tragic ending rather than to discover an alternative to it. Similarly, Boccaccio's contradictory treatment of Fortune may well have seemed chaotic to someone of Chaucer's Boethian convictions, and yet it is one of the chief means by which Boccaccio addresses the major issue of his work. Boccaccio produces an extraordinary number of variations on the two basic plots of an arbitrary Fortune abusing the human victim and of a just Fortune punishing the human sinner.

In the introduction to the whole work, Boccaccio identifies Fortune with God and suggests that the conception of a separate, arbitrary power is a human error (Fol. i^r; Hall, p. 1); but in his first tale, the story of Adam and Eve, he presents arbitrary Fortune as real and one of the sorry consequences of sin and crime

(Fol. i^v; Hall, p. 4). The realm over which Fortune holds sway is also variously described. At one point (Fol. lviii^r; Hall, p. 137) Boccaccio characterizes Fortune as the administrator of all mortal affairs, and in story after story, such as those of Priam, Agamemnon, Hannibal, and Samson, he dramatizes her absolute power. Yet in his account of the philosopher Callisthenes, tutor to Alexander, Boccaccio claims that Fortune has no power over the inner man—her control of worldly goods may be scorned for they are only trivia anyway. His stories deal with the winning and losing of such trivia, he says, only because most men can be moved by such tales, while they cannot grasp the higher truth of the sufficiency of the inner man. A third account of Fortune's power, in Boccaccio's discussions of poverty (Fol. x^{r-v} and Fol. xxii^v–xxiii^v; Hall, pp. 36–38 and 67–72), is still different. Here we are told that Fortune cannot buffet any man, wise or foolish; the ancients were mistaken in giving her power over both success and failure. Actually, she can distribute only favors; misfortunes are chained to a stake from which only the individual can unleash them.

The motivations ascribed to Fortune are similarly confused. Most frequently, she is the traditional unstable and arbitrary force, envious of all human success and oblivious of all human worth, a character epitomized in her wavering between Caesar and Pompey. Occasionally, however, as in the story of Walter, Duke of Athens, she is presented as the punisher of vice, executrice of God's judgment. Still another portrayal, in her face to face confrontation with the author as narrator (Fol. lviii^{r-v}; Hall, pp. 137–143), represents her as desiring to educate man and, though not specifically linked to the divine, as wishing to wean him away from earthly attachments.

Not surprisingly, Boccaccio's inconsistent portrayals of Fortune lead to contradictory versions of man's personal responsibility for his fate. Simply stated, the persistent theme of his work is the radical instability of all human happiness irrespective of personal worth or distinction. More specifically, Boccaccio sometimes suggests that preeminence of any sort leads inevitably to ruin: the heights invite the depths. In this view, as Boccaccio says explicitly in the story of the admired Zenobia, the actor incurs no special responsibility for his fall; he is merely the victim of an immutable law of the universe. On the other hand, the fable of Poverty's fight with Fortune attributes man's misfortune to his own rejection of the contemplative life associated with Poverty, and his favoring instead the active life of worldly involvement. Thus while it sometimes appears that man can do nothing to avoid the blows of Fortune, at other times Boccaccio claims that only the heights are vulnerable; the humble station is always secure. In urging his reader to choose poverty, however, Boccaccio seems to vacillate between recommending mere safety and recommending legitimate ascetic values. Moreover, when writing of his most admired characters, he consistently rejects this characterization of the active life as the cause of tragedy. The famous case is Alcibiades. Here Boccaccio identifies ambition and the tendency to overreach one's grasp as an integral part of spiritual nobility instead of a deviation from the ideal of poverty. Anyone can be unhappy, Boccaccio says, but only the noble can in the process earn a fame that will outlive their mortal defeat. Ultimately the greatest sin is not ambition but sloth, and Boccaccio's chief villains are the sensualist Sardanapalus and others of his ilk. This view is most powerfully confirmed in the dramatization of Boccaccio's own temptation to sloth and his rebuke by Petrarch (Fol. xc^{r-v}; Hall, pp. 202–207).[11] If from this complexity there does not emerge a coherent conception of the tragic, at least Boccaccio speaks clearly concerning an elite group of the talented and powerful. They cannot escape the inevitable blows of Fortune, but they can avoid the vices that would call down such blows as punishments and they can practice the virtues that will earn fame—a gift far outweighing the worst Fortune can do (Fol. cxvii^r; Hall, p. 243).

Strangely, Boccaccio's multiple and contradictory theories are

11. Page 186 of the facsimile, the first of two folio pages marked xc.

both the weakness and the strength of his work. The weakness is apparent enough; the strength lies in the evidence these theories provide of his attempt to probe the causes of human action and especially of tragic experience. But unable, it would seem, to discover a nexus of interacting forces, he resorts to considering serially and in isolation from each other a contradictory variety of explanations for man's fate. This instability of content in Boccaccio's work is considerably masked, however, by a rigidity of form. Although Boccaccio often gives extraordinarily full accounts of complex biographies, all the details are nudged into the rise-and-fall pattern—a pattern so predictable that it is not always necessary to tell the story; a mere listing of famous names may be sufficient. Boccaccio imitates this already standard feature of some tragical stories in the many chapters in which hordes of complaining souls appear briefly before him in his vision. The meaning and the moral of their experience, confused though it is by Boccaccio's theoretical inconsistencies, already resides in the pattern; the form hardly needs the content, and sheer quantity becomes more important than exposition. As Boccaccio explains (Fol. xiii^r; Hall, p. 48), he omits no example that might prove effective and intends his stories to impress his readers just as a constant flow of water will penetrate the hardest stone.

The union of unstable content and rigid form is paradoxical but, I believe, explicable. Both elements are, in their different ways, evidences of Boccaccio's determination to find meaning in his materials. On the one hand, he runs through the repertoire of late classical and medieval theories about man's relation to Fortune; on the other, he relies on a structural formula that seems guaranteed to insure that the intricacies of any human career can be reduced to an intelligible pattern. His materials must subserve the heavily didactic purpose of the work, and this didacticism in turn reflects Boccaccio's faith in the power of man's unaided intellect to discover meaning in his own history and to put it to profitable use. In his dialogue with Fortune (Fol. lviii^v; Hall, p. 139), he complains that Fortune herself does not warn men but strikes them senseless. But Boccaccio's moralized history is intended to enable men to advance from being mere victims of events to becoming shapers of their own destinies.

An important consequence of Boccaccio's search for meaning is a potentially radical splitting off of the mundane sphere of man's experience from the transcendent sphere of divine action. In his confrontation with Fortune, Boccaccio claims that the limitations of his own talent have led him to deal only with mortal affairs. He does not have the feathers of a bird that might enable him to penetrate the Heavens and view God's secrets, he says, in what may be another echo of the *Consolation* (Fol. lviii^r. 33–39; Hall, pp. 138–139).[12] Nor does he have the grandeur of words or the depth of understanding to disclose these truths to men. Other passages suggest, though, that this alleged limitation of talent is related to a deeper predilection of the author's, because Boccaccio would have men come to a richer understanding of their existence not through divine revelation but through their own observations. As he says in a discussion of human blindness:

Etsi caelum spectare taedet / Si deu[m] audire / saltem quae coram vertuntur cotidie prospectemus. [Fol. xxvii^r. 37–38]

Although we are weary of regarding the Heavens and listening to God, at least every day we should be intent upon those things that are come right in front of our eyes. [Hall, p. 87]

Such an act of seeing is dramatized in Boccaccio's own careful sifting of the various and often contradictory versions of the stories he tells. The main thrust of the work's overt didacticism is to engage the reader in his own act of seeing by studying these examples and their relevance to his condition. But in this contemplation of historical and personal experience, the reader is neither directed, nor in any way required, to take account of a

12. *Cons. Philos.*, 4. met. i.

divine sphere, either as the wholly transcendent alternative to a contemptible world or as the completion and perfection of a good but mutable world. At the same time the only worldliness that is rejected with conviction is that sloth which prevents a man from achieving his full humanistic development.[13]

A reader like myself, for whom the Chaucerian vision is a customary point of departure, does not at once find Boccaccio's work congenial but is soon convinced, nevertheless, of his considerable achievement in the *De Casibus*. In contrast readers who readily admire Boccaccio's work, perhaps partly because they think they see later ideas of tragedy foreshadowed there, need to consider the possibility that Chaucer, necessarily approaching the work from a different perspective, may have had legitimate reasons for finding fault with it. If Chaucer interpreted Boethius' *Consolation* in the same vein as Jean de Meun did, the *De Casibus* must have seemed to him a philosophically chaotic work that does not escape the worldliness it sets out to condemn. That is, the work itself, and not just its characters, attaches great significance to material prosperity and adversity and laments man's inability thoroughly to enjoy the one or wholly to avoid the other. But I think Chaucer would have been prepared to recognize worldliness of another sort in the *De Casibus* as well: a worldliness that consists not so much in the choice of specific worldly goods in preference to God as in the loss of a sense of connection between the human and the divine.

13. At the conclusion of his discussion of the *Decameron*, Eric Auerbach says: "The worldliness of men like Boccaccio was still too insecure and unsupported to serve, after the fashion of Dante's figural interpretation, as a basis on which the world could be ordered, interpreted, and represented as a reality and as a whole." See *Mimesis: The Representation of Reality in Western Literature*, trans. Willard Trask (1953; rpt. New York: Anchor, 1957), pp. 202–203. But Vittore Branca, some of whose studies are now available in English in *Boccaccio: The Man and His Works* (New York: New York University Press, 1976), dismisses Auerbach's view and emphasizes the likenesses between Dante and Boccaccio. See pp. 215–216 and 222, n25.

It is tantalizing to consider why, in the *Canterbury Tales,* Chaucer assigned his own parodic imitation of the *De Casibus* to a character who "leet olde thynges pace, / And heeld after the newe world the space" (*CT,* I.175–176).[14] Of course, in so describing the Monk, the narrator of the *General Prologue* refers specifically to the Monk's rejection of "The reule of seint Maure or of seint Beneit" (173). But this reference serves only to define "olde thynges," and then perhaps in only one sense, and does not interpret that striking phrase "the newe world." It is not necessary to suppose that Chaucer had some intimation of an imminent collapse of the medieval Christian world view. Rather Chaucer probably saw the tendency to construct a "new" man-centered "world" as a persistent temptation of and threat to the Christian life. The world, with its sorrows and its joys, its problems and its pleasures, is so involving and heaven is so distant. "The hevene is ferr, the world is nyh," as John Gower puts it.[15] The narrator of the *Tales,* parroting the Monk, turns the commonplace into a problem: "How shal the world be served?" (187). The fact that the Monk may stress service partly to mask what is mere self-indulgence does not invalidate the question. Merely rhetorical for the seduced narrator, the question is genuine, and to some extent open-ended, for Chaucer and articulates a problem reflected in all his pilgrims. And their typical response is much like Boccaccio's: compartmentalization, the splitting off of the human from the divine.[16]

Since a fully secular view of man had not in Chaucer's time acquired those philosophical underpinnings that make it now a viable position, it could only seem an aberration—one that

14. All references to the *Canterbury Tales* are taken from Robinson's second edition of the *Works.*

15. Line 261 of the "Prologue" to the *Confessio Amantis,* ed. G. C. Macaulay in *The Works of John Gower,* vol. 1 (Oxford: Clarendon, 1901).

16. E.g., the Knight who "foughten for oure feith" (I.62) refuses to speculate on the immortality of souls, preferring to leave that question to "divinistres" (I.2811).

would cut a man off from the roots of his true identity and set him adrift in a universe suddenly rendered meaningless. By making the character who epitomizes this situation a monk, Chaucer contrasts in the strongest possible terms the fragmentation and insecurity of the "new" man with the wholeness and self-assurance of a traditional world view, even one so much dishonored in practice as the monastic ideal.[17] The furs, the gold, the shining head, the fine horse bespeak a smug self-confidence, but one belied by the eyes "stepe, and rollynge in his heed, / That stemed as a forneys of a leed" (201–202). Inwardly, the soul is adrift, if not the victim of a hellish desperation. Chaucer links a genre ambivalent in its worldliness to a similarly ambivalent soul, and thus, to use C. S. Lewis' term, "medievalizes" Boccaccio's work.[18] In Chaucer's tale the concept of *de casibus* tragedy is measured against the larger context of a Boethian and Christian philosophy, just as the old definition in the *Consolation* is subsumed by Philosophy's enveloping and hostile argument, and just as the tragical narratives of Jean de Meun's *Roman* are surrounded by Reason's Boethian disquisitions. One of the most important aspects of this "medievalization" is Chaucer's implied comparison of the literary, *de casibus* concepts of a fall and of pride with the theological concepts of the same names.

Several critics, of whom Robert E. Kaske may be taken as representative,[19] have already usefully analyzed the conception of Fortune in the *Monk's Tale* and traced its deficiencies prin-

17. Cf. Robert B. White, Jr., "Chaucer's Daun Piers and the Rule of St. Benedict: The Failure of an Ideal," *JEGP,* 70 (1971), 13–30.

18. Lewis, "What Chaucer Really Did to *Il Filostrato*," *Essays and Studies,* 17 (1932), 56–75. On the Monk's worldliness, see Jack B. Oruch, "Chaucer's Worldly Monk," *Criticism,* 8 (1966), 280–288; William C. Strange, "*The Monk's Tale:* A Generous View," *Chaucer Review,* 1 (1967), 167–180; and David E. Berndt, "Monastic Accidia and Chaucer's Characterization of Daun Piers," *Studies in Philology,* 68 (1971), 435–450.

19. "The Knight's Interruption of the *Monk's Tale*," *ELH,* 24 (1957), 249–268.

cipally to the Monk's own worldliness. Because of his attachment to worldly prosperity and his obsessive fear of losing it, the Monk, so the argument goes, fails to grasp the Boethian truth that all fortune is ultimately good fortune, that Fortune is the minister of God's providence. It is important to see, however, that once the concept of a two-faced Fortune who dispenses actual goods and evils is discredited, neither the innocent nor the pridefully guilty can be said to experience either a rise or a fall, for this faulty conception of Fortune provides the very measure by which rises and falls are defined. If these three interrelated concepts—of Fortune, of pride as a tragic flaw, and of a fall as a fatal dénouement—are all philosophically faulty, then the Monk's very definition of tragedy must be judged an erroneous interpretation of human experience. I prefer to emphasize the as yet not fully explored deficiencies of the genre rather than the admitted deficiencies of the teller.

The concept of a fall appears emphatically in the opening tale of Lucifer where the word occurs twice (VII.2002, 2006).[20] The two-part structure of Lucifer's career is sharply outlined; he fell from high degree to hell "where he yet is inne." The changing of his name from Lucifer to Satan symbolizes the irreversible change in his nature, and the name "Satan" also suggests his continuing role as an agent of evil, one justification for his eternal damnation. In contrast the word "fall" does not appear at all in the story of Adam, who, says the Monk, "Was dryven out of hys hye prosperitee / To labour, and to helle, and to meschaunce" (2013–2014). The disproportion among the nouns in the last line and their anticlimactic order signal the Monk's inability to shape the story into the prosperity-to-wretchedness pattern. And for good reasons. As George Pace has carefully demonstrated, in the very word "helle," Chaucer reminds his audience of the harrowing of hell by the crucified Christ.[21] Adam's story cannot ac-

20. Lucifer's story is a Chaucerian addition; as we have seen, Boccaccio began with Adam.

21. "Adam's Hell," *PMLA,* 78 (1963), 25–35.

curately be provided with a wholly catastrophic ending and, by the omission of any mention of a fall here, Chaucer suggests that the tragic concept of a fall is incompatible with the theological concept of *the* Fall.

Ironically, there is a single, unique career fitting the old tragic pattern and that is Lucifer's. Lucifer knew the Good directly and rejected it; he could not, like man, be deceived by confusing a partial good with the Good. Also there was no external influence of fate to limit the free action of his will, for "Fortune may noon angel dere" (2001). Lucifer's choice was totally free and so he is held totally responsible by a just God. Chaucer shows that two of the central concepts of "tragedye," an irredeemable fall and a universe in which Fortune holds sway, are theologically incompatible. It is partly because man is subject to Fortune that the just God turns His face of mercy toward mankind. For the Christian, a fall is not the end of a story but the beginning. The Monk was unknowingly accurate when he said that labor follows the Fall. Now man must work out his salvation, and in this work he always has the aid of two "remedies" against Fortune: the power to make his own responsible choices and the power of Christ's death and resurrection. Chaucer's Christian vision does not eliminate tragedy, but presents it as only one possible outcome of man's exercise of free will as it is impinged upon by both Fortune and grace. Only for Lucifer, who was "nat a man" (2000), is a unique fall the inevitable and irrevocable end.

The word "fall" itself or some formula directly suggestive of it appears in ten of the other fifteen stories,[22] but the human careers the Monk describes are incommensurate with Satan's and thus the imposition of the *de casibus* structure inevitably distorts them. The Monk misses the possibility of a spiritual victory in Samson's defeat, while at the other extreme, he ignores the fact

22. Samson, 2078; Hercules, 2138, 2142; Balthasar, 2189; Cenobia, 2349; Peter of Spain, 2376; Barnabo, 2401–2402; Ugolino, 2457; Nero, 2526; Antiochus, 2581; and Caesar, 2672.

that Nero is morally at his nadir when he is materially at his height (2463–2467). Passing over Nabugodonosor's repentance, the Monk joins his career to his son Balthasar's so that this narrative unit too may end with a fall. In the stories of Pompey and Caesar, the cause of one man's fall becomes the occasion for another's rise. In Barnabo's case, the mere fact of violent death must suffice to make a fall, since the Monk admits "why, ne how, noot I that thou were slawe" (2406). And the Monk seems to think that the essence of Zenobia's fall consists in her demotion to woman's estate: she who once bore a scepter must now bear a distaff (2373–2374). Harry Bailey finally reduces the theme to bathos when he complains that the Monk's stories have almost made him fall asleep and fall off his horse (2797). The cause of these anomalies and absurdities lies not just with the Monk, however, but with his chosen genre.

In six of the tales, the hero's fall is rationalized as the consequence of pride and is thereby given a coloring of orthodox morality.[23] Yet once again Chaucer shows that the literary concept may not necessarily be compatible with the theological concept. Pride is not mentioned in the Monk's accounts of either Lucifer or Adam, contexts in which its theological significance as the rebellion of the creature against the Creator might have been established. Where it does appear, it constitutes not a moral condition "withinne the herte of man," as the Parson later describes it (X.408), but only a mistake, a misjudgment of one's power in a universe where the chief value is power.

The monk's heroes are chosen so that we may "Witnesse on alle thise conqueroures stronge" (2726) and in all his stories the Monk evades the task of moral evaluation he explicitly refuses in Zenobia's case: to consider "Why she conquered, and what title had therto" (2322). We are not surprised to learn that Fortune is perceived in terms of power or that her actions, such

23. Nabugodonosor, 2159, 2167; Balthasar, 2186, 2188, 2212, 2223; Nero, 2472, 2520; Antiochus, 2577, 2580, 2583, 2590, 2609, 2630; and Olofernes, 2555.

as her attack on Nero, are motivated by jealousy of that power. It is surprising, though, to find that the God of the Monk's universe is only another powerful tyrant. Nabugodonosor, having been turned into a beast by God and then released, "evere his lyf in feere / Was . . . to doon amys or moore trespace" (2179–2180); and Antiochus "knew God lord of every creature" (2622), not through any contemplation of God's beneficence, but by experiencing in his own stinking body "The wreche of God" (2615). In such a world pride consists of an overconfidence in one's own power that exposes one to the cruel and envious blows of the greater tyrants, Fortune and God. The typical form of this overconfidence is the belief that one has been able to co-opt, for one's own purposes, the turning of Fortune's wheel. In the Monk's reiteration of the tragic formula, the last lines prove to be an accurate gloss on the immediately preceding term, "proude": "For whan men trusteth hire [Fortune], thanne wol she faille" (2764–2765).

Morally there is little to choose between in the two typical plots of "tragedye": the overthrow of the proud man, on the one hand, and the arbitrary destruction of innocent and guilty alike on the other. It has been common for critics to praise the first type, either as the more pious, from a medieval point of view, or as the more rational, from a renaissance point of view— that is, in so far as it brings judgment and punishment into this world instead of reserving it for the next.[24] But as we have just seen, the piety can be thoroughly specious. The rationality, moreover, can be blasphemous, for in the very rush to judgment, the tragedian of such a tale, from an orthodox perspective, usurps divine prerogatives by presuming to read divine judgments in wordly events. The tragedian seizes on a single event in a char-

---

24. See D. W. Robertson, "Chaucerian Tragedy," *ELH*, 19 (1952), rpt. in *Chau. Crit. II*, pp. 86–121; William Matthews, *The Tragedy of Arthur* (Berkeley: University of California Press, 1960), pp. 115–120; Farnham, *Medieval Heritage*, pp. 115–116 and 290–291; Kaske, "Interruption," 262; Strange, "Generous View," 169.

acter's life as rendering a judgment on the entire life; he presents that judgment as final, usually fatal, and denies to man the power to make any human response to the event. Man neither learns nor repents, nor is he able to meet material loss with spiritual possession. He is held mercilessly responsible for his free acts before the fall but allowed no exercise of free will after the fall.

It is inevitable that such a vision should produce that antithetical image of itself in which man is the innocent victim of an arbitrary turn of Fortune's wheel. This antiversion exposes to full view the closed system of a world in which man has every chance of failing and no chance of growing. He rises and he falls; no other pattern is possible. As the antiversion makes virtually explicit, the government of this tragic world is in the hands of a force totally alien to man; thus its judgments are inevitably horrifying, whether they are construed as "just" or arbitrary. The fall of the proud man emphasizes man's freedom but at the expense of making that freedom a curse in a punitive and vengeful universe. The turn of Fortune's wheel emphasizes fate and relieves man of responsibility but at the expense of making him a pathetic, helpless victim deprived of his dignity. The two plots, one with its overlay of specious morality, and the other with its cynicism and despair, are inextricably linked in their fundamental representation of man as alienated both from the inner self and from the outer world.

Although the Monk's stories are dressed out in all sorts of moralistic trappings, they are fundamentally amoral. The Monk worships worldly power and yet is wracked by the knowledge that all human power must be both limited and temporary. Following the disappointment in man's power comes terror, for the only alternative in a universe like the Monk's is the tyrannical power of Fortune or the no-less-paralyzing power of a tyrant God. The rigid structure and pseudomoralistic fervor typical of the *de casibus* story as the Monk uses them constitute an implicit plea for some measure of safety and control in a chaotic universe.

The narrative structure of numerous exempla by which others may "Be war" (1998) and the heterogeneous bits of advice—to avoid the snares of women, to seek self-knowledge—are symptomatic. But this fragile moralizing cannot wholly shut out for the Monk the horrifying vision of a totally amoral universe. The Fortune that casually raises up a man like Nero and just as casually hurls him down is more horrifying than the human tyrant himself. Even the vicious Nero becomes pitiable as he desperately seeks a way to die. Overtly moralized as an expression of just judgment, death is ultimately revealed to be, for Chaucer's *de casibus* tragedian, the only escape from the amoral tyranny of Fortune. What had been intellectual confusion in Boccaccio's work becomes in Chaucer's interpretation a panic of existential proportions.

Thus the *de casibus* vision is seen to embrace, and disguise, both a thoroughly materialistic commitment to the world and a violent, fearful recoil from the world, and the attraction of a man like the Monk to the genre becomes intelligible. There is no denying, of course, that the Monk's choice of material is at first surprising. Clearly, the Host did not expect to hear from the "tredefowel aright" he playfully addresses in the Prologue (1945) stories about "how Fortune covered with a clowde / I noot nevere what" (2782–2783).[25] But the Host's subsequent plea that the Monk "sey somwhat of huntyng" (2805) reassures us that we are dealing with the same monastic we met at the Tabard Inn, that Chaucer's characterization is not inconsistent but complex. The old critical problem of the "two Monks" actually arose from a misapprehension of the Monk of the *General Prologue* as a contented hedonist.[26] He is, rather, a defiant, posturing, and joyless hedonist, well armed with specious arguments for his way

25. The Monk's vigorous physical appearance may be misleading. Cf. the fearful attitudes toward both male and female sexuality expressed in his tale: 2091–2094, 2279–2294; 2483–2494, and 2711–2715.

26. Joella Owens Brown, "Chaucer's Daun Piers: One Monk or Two?" *Criticism*, 6 (1964), 44–52; and Berndt, "Accidia," 446.

of life. Having rejected the "olde thynges" of true asceticism, the Monk ends up embracing a perverted form of it in worldly pessimism.[27] By committing himself to the "newe world," the Monk has exposed himself to those very fears and frustration that the *de casibus* form seemed to Chaucer to embody.

The Monk's reiteration of the tragic definition, whether Chaucer ultimately intended to give it a medial or a final position among the tales,[28] must bear the weight of these accumulating literary and spiritual ambiguities. Chaucer makes this clear by his careful reworking of the tragic definition as he found it in Boethius' *Consolation:*

> Tragediës *noon* oother maner thyng
> *Ne kan* in syngyng crie *ne* biwaille
> *But that* Fortune alwey wole assaille
> With unwar strook the regnes that been proude.
>
> [2761–2764; italics mine]

No form of the verb "to be able" appears in the Latin text, or in the French translation by Jean de Meun that Chaucer used, or in Chaucer's own Middle English translation of the passage.[29] With the use of the three negatives and the introduction of the verb "kan," Chaucer emphatically asserts the limitations of such "tragedyes." A genre that can only "biwaille," and not deepen insight, and bewail only the deeds of Fortune and not those of men, cannot provide a sufficient remedy for worldliness or any spiritual illness. Ironically, a genre that has always been characterized by its didactic pretensions is shown to be deficient specifically in its ability to teach. Even where the pedagogical instrument is flawed, however, something may yet be learned by the astute pupil, as the *Canterbury Tales* demonstrates over and

27. E. T. Donaldson, *Chaucer's Poetry: An Anthology for the Modern Reader* (New York: Ronald Press, 1958), p. 939.

28. See Robinson's Explanatory Note, pp. 746–747, and Donald K. Fry, "The Ending of the *Monk's Tale*," *JEGP*, 71 (1973), 355–364.

29. In the Latin text, the verb is "deflete," and in Jean de Meun's French translation, "pleure."

over again. The complex responses of the Knight and the Host to the Monk's vignettes reveal both that the deficiencies of "tragedye" are not absolute and that something may be, and should be, learned from them.

The Knight, echoing the conventional medieval definition of comedy, announces that he prefers stories in which "a man hath been in povre estaat, / And clymbeth up and wexeth fortunat, / And there abideth in prosperitee" (2775–2777). Such stories expose the extraordinary narrowness of the Monk's vision by reminding us of an aspect of reality wholly excluded from the Monk's stories: the fact that man is sometimes able to overcome obstacles, to translate his intentions successfully into actions, to control his environment. Thus the universe is not merely a great mechanism for cranking out catastrophes. At the same time, the assignment of this celebration of comedy to the Knight should serve as a warning because, although the Knight cultivates an optimistic outlook, his own tale suggests that his experience has often been closer to the sort depicted in the temples of his "noble theatre" (I.1885). Indeed it is probably the grimness of his actuality that motivates his determined optimism.[30] The danger of his triumphal comic literature, then, lies in the encouragement it offers to seek mere escape from the heterogeneous sufferings of actual life.[31]

This danger is brought more emphatically to our attention by

30. Fry, 265–266, summarizes the variety of motives that have been found for the Knight's interruption—boredom, naive literary taste, dissatisfaction with the Monk's philosophy—and suggests that the Knight sees in the tale, and reacts to, a prediction of his own fall.

31. Contrast the Knight's description of the fortunate who "abideth in prosperitee" with Reason's Boethian observation, at the end of the tragical narratives in Jean de Meun's *Roman,* that even the happy are never entirely so. Helen Corsa, *Chaucer: Poet of Mirth and Morality* (Notre Dame: University of Notre Dame Press, 1964), pp. 97–98 and 210, attributes the Knight's definition of comedy to Chaucer, while Kaske, "Interruption," 267, thinks the Knight's projected comedy and his tale represent the two possibilities "for a true literary presentation of Boethian fortune as it affects good men."

the Host's characteristically blunt expansion on the Knight's remarks: "Pardee, no remedie / It is for to biwaille ne compleyne / That that is doon, and als it is a peyne, / As ye han seyd, to heere of hevynesse" (2784–2787). In part the Host makes explicit, in commonsensical terms, Chaucer's own critique of the didactic deficiency of a literature that can only complain. Yet we notice that the Host's position is more extreme than the Knight's; the Knight will tolerate a "litel hevynesse" (2769), but the Host will have none. His apparent recommendation that we totally suppress reports of the darker realities of life is probably intended to provoke us into seeing that our rejection of the Monk's "tragedyes" could be too absolute.[32] For the Harry Baileys of the world, "tragedye" could serve, as Robert Heilman says of the literature of disaster in general, as "a rebuke to thoughtless security in the world, [and] to dreams of invulnerability . . . [as] a reminder of limits and liabilities . . . [of] the physical forces . . . that forever elude our wiliest efforts to bend them permanently to our will . . . [and of] the irreducible remnant of irrationality" in the universe.[33] In other words, Chaucer's *Monk's Tale* is meant to serve the same purpose as Philosophy's citation of the old tragic definition in the *Consolation*. Placing the definition in the mouth of a putative Fortune whom she impersonates, and temporarily adopting Fortune's interpretation of man's life, Philosophy teaches Boethius that change and loss are the common and inescapable experiences of all men. The Monk's "tragedyes," like the old definition to which they are indebted, represent a fundamentally erroneous interpretation of human experience from which Chaucer, like Philosophy, extracts a part of the truth.

32. Alan Gaylord, "Sentence and Solaas in Fragment VII of the *Canterbury Tales:* Harry Bailey as Horseback Editor," *PMLA,* 82 (1967), 31–33.
33. Robert Heilman, *Tragedy and Melodrama: Versions of Experience* (Seattle: University of Washington Press, 1968), p. 35.

Obviously, though, error has its limits as a didactic device. It is unlikely, for example, that the Knight will learn anything from the "tragedyes," if his definition of comedy can be taken as revealing the way he prefers to structure experience, for here again the crucial change is a purely external one; again a single act is selected as the basis for rendering a universal judgment. Such a comedian, no less than the Monkish tragedian, would seek to fix the significance of a life in a single moment and thus implicitly deny the continuing reality and responsibility of freedom. The justice, too, of this comic world would prove to be as specious as the Monk's tragic justice. If the turn of Fortune's wheel were to be emphasized, we would be treated to the spectacle of the elevation of the worthy and the unworthy alike. If the comic plot were to be rationalized as a demonstration of virtue rewarded, we can be fairly sure that just as the Monk's pride was no vice, so the comedian's virtue would turn out to be little more than skillful opportunism. The Knight's comedy and the Monk's tragedy are almost mirror images of each other, and the "tragedyes" cannot challenge errors in which they themselves participate.[34]

The care that Chaucer has clearly taken to evaluate "tragedye" inevitably raises two final questions: did Chaucer think it possible to construct a philosophically and theologically sound tragedy, and if so, what would such a genuine Chaucerian tragedy be like? The answer to the first question is, I think, clearly "yes." Considering the slighter evidence first, we may note that if the Monk's stories are taken to imply a rejection of all possible tragedies, the Knight's definition must be read as implying a rejection of all possible comedies, a most unlikely outcome. But Chaucer has also incorporated into the Monk's

---

34. Heilman, pp. 82–87, remarks that the drama of disaster and the drama of triumph "are not different genres at all, but simply alternative forms of melodrama in which the ways of formulating experience are fundamentally the same."

performance a more direct hint that the Monk's stories had potential meanings that the Monk neglected to develop, for the Monk made his gravest error at the very beginning when he decided to present his stories not in chronological order but in random succession (1984–1990). With his characters thus wrenched out of their settings and their actions wrenched out of their situational contexts, it became all too easy to imprison their experiences in a formula—and all but impossible to study what must be the center of mature tragedy and comedy, the reality and mystery of human choice.

The trouble cannot be remedied, however, merely by elaborating the Monk's narratives in more leisurely and more circumstantial detail, as is sometimes suggested, particulary in comparisons of the *Monk's Tale* with *Troilus and Criseyde*.[35] Rather Chaucer's critique of the structure of "tragedye" both shows that genuine tragedy must have a different structure and indicates, by inversion, what that structure must be. Genuine Chaucerian tragedy would treat principally the deeds of men, not of Fortune; would focus on inner spiritual change rather than on outer material change; would represent man, not as now the victim of his own freedom, now the plaything of Fortune, but as always simultaneously fated and free; would explore seriously the interplay of character and action instead of having recourse to a semimagical tragic flaw; and finally, instead of relying on a formula to provide a priori evaluations, would itself confront the task and agony of judgment. Since we cannot date with certainty the original composition and the possible revisions of the *Monk's Tale*,[36] we cannot know whether it represents for Chaucer in part

35. E.g., S. S. Hussey's suggestion in "The Difficult Fifth Book of *Troilus and Criseyde*," *Modern Language Review,* 67 (1972), 728, that Chaucer refined *de casibus* tragedy in the *Troilus* by showing Troilus' descent from Fortune's wheel in detail.

36. On the date of the *Monk's Tale,* see F. N. Robinson's Explanatory Note, p. 746. Chaucer's careful rephrasing of the tragic definition may indicate that that part of the *Tale* was written or rewritten after his *Boece.*

a ground-clearing exercise preparatory to the composition of *Troilus* or in part a retrospective exercise in which he rehearses what he learned in writing *Troilus*. But in either case, as Chaucer's most sharply focused critique of *de casibus* tragedy, the *Monk's Tale* provides the modern reader with a uniquely useful prolegomenon to the reading of *Troilus and Criseyde*.

4

"Litel myn tragedye": The Narrator of *Troilus and Criseyde*

The kind of plot that Chaucer finally chose as the vehicle for the elaboration of his own concept of tragedy is very different from the sort cited by Boethius, prescribed by the theorists, and elaborated by Jean de Meun, Boccaccio, and Chaucer himself in his *Monk's Tale*. The "matere" of *Troilus and Criseyde* is not the rise and fall of a great prince, but love. It is an essential part of Chaucer's accomplishment to have brought love and tragedy together. Perhaps the combination, and the choice of the story of Troilus and Criseyde in particular, was sparked by the quasi-tragic rhetoric, in the *de casibus* mode, at the end of Boccaccio's *Il Filostrato* (1335?). There the narrator attributes Diomede's success and Troilo's sorrow to the movements of Fortune (8. st. 25) and exclaims at the miserable end to which Troilo and his royal promise have come (st. 28). The hint is slight, but Chaucer may have seized upon it just as he seized upon Boccaccio's inconsequential use of Adam's fall in the *De Casibus*. Moreover, he may already have been thinking of the relationship of love and tragedy as problematical. In the *Consolation of Philosophy* the prisoner's depiction of a world governed by Fortune is confronted by Philosophy's depiction of a world governed ultimately by love, but in such a way as seemingly to eliminate the possibility of any meaningful tragedy from this world of love. Then, too, for Boethius, writing six hundred years before the birth of modern European literature, sexual love was little more than lust ("corporis voluptatibus" ["delyces of body"], 3. pr. vii. 1; 1) and deserving of less attention than the desire for fame in his antitragic revaluation of earthly goods. Jean de Meun's *Roman de la Rose* does place the traditional materials of tragical story within the context of an extensive study of love's varieties. Jean recommends friendship as a love aligned with Nature and Reason, but he will not admit romantic love to be anything other than Boethius' lust now grown more dangerous by the accretion of elaborate fantasies concerning its preeminence among all human experiences. It can easily be dismissed as a gift of Fortune whose loss cannot, in Boethian terms, be tragic. Thus the suggestion for an integrated treatment of the tragic tradition with modern conceptions of love lay in at least two of Chaucer's principal sources.

Chaucer's decision to treat tragically the love story of Troilus and Criseyde could not have been only programmatic, though—a response to issues posed, perhaps over a long period of time, in his reading. His decision, it seems to me, must also have been based on an intuitive grasp of the tragical potential of the story itself, an original insight not found in Boccaccio's version or in earlier treatments by Benoit de Sainte-Maure and Guido delle Colonne. But the progressive clarification of this intuition would have had to proceed hand in hand with the development of a new concept of tragedy. Chaucer could not merely discover in or impose upon this new material the familiar *de casibus* structure of meaning, for the traditional concept of tragedy had already been discredited for him by Boethius. He had to shape a new tragic structure as he attempted to draw out the tragic potential in his story. The narrator of *Troilus and Criseyde* may well have been born partly out of the complexity of this creative struggle. Like Chaucer, the narrator is both love poet and tragedian; he perceives, indistinctly, the germ of authentic tragedy in his "matere"; and he is obstructed in his search for tragic meaning by the traditional concept. Unlike Chaucer, however, the narrator is unaware of the long-standing problem in integrating love and tragedy; he never directly questions the traditional concept of tragedy; and consequently, he never achieves either a fully unified interpretation of his material or a full reconciliation of his two potentially conflicting roles. In the narrator Chaucer may have preserved a version of some early stage of his own development as love poet and tragedian, a stage close to the literary experience of his medieval audience. Thus through the narrator Chaucer engages his audience's conventional ideas of love and tragedy while, through his own manipulations of the narrator, he draws his audience into a Boethian transformation of images.[1]

The recognition that the narrator has in some sense a double relationship to his material is almost twenty years old. E. T. Donaldson offered one formula for that relationship when he described the narrator as both an "historian whose knowledge of the story is wholly book-derived" and as "an invisible yet omnipresent participant in the action."[2] In the first role the narrator deals with "incontrovertible fact," and in the latter with "equally incontrovertible emotional experience." Yet it proved difficult for Donaldson to uphold consistently the supposed equality of emotional experience, as for example when he speaks of the historian as one who "knows the truth." The truth comes to be equated with the version of events recorded in the old books and confounded with what I would distinguish as the narrator's tragic interpretation of those events. As a result when the narrator questions the truthfulness of the old books (4.19–21), he is said to have become too "emotionally involved" with his story,

1. Cf. Theodore A. Stroud, "Boethius' Influence on Chaucer's *Troilus*," *Modern Philology*, 49 (1951–1952), rpt. in *Chau. Crit. II*, pp. 126–128; John Steadman, *Disembodied Laughter: Troilus and the Apotheosis Tradition* (Berkeley: University of California Press, 1972), pp. 88–111; and Paul Ruggiers, "Notes toward a Theory of Tragedy in Chaucer," *Chaucer Review*, 8 (1973), 93.

2. *Chaucer's Poetry: An Anthology for the Modern Reader* (New York: Ronald Press, 1958), pp. 966–967; and cf. his "The Ending of Chaucer's *Troilus*," *Early English and Norse Studies: Presented to Hugh Smith in Honour of His Sixtieth Birthday*, eds. Arthur Brown and Peter Foote (London: Methuen, 1963), pp. 33–35.

and the value of participation as opposed to book learning almost evaporates. It is partly because of this difficulty in the reader's preserving a real duality of perspective that I prefer to distinguish instead between the *de casibus* tragedian and the poet of love. These are titles, and corresponding functions, that the narrator chooses for himself when he outlines Troilus' career on the model of *de casibus* story (1.1–5), refers to his book as a "trage-dye," (5.1786), and describes himself as the servant of the servants of love (1.15) and as the "clerk" of Venus (3.40–41). Both are literary roles involving specific conventions for the treatment of character and event. Each dictates to the narrator *a way of looking at* his material and with this understanding we will be less likely, I think, to confuse either perspective with the simple truth.

The chief purpose of Chaucer's strategy in giving the narrator two sets of conventions to work with is precisely to focus attention on the literary instruments themselves. The narrator's personal limitations, so often described and sometimes exaggerated by critics, intersect with the limitations of these instruments. The conventions of love and tragedy that he has inherited do not permit him to represent the whole truth of events, for each type of story selects for treatment only a small part of the whole reality of any event but treats that small part as if it were the whole. This exclusiveness makes it difficult for the artist to make simultaneous use of the two sets of conventions. And indeed, the narrator tends to use them serially rather than simultaneously. Although he invokes *de casibus* theory briefly in his opening description of Troilus' career, Books 1 through 3 are governed essentially by the conventions of love story. Books 4 and 5, on the other hand, are governed by the conventions of *de casibus* tragedy, as signaled by the invocation of the emblem of Fortune's wheel (4.1–11).

This juxtaposition of conventions reveals the fallibility of both. The *de casibus* world—dealing as it does with power, riches, and fame—is always a public world and, by asserting that reality, it reveals the limited scope of that private sphere lovers seek to create and dwell in. Moreover, the *de casibus* perspective asserts the reality of fate, of external forces beyond the lovers' control; the lovers may complain of the power exercised over them by the God of Love, but it is nothing compared with the force exercised by fathers, social conventions, parliaments, and wars. (We may admit these corrective values in *de casibus* tragedy purely as a literature of disaster without withdrawing our objections to it as genuine tragedy.) In the mutual correction of the two genres, the critique of *de casibus* values offered by the love story seems to me to be the much more devastating one, however. For instance, the narrator's conventions of love story explore, often minutely, interior life and change while the *de casibus* story tends to focus exclusively on external event and change. Also, the fundamental tenet of *de casibus* tragedy, that man lives in an alien universe, is challenged by the lovers' claim that love puts them in contact with a power larger than themselves in a universe aligned with their own natures. Although the conventions of love are by no means immune from Chaucer's implied criticisms in Books 1 through 3, still, especially as improved upon by the narrator, they confer a complexity and richness upon the characters and the plot that cannot be undone and that exposes the relative poverty of the *de casibus* conception so belatedly reintroduced in Book 4.

Ultimately, there emerges from the narrator's struggle with these two sets of conventions something transcending both: a profound treatment of human love, which is both tragic in a new sense and, unexpectedly, comic as well. To arrive at this conclusion, though, it is necessary to retrace the sequence in which the narrator uses these conventions in his creative storytelling. Following the structure of Chaucer's poem, we must approach an evaluation of the narrator's performance as tragedian through a prior consideration of his performance as poet of love.

One of the most important facts about the narrator's role as poet of love is that it develops. At the beginning of his work, as reflected in the prologue to Book 1 (1–56), the narrator has only a superficial idea of what the role will require of him. Although he speaks at length about his compassion for lovers and his willingness to serve them, he seems really to be in flight from love itself. I refer not just to the narrator's statement of his "unliklynesse" for love but to the overwhelming emphasis in the passage on the pain and unhappiness of love. Consequently, the god of love, a rather faint presence here from whom the narrator seems glad to keep his distance, appears as essentially a fearful figure. Indeed, later, as the narrator describes how the fire of love burns Troilus, he expresses the hope that he may be spared such an experience (1.435–436). Perhaps, like the narrator of *The Parliament of Fowls* (8–14), he is overimpressed by love's sufferings, as he has read about them in books, because he cannot balance these accounts with any firsthand experience of love's rewards. Yet the narrator recognizes, though dimly, that it is necessary to be related to love in some way in order to advance one's soul (47–49). So his alliance with the servants of love (15) seems to be partially a substitute for a relationship with the fearful lord himself. Furthermore, he seems to see these servants as essentially love's victims and dedicates himself to write only of their woes and not their joys (10–11, 49). But, like the narrator of *The Book of the Duchess,* he initially thinks it possible to console those in distress without sharing their pain; paradoxically, even in his association with lovers' woes, he seems both to expect and to seek immunity from personal suffering. As John Lawlor has remarked, the narrator's "sory chere" for a "sorwful tale" (12–14) has all the remoteness of a merely decorous response.[3] The narrator's brotherhood with all lovers is still for him only a figure of speech—"*As though* I were hire owne brother dere" (51; italics mine)—and not a felt reality.

3. John Lawlor, *Chaucer* (New York: Harper and Row, 1969), pp. 55–57.

Initially the narrator's credentials as a poet of love are ambiguous at best; in fact, those credentials are yet to be earned, and they can be earned only through the experience of telling his story. The prologues to Books 2 and 3 serve to clarify what those credentials are and are not. In Book 2 the narrator may seem at first only to further disqualify himself as a poet of love. What could be more inappropriate than to "speeke of love unfelyngly" (19). Yet the narrator can do no better because he has no more experience of love than the blind man has of color (20–21); he lays claim only to a talent for translating Latin. Moreover, he seems to continue his flight from love, as he seeks to avoid not only pain but responsibility: aesthetic responsibility for lame words and false hues but also, we may suspect, moral responsibility for judging conduct. But although the narrator's assertion that "In sondry londes, sondry ben usages" (28) in love may seem at first to be just another strategy of excuse, it is here, I believe, that we may begin to discern one of the narrator's positive qualifications. Precisely because he is not an active lover, the narrator feels no allegiance to any particular customs of courtship, either those of his characters or those of his contemporaries. With something like the breadth and disinterestedness of vision appropriate to Clio, Muse of history and patroness of his second book, the narrator recognizes the essential relativity of social mores and takes an important step toward defining himself not merely as a poet of courtly love but as a poet of Love. Not the courtly road to Rome, but Rome itself is his true subject (36–37). Ultimately, the narrator will give his allegiance not to his contemporaries who suffer in love, to his characters, to either's customs in love, nor even to his old books, but to something larger than these. Meanwhile it is important to see how absolutely and how rightly the narrator rules out here any prospect of a change in his own "unliklynesse" for romantic love. Rather the stature he achieves as poet of love will come partly in spite of, partly because of, this very "unliklynesse."

In the Prologue to Book 3 the narrator who in Book 1 anticipated speaking only of the woe in love now prays to Venus and

Calliope to help him describe the joy in love. It may be argued that this change in orientation is simply an example of the narrator's characteristic tendency to vacillate between the long and short view of his plot. In Book 1 the narrator had clearly in mind Troilus' later unhappiness in love, while here he thinks only of Troilus' imminent but short-lived happiness. Considered from the point of view of the narrator's development as love poet, however, Book 3 clearly represents the profounder view. In Book 1 the narrator addressed lovers directly but spoke of the fearful god of love only in the third person. Now he enters into a new relationship with love as he addresses it directly, reverentially, and at length in its manifestation as Venus (here not only the goddess of sexual attraction but also the principle of universal Platonic unity). Love is now perceived as a force operating on several levels, from the cosmic to the superhuman, or mythological, to the human.[4] As the narrator's concept of love changes, so does his self-concept. He now describes himself not as the servant of the servants of Love (1.15) but as the "clerk" of Venus (3.40–41). Actually, in suggesting a quasi-priestly function, the narrator's new self-description expresses a meaning latent in the earlier one, which is itself an echo of the papal title "servus servorum Dei." The narrator now defines a relationship for himself not just to lovers but to love itself. Implicitly, he dedicates himself not merely to serve others on terms they may set, but to instruct them also, and to offer instruction not only in the "usages" of love but in its moral and philosophical dimensions.[5]

4. Robert Jordan, *Chaucer and the Shape of Creation* (Cambridge, Mass.: Harvard University Press, 1967), pp. 84–85, has analyzed this descending structure in the elements of the narrator's eulogy of Venus.

5. As Root notes, p. 466, lines 39–49 are original with Chaucer. Cf. *The House of Fame*, 1487, where Chaucer describes Ovid as "Venus clerk" and see "The Clerk of Venus: Chaucer and Medieval Romance" in *The Learned and the Lewed: Studies in Chaucer and Medieval Literature*, ed. Larry D. Benson (Cambridge, Mass.: Harvard University Press, 1974), pp. 31–43, where R. T. Lenaghan describes the double authority of the clerk as love poet and moralist.

In addition, the narrator opens himself to change as he prays to Venus, "in my naked herte sentement / Inhielde" (43–44). The nakedness of his heart is not, I think, just another reference to his personal inexperience but a striking metaphor for his voluntary exposure of himself to a new influence. Nor is the "sentement" he now prays for merely equivalent to that feeling in love which springs from experience (cf. 2.19); it is, rather, a complex intellectual as well as emotional insight proportionate to his more profound conception of love. It is important to recognize that one may acquire "sentement" in this second sense without ever acquiring it in its more mundane first sense. Indeed romantic love may prove an obstacle to this profounder "sentement" since it can be so immediately and totally absorbing in its own right.[6] Thus the need for just such priestly poets of love as the narrator who can mediate between realities, who can remind lovers that their experience is part of a larger drama of cosmic import. The narrator begins his work as an outsider, but he does not remain one; he discovers a kind of love that embraces all men and within which he has a specific and exalted role to play.

A narrator who goes through a process of development is necessarily a fallible narrator; a capacity for change is also, from one point of view, a capacity for imperfection. Nor does this narrator, in spite of progress, ever achieve a state of finished perfection. As a consequence his performance, as both historian of love (Book 2) and clerk of love (Book 3), imposes on the audience the task of correcting and completing his work.[7] As the narrator

6. At the height of his happiness, Troilus understandably believes romantic experience to be essential to all; but the narrator breaks in to modify his hero's view: "For soth to seyn, *he* lost held *every* wyght / But if he were in loves heigh servise, / *I* mene folk that oughte it ben of right" (3.1793–1795; italics mine).

7. For excellent general discussions of the role of the audience in *Troilus*, see Robert O. Payne, *The Key of Remembrance: A Study of Chaucer's Poetics* (New Haven: Yale University Press, 1963), pp. 227 ff., and Dieter Mehl, "The Audience of Chaucer's *Troilus and Criseyde*," in *Chaucer and Middle English Studies in Honour of Rossell Hope Robbins*, ed. Beryl Rowland (London: Allen & Unwin, 1974), pp. 173–189.

himself says with respect to his language, the audience should strive both to "maken diminucioun" and "tencresce" his depiction of love (3.1408–1413). Modern readers of Chaucer have been quick to respond to the need for "diminishing" the love the narrator portrays by conducting an ethical critique of courtly customs, the need for which the narrator either avoids or does not understand.

As we have already seen, his narrative takes us behind the scenes of such courtly poses as the lover's professed humility and allows us to watch Troilus laughing as he describes his own unworthiness in a love letter to Criseyde (2.1077–1078). It also allows issues on which courtly poetry is usually silent, issues such as the moral standing of the friend or go-between, to come to the surface for discussion (3.246–287). Since the narrator does not respond to these ambiguities, the work of judgment passes to the audience. But there is little need to expand on this theme; readers of Chaucer have embraced this task all too fervently, partly perhaps because of the pleasure of having discovered it for themselves, partly because of the sense of superiority to the narrator that it confers on them. Yet since, as we have seen, the narrator is not committed to the courtly "usages," it is certainly a mistake to concentrate heavily or exclusively on this task as though it could reveal or exhaust all the poems' implications. At least the reader's critique of courtly customs ought to be presented as exemplary, that is, as a model of the critique that might be made of any "usage" in love. Certainly Chaucer and his audience were humorously aware that courtly conventions were not really indigenous to ancient Troy but rather to their own recent Christian-European past.[8] And even if those conventions already seemed a bit archaic in the late fourteenth century, they were still uncomfortably familiar enough to make Chaucer's real point: that all "usages" in love tend to be endemically tainted

8. Cf. Donald R. Howard, *The Three Temptations: Medieval Man in Search of the World* (Princeton: Princeton University Press, 1966), pp. 115–118.

with a narcissism antithetical to genuine love and with the faults it brings in its train—deception, self-deception, exploitation, and even cruelty.

It is unfortunate that the "diminishing" of courtly customs has so much distracted Chaucer's audience from their other task of "increasing" the depiction of love by supplying feeling. This need is not less real or important simply because the narrator has identified it. The very opening lines of Book 2 dramatize the narrator's lack of feeling as he describes Troilus' sorrow in tired Petrarchan conceits and then flatly explicates his own metaphors: "This see clepe I the tempestous matere / Of desespoir that Troilus was inne" (5–6). The proper correction of this passage requires two responses. On the one hand, its overt artificiality ought to encourage us, if we have not done so already, to puncture Troilus' own exaggerated stylization of his woe in Book 1. The courtly lover's protestation that he is dying of love cannot, of course, be taken at face value. On the other hand, Troilus is going through an experience whose power to seize, shake, nearly paralyze, and sometimes obsess, sometimes transform, anyone who has ever fallen in love can vouch for. This is a dimension of the story that the narrator clearly does not and cannot feel, and therefore one that the audience must augment. Indeed, since the audience has already had many opportunities in Book 1 to perceive and expose Troilus' artificially worked up emotions, and since Chaucer has placed this Petrarchan passage in juxtaposition with the narrator's description of his personal limitation, I suspect that Chaucer's chief concern at this point is to emphasize the genuine need for the second response: to supply the feeling that is missing in the narrator's depiction of love.

To do this would require drawing on both experience and imagination, allowing them alternately to be guided by the text and to complete the text. Such participation, however, would bring us dangerously close to being on an equal footing with the narrator and his characters. Many readers have preferred instead to enjoy a sense of superiority, to exercise control by analyzing the ironies and deficiencies of human love. But excessive "diminishing" of the narrator's concept and language of love diminishes us, too, by denying some of what we already know about love and by aborting the opportunity the poem offers to contemplate love in an act that fully engages both the emotions and the intellect.

The claims that the narrator as clerk of Venus makes for the spiritual significance of love also require "diminishing" and "increasing." These claims are advanced by the religious and theological language that both the narrator and his characters use so heavily in describing human love. Troilus' falling in love, for example, is characterized as a conversion, and he is said to vacillate between despair and hope; Criseyde is portrayed as a source of grace and as having life-saving and life-restoring powers; and the lovers' union is described as bliss or heaven. Clearly such language poses the danger of idolatry: the possibility that an imperfect human good might be mistaken for a perfect divine good, that man's experience of love in this world might become its own end instead of a means directing man to his true end. And since the narrator does not advert to this danger in courtly usage, anymore than he responds to its ethical ambiguities, the reader must supply the critique. That critique, however, should include an analysis not only of how such idolatry misrepresents divine love but also of how it defaces human love.

Troilus' progress in love suggests that the danger of idolatry is greatest when the love is most narcissistic.[9] As his first Petrarchan song of love suggests, Troilus is at first fascinated by love as a wholly individualistic and interior experience. It is also at this stage, however, that Troilus thinks of Criseyde as a goddess (1.425–427), truly an idol of the mind; she is inappropriately venerated and reduced to a mere image subserving Troilus' fantasy life. But Troilus' hymn to Venus and Cupid on the night

9. See Chap. 5 for a detailed analysis.

of the consummation shows both a new mutuality in his love for Criseyde and a theological redefinition of himself as the human subject, not of a lady, but of gods who dispense grace beyond his deserts (3.1254ff.). Finally, in his climactic hymn to love, his conception of love becomes cosmic, a force that embraces Criseyde, himself, other lovers, and all creation (3.1744–1771). Thus Troilus' development suggests that the tendency to idolatry is overcome, if at all, at an early stage—at the same time that the danger of narcissistic self-absorption is passed. Genuinely mutual human love is naturally outward flowing: it embraces the beloved first and then the cosmos. This is not idolatry but, even in a pagan like Troilus, a form of worship.[10] Chaucer's poem, then, does criticize idolatry in love although its chief target is not Troilus, who eventually passes the test and, as a pagan without revelation, could never be culpable in the same way as a Christian anyway.[11] We must continually recall that Chaucer's anachronistic attribution of courtly "usages" to ancient Trojans always really points the finger at his contemporary audience. It was Christian Europe that developed the courtly theology of love. Troilus might distort his own potential for human love by narcissistic self-absorption, but only a Christian could in addition be guilty of blasphemy and heresy.

Yet just as the pagan can never err so seriously as the Christian, neither can he ever know the truth of love so completely as the Christian. Liable to more grievous sin, the narrator's Christian audience is also in a position "tencresce" his claims for the spiritual potential of love beyond anything his pagan characters could suspect. Actually the narrator and his hero arrive at essentially the same conception of love here in Book 3, as the narrator's hymn to Venus and Troilus' hymn—both adapted from the same Boethian metrum (2. met. viii)—suggest. This

10. As Theodore Stroud says in "Boethius' Influence," *Chau. Crit. II*, p. 130: "How could [Troilus] be more philosophical—in Troy?"
11. See Chap. 5, n10 for my discussion of Troilus' address to Criseyde's house (5.540–553), a passage that some critics regard as proof of the persistently idolatrous nature of Troilus' love.

conception is not wrong, but it is incomplete for, under the Christian dispensation, love is not only a force, but a Person; in addition to being a principle of harmony in this world, love is the way to and the essence of eternal life in a transcendent world. As a pagan, Troilus knows no more and no better than his Platonic hymn. The Christian narrator does know better but, because of his characteristic inability to apply more than one perspective at a time, and perhaps because of his intention to be faithful to "olde [*pagan*] clerkes speche / In poetrie" (5.1854–1855), he fails to articulate here the reconciliation of Christian truth with Platonic wisdom. He remembers to invoke the love of Christ only after his use of *de casibus* conventions has interfered, as we shall see, to obscure the possibility of such a reconciliation. Meanwhile the task falls on the audience and it is a very difficult one, because it is a delicate matter to "increase" the spiritual claims of human love without falling, or seeming to fall, into that very idolatry we are also called upon to "diminish." Chaucer dramatizes the complexity of the task, I believe, in the two responses to Troilus and Criseyde's nights of love that he assigns to the narrator in Book 3.

On the first night of love the emphasis of the narrator's account falls understandably on the ecstasy of sexual union. The narrator revives the theme of his own romantic inexperience, saying he cannot describe the least of the lovers' joys; and he appeals to those in his audience who have themselves been "at the feste" to judge their happiness (1310–1313). He then bursts into a personal response to the scene that must be counted as one of the poem's most surprising moments:

> O blisful nyght, of hem so longe isought,
> How blithe unto hem bothe two thow weere!
> Why ne hadde I swich oon with my soule ybought,
> Ye, or the leeste joie that was there? [1317–1320]

The narrator who initially fled from the god of love is so moved by his story that he now experiences a very poignant sense of the good he has missed. Perhaps it is just because he has missed it that he overvalues it here, endowing it with all the magic that imagination coupled with inexperience can conjure up. Sexual fulfillment appears as an absolute good, an end in itself to be pursued even to the possible detriment of the soul's true good. This is the narrator's own personal version of the temptation to idolatry and it serves as a reminder to the audience of the necessity to "diminish" the depiction of love. If the narrator were to pursue actual sexual experience, he would be deflected from his true quasi-priestly role of identifying and interpreting for others the transcendent implications of love. The temptation seems to be fleeting, however, and in the narrator's reaction to the lovers' second night of love we have, I believe, one of his moments of supreme accomplishment as priest of love and the reader's climactic experience of "increasing" the poem's depiction of love.[12]

It is a significant fact often overlooked that Book 3 does contain accounts of two nights of love. The first night, which is for Pandarus the goal he has long sought (3.1582), is not the whole story for the lovers. The account of the second night is included to help define their love as embracing more than sexual passion; even on the merely human level, it suggests that sex is not an end in itself but a means for building up the mutuality of true affection:

> And bothe, ywys, they hadde, and so they wende,
> As muche joie as herte may comprende.
>
> This is no litel thyng of for to seye;
> This passeth every wit for to devyse;
> For eche of hem gan otheres lust obeye. [1686–1690]

---

12. As Charles A. Owen, Jr. points out, the narrator's request to the audience "tencresce or maken diminucioun / Of my langage" originally followed immediately on the narrator's temptation to sell his soul (i.e., in Root's edition, after stanza 189). Later Chaucer moved it to the end of his account of the lovers' first night (after stanza 200), so that it now stands in a somewhat more independent position between a passage that requires "diminishing" (1317–1320) and a passage (1691–1694) that requires "increasing." See Owen's "Minor Changes in Chaucer's *Troilus and Criseyde*" in *Chaucer and Middle English Studies,* pp. 314–318.

In response the narrator this time implicitly compares himself, not with those who have been "at the feste," but with other clerks:

> Felicite, which that thise clerkes wise
> Comenden so, ne may nat here suffise.
> This joie may nat writen be with inke;
> This passeth al that herte may bythynke. [1691–1694]

The narrator struggles to comprehend the highest reaches of human love and finds the guidance provided by books wanting; he discovers a gap between the experience of his characters and the definitions of philosophers. Tutored by his own experience as storyteller, he wisely recognizes a dimension of love that lies beyond the powers of human description.

But if the "felicite" abstractly defined by clerks will not suffice to render the love of Troilus and Criseyde, it will certainly not suffice to describe, as it was intended to, the love of the soul and its Creator. This passage, unlike the narrator's response to the first night of love, does not so much set up an opposition between human love and soul's good as it opens the epistemological question of how limited human beings are to come to understand the nature of their own transcendent good. The narrator's principal contribution is the suggestion that "felicite," in addition to being an idea, something that can be defined by clerks and recorded in ink, is always and ultimately an experience. It is for this very reason—though the narrator does not make this connection—that human love can give men and women a foretaste of divine love. The actual experience of the "feste" of romantic love is neither indispensable nor in itself sufficient, however. What is necessary is a profound contemplation of the experience of human love, such as the quasi-priestly narrator achieves here and helps his readers to achieve. Inspired by the human excellence of Troilus and Criseyde's love and by the narrator's struggle to comprehend it, the reader who would rightly "increase" the depiction of love will rise to a contemplation of that ultimate "felicite" in which, except by such analogies and simulacra, all persons must, in this life, be inexperienced.[13]

Through the work of "increasing" and "diminishing" the narrator's depiction of love, then, the audience should discover both the excellences of human and divine love, and their narcissistic and idolatrous distortions. These excellences and distortions may seemingly threaten to cancel each other out, however. The most striking example of this threat is the juxtaposition of the narrator's prayer to Venus with the scene of the lovers' first meeting at Pandarus' house. The juxtaposition is forced by the narrator's unusual decision to divide the presentation of the scene between two books. The account at the end of Book 2 of Pandarus' elaborate shuffling of persons in and out of Troilus' room so as to assure, unbeknown to the others, a private interview between the lovers makes a strange preparation for the narrator's exalted tribute to Venus in the prologue to Book 3. And the descent is swift and extreme as we turn from the narrator's prayer for the transformation of his "naked herte" to his hero's rehearsal of the line he will use to ensnare the object of his infatuation (50–55). Yet as subsequent events reveal, it is this very infatuation, tainted at first by the lovers' mutual dependence on courtly "usages" and by the interventions of Pandarus, that comes to serve as an image of "felicite." This could not happen if love were, as in the classical pagan conception, merely a force with the power to compel man's participation. Actually, one of the profoundest insights of the courtly ideal is its recognition that even on the human level love also has the power, the "grace," to make man worthy of that participation.[14] Both the idea and the terminology are, of course, bor-

13. Cf. Anselm's *Monologion* 65, trans. Sidney Norton Deane, *St. Anselm: Basic Writings,* 2d ed. (La Salle, Ill.: Open Court Publishing Company, 1962), pp. 129–131: "[Being] is that ineffable, because it is incapable of description in words or by any other means; and, at the same time, an inference regarding it, which can be reached by the instruction of reason or in some other way, as it were in a riddle, is not therefore necessarily false."

14. The subject of worthiness is introduced by Troilus himself just

rowed from the Christian theology of divine love. It would be wrong, then, whether we are speaking of things divine or human, to estimate the potentialities of man's love by reference only to his necessarily deficient works. On the other hand, it would be presumptuous to rely wholly on the action of grace and absolve the lover of responsibility for his works. So just as the realities of grace and works do not finally contradict each other or cancel each other out, neither do the excellences and distortions of love. The reader's final vision of love must hold them all in delicate balance.[15] What could be further from the crude opposition of judgments on which the *de casibus* tragedy depends: an undeserved exaltation of worldly goods followed by a total rejection of them as worthless? The reader who has performed even a small part of the work of discrimination that the love story and its narrator have so far demanded has been wholly unfitted to behave as the *de casibus* conventions require.[16]

The audience's intricate education in love should produce not a sense of disdainful superiority to the narrator but a feeling of gratitude toward him, for it is the narrator's very imperfection that makes the audience's progress possible. Both the narrator's growth in his role as poet of love and his continuing limitations in that role help to guide the reader's responses. Moreover, the

---

prior to his first meeting with Criseyde when he asks Helen and Diomede to read a letter and decide "If swych a man was worthi to ben ded" (2.1699). The questions of who deserves to be loved and who deserves to die are similarly linked in the *Knight's Tale*.

15. For discussions of how Chaucer's narrative methods typically affirm multiple and seemingly contradictory positions, see Donaldson, "The Ending of Chaucer's *Troilus*," *passim*, and Peter Elbow, "Two Boethian Speeches in *Troilus and Criseyde* and Chaucerian Irony" in *Literary Criticism and Historical Understanding: Selected Papers from the English Institute*, comp. Phillip Damon (New York: Columbia University Press, 1967), pp. 85–107.

16. The work of "increasing" and "diminishing" the depiction of love provides a good example, I believe, of how, in Howard's words, "Chaucer's fragmented self-presentation [i.e., through his narrator-masks] leads us to grasp two truths at once—that evil lurks beneath good appearances, but that good lies beneath evil." See "Chaucer the Man," *PMLA*, 80 (1965), 343.

narrator's progress, if not as full as the reader's can be, is sufficiently real and extensive to provoke a wholly new critical question as we turn to Book 4. Whatever the narrator's tragic intentions when he began his work (1.1–5), why does he persist here in reimposing the *de casibus* scheme on a plot that he himself has now done so much to develop in an antithetical direction? My first answer is that the narrator is still responding to an initial and profoundly true insight into his materials—simply that this love story, in some sense, involves a great tragedy. Second, the narrator's new experience of love in the course of telling his story has undoubtedly strengthened in him certain sentiments closely allied to the tragic, particularly the poignancy of loss. His discovery of the joy of love can only have deepened his initially shallow appreciation of the agony of love: "By his contrarie is every thyng declared" (1.637). The *de casibus* formula is particularly well suited to express and bewail the experience of loss. If the narrator does not distinguish between such a literature of disaster and genuine tragedy, he is simply representative in this of medieval artists and readers. Indeed, most modern readers have been willing to follow the narrator in his extraordinary leap from the celebrations of love to the lamentations of *de casibus* tragedy. They grant him an unquestioned authority as tragedian that almost no one grants him as poet of love.

Yet the narrator's performance in this second role stands as much in need of correction as his performance in the first. In the *Monk's Tale,* the deficiencies of conventional *de casibus* theory were shown up by the Monk's very "success" in applying it rigidly to his materials. In *Troilus and Criseyde* the deficiencies appear because of the narrator's inability to fit already complexly elaborated materials to the theory. Contradictions multiply partly because of the narrator's humorous ineptitude as a storyteller, but also because of his sensitivity as the priest of love. Through the narrator's characteristic weaknesses and strengths, then, we come to see that the chief deficiency lies in the tragic theory itself. The *de casibus* form cannot give us an accurate and adequate account of this story's genuine tragedy because the form itself embodies a narrow and in some respects distorted vision of human experience. Thus, despite the narrator's continuing confidence in his tragic theory, the generic nature of the work becomes for the reader something to be defined only as the meaning of the tale itself unfolds.

The narrator's opening description of his work casts the story in the *de casibus* mold in an apparently simple statement qualified by its own inherent contradictions:

> The double sorwe of Troilus to tellen,
> That was the kyng Priamus sone of Troye,
> In lovynge how his aventures fellen
> Fro wo to wele, and after out of joie,
> My purpos is, or that I parte fro ye. [1.1–5]

Plainly, the shaping assumption here is the familiar one: that tragedy is the story of the fall from prosperity to wretchedness of a man of high degree. Yet we note the striking deviation that the "aventures" of this king's son have to do, not with material success of any sort, but with loving. Love is an anomaly as the subject of a *de casibus* tragedy. But I think Chaucer would have put it the other way around. *De casibus* tragedy, with its motives of power and possession, is the anomaly, a distortion of man's career in a Boethian universe governed ultimately by Love. Consequently, even on a mundane level, it must distort the figures of both lover and beloved. The rising action of this story can be fitted to the *de casibus* pattern only if we define Troilus' achievement narrowly and inaccurately as the conquest of Criseyde. In fact, though, Troilus has not only chosen a beloved and earned her love; he has also chosen, after some trial and error, a *way* of loving, and he has progressed through a number of increasingly profound *conceptions* of love. As the nature of these changes implies, his development is more complex than the *de casibus* hero's, because it is more inward; he has been changed emotionally, morally, and spiritually. Indeed the narrator concludes the action of Book 3 by dwelling on the transformation of Troilus (1800–1806). But if this description, partly couched as it is in courtly language, should seem suspect, the reader may have recourse to still weightier evidence: his own experience in "increasing" and "diminishing" the depiction of love, for the reader's experience and Troilus' overlap to some extent as the action requires both to plumb the meaning of love. Troilus, as a pagan, does not and cannot hope to attain to the full vision of love available to the medieval Christian audience. And yet Chaucer's readers, including his post-Christian readers, can know, with the certitude of personal experience, that what Troilus has achieved cannot be lost as material goods are lost; his "prosperite" in love cannot conceivably be reversed by the kind of fall characteristic of *de casibus* tragedy.

If the prosperity that Troilus achieves is more than the possession of Criseyde, Criseyde herself is more than a material good to be possessed. She comes to have a weight and a significance in the tale that the narrator's conventions have prepared him to grant only to his hero. As the narrator emphasizes, his tale concerns the King's son "in special"; the "matere" is "*his* joie," "*his* cares," "*his* werk": everything else is "collateral" (1.260–266; italics mine). Nevertheless, from the very beginning, the competition between the hero and the heroine for the narrator's and the audience's interest is an issue.[17] As the narrator attempts to clear a way to his "matere," he makes what might be considered several false starts, speaking first of the causes of the war, then of Calkas' treachery, Criseyde's danger, and finally the conduct of the war (1.57–147). It is Criseyde who receives the most significant development in this section and who thus makes a claim on the audience's sympathy, even before Troilus actually

17. The competition was reflected early in the varying titles given to the work (see Root's edition, xi) and is still reflected in criticism. See, e.g., Donaldson, *Chaucer's Poetry*, p. 973, and Ida Gordon, *The Double Sorrow of Troilus: A Study of Ambiguities in Troilus and Criseyde* (Oxford: Clarendon, 1970), p. 113.

appears on the scene. In the temple scene, too, the elaborate descriptions of Criseyde (169–182 and 281–294) compete with the depiction of Troilus for our attention. The decisive factor that challenges Troilus' theoretically exclusive status, however, is the complex development of Criseyde in Book 2.

The woman who is primarily an image in the mirror of Troilus' mind in Book 1 (365–366) assumes her own independent reality as a citizen of doomed Troy and as head of a household, but most significantly, as an experiencing subject of love. In the courtly tradition this last privilege is almost exclusively reserved to the male, for whom the female is merely the object of love. But Criseyde undergoes a psychomachy of love that is, in fact, of a profounder nature than Troilus' highly conventionalized sufferings in Book 1.[18] It may be that the narrator's ecstatic prayer to Venus (Prologue, Book 3), so different from his earlier unfeeling response (Prologue, Book 2), is inspired in part by the new depths conferred upon the love theme by the heroine's emergence as a center of experience equal with the hero. Once their joint importance has been sealed by the consummation scene, the narrator makes transitions between his two characters as between equals (3.1583, 5.687, 1100), although he had earlier treated accounts of Criseyde's actions as digressions from the story of his hero (2.687, 932). On the other hand, the narrator is characteristically unclear about his own deviations from convention and persists in opening and closing each book by focusing on his hero. Thus a growing tension develops, climaxing in Book 5, between the heroine's conventional role, which the narrator in large measure theoretically adheres to, and Criseyde's actual felt presence, which the narrator's practice has helped to create. Once we as readers register that presence, however, we are com-

18. In her survey of courtly literature in *Woman as Image in Medieval Literature* (New York: Columbia University Press, 1975), pp. 65–98, Joan M. Ferrante finds that in both lyrics and romances woman is typically treated, not in her own right, but as the representative of some reality within the man: the force of love working in him or his own ideal self. The works of Marie de France provide the single exception.

mitted to an interest in Criseyde, not merely as someone whom the hero loves and loses, but as someone who herself experiences both love and loss. Only the greatest violence to Criseyde's reality could reduce her to a representative of the unstable goods of *de casibus* tragedy. Her equality, which the narrator himself has helped to confer upon her, shatters the solipsistic focus on the hero of the "litel tragedye" the narrator still attempts to complete.

As this analysis suggests, we must deal throughout the work with two sets of contradictions. There are contradictions between the narrator's overt patternings and the traditional *de casibus* structure, although the narrator seems unaware of them; and there are further contradictions between the narrator's patternings and Chaucer's. This kind of dual contradiction is well exemplified by yet another anomaly in the narrator's opening description of his tragical purpose: the "double sorwe" of Troilus. The narrator seems unaware that this very multiplicity of sorrows squarely challenges the *de casibus* assumptions. *De casibus* tragedy has no way of recognizing sorrows that do not constitute falls, and by definition its fall must be a unique event. This exposure of how ill equipped the *de casibus* theory is to deal with the complexities of human life is at once so simple and so profound as to be almost hilarious. The narrator, however, is commonsensical and compassionate enough to know something of life's diverse sorrows, and at the same time inconsistent enough not to notice that his theory cannot accommodate such diversity. His story will have, he thinks, a fall and that seems sufficient to him to characterize it as a "tragedye." Actually, the narrator characterizes both of Troilus' sorrows as falls. He is merely being humorous, though, when he treats Troilus' falling in love as an instance of the downfall of the proud; he intends to be serious only when he treats Troilus' loss of Criseyde as an exemplum of arbitrary Fortune's turning wheel. But the narrator's initial joke gives Chaucer the opportunity to lay the foundation for his ultimate rejection of the narrator's later, sober, tragic interpretation. Chaucer realizes that it is impossible to make an adequate analysis of one of the interlinked *de casibus* plots in isolation from the other. A critique of the emblem of Fortune's turning wheel requires a complementary critique of the theme of the proud man's overthrow.

Chaucer rejects the tragic scheme that would have a totally alien force utterly overwhelm a man in punishment of some fault. Yet he acknowledges that something analogous does happen in human life. In his account of Troilus' falling in love, Chaucer gives us his own version of what happens when a man is directly acted upon by a force greater than himself, a conception substantially different from the *de casibus* scheme. First, the greater force does not punish, but corrects, essentially offering man an opportunity to learn. Second, the correction concerns not vicious sins but such faults as may arise from moral blindness of some sort. Most important of all, this force is not wholly alien to the man it acts upon and does not contradict his free will. Chaucer describes Troilus' falling in love in three stages, and in each successive stage Troilus' own free action becomes more important.

In the first stage Troilus is unconsciously rendered ready for love by the arrow of the God of Love (1.206–210). But the God of Love's power over Troilus arises from the fact that Love is part of Troilus' own nature, "the lawe of kynde" (238). His haughty will experiences contradiction, but by his own heart (226–231). In the second stage, Troilus, still "pleyinge" (267) and unaware of his new vulnerability, enters the temple and is affected by a specific stimulus and occasion for love: Criseyde.

> And of *hire look* in him ther gan to quyken
> So gret desir, and swiche affeccioun,
> That in his hertes botme gan to stiken
> Of hir *his fixe and depe impressioun.* [1.295–298; italics mine]

Here, as throughout this scene, Chaucer carefully balances the two effective agencies: Troilus' own active work of perception and response, as well as the power of Criseyde's beauty and personality. Then in the third stage, Troilus retires to the privacy of his chamber where he makes "a mirour of his mynde" (365) and contemplates his image of Criseyde. Now he accepts and confirms Love's unconscious and conscious actions on him by making two matching decisions:

> Thus took he purpos loves craft to suwe,
>
> . . .
>
> [And] with good hope he gan fully assente
> Criseyde for to love, and nought repente. [1.379, 391–392][19]

Finally, Troilus' falling in love is revealed to be not the expected punishment for pride but the beginning of a transformation that cures pride. Instead of humiliation he finds humility. The narrator emphasizes this result in an entire stanza devoted to describing the new Troilus purged, significantly, of pride, the supposed vice of the *de casibus* hero (3.1800–1806).

Chaucer's analysis of falling in love shows that the world is not as punitive as the *de casibus* plot of the proud man's fall represents it to be. Free will need not be a curse, a limited power of man's that only exposes him to the harsh judgment of a greater power. It can be a means of growth, of self-fulfillment, that is in harmony with the greater forces of the universe. Moreover, we see Chaucer's hand in the placement of the stanza describing the reformed Troilus. It occurs at the very end of Book 3 in close and significant juxtaposition with the opening of Book 4 where the narrator introduces his characterization of Troilus' second sorrow as a fall from Fortune's wheel. The credibility of this traditional emblem is undercut by Chaucer's pointed and timely reminder that the evolving rhythm of Troilus' career is one that the *de casibus* assumptions could not have predicted. Moreover, if the universe is not as rigid and punitive as the first *de casibus* plot of the overthrow of the proud would have it, neither is it as chaotic and arbitrary as the second *de casibus* plot of the

19. Troilus' experience follows the familiar and profound pattern of the Black Knight's dedication first to the craft of love and then to Good Fair White (*The Book of the Duchess*, 791 and 835–841).

arbitrary turn of the wheel would have it. Freedom is not all, nor is fate all. The two *de casibus* plots tend to swing wildly from one view to the other, in reaction against each other. But Chaucer keeps a constant and fine balance between freedom and fate, always affirming the one without denying the other. The *de casibus* tragedian who perceives freedom as a curse is all too likely to fling it off and portray man as Fortune's helpless and pathetic victim. The man who experiences freedom as a means of achieving inner-directed growth will also be willing to accept, even in adversities beyond his control, the responsibility that freedom entails.

One of the most striking characteristics of the traditional emblem with which Book 4 opens is the clarity and simplicity of the visual image it suggests:

> From Troilus [Fortune] gan hire brighte face
> Awey to wrythe, and took of hym non heede,
> But caste hym clene oute of his lady grace,
> And on hire whiel she sette up Diomede. [4.8–11]

But the use of such clear and simple imagery constitutes a retreat from the complexities of human experience. Only Fortune is portrayed as active; the human actors are reduced to pawns. It is true that in so far as Criseyde's exchange is something neither she nor Troilus could foresee nor wholly control, it appears under the aspect of fate. But Chaucer shows that it is also the complex result of free choices made by several persons: Hector, Calkas, the Greeks, the Trojan parliament, the Trojan people, and finally, Criseyde and Troilus themselves. Criseyde's infidelity is an event in which we feel the hand of fate even more heavily and yet must finally recognize even more soberly the action of free will.[20] Nor should we overlook the fact that Diomede, a man who never forgets himself (5.94–98), is not merely the passive beneficiary of Fortune. These free actions of the secondary figures are neglected because of a distorted emphasis on the fate of the

20. See Chap. 6.

hero alone. To Troilus' credit, however, he finally comes to see that Criseyde's infidelity is not only a loss for him, but in a more essential way, a loss for Criseyde—of honor, faith, name (5.1674–1687). Moreover, Troilus is not utterly crushed and left without "remedies," both good and bad. On the positive side, he freely continues to love Criseyde (5.1696–1698); on the negative side, he seeks revenge against Diomede. The narrator's use of Fortune's wheel contradicts the truth that human beings, even in adversity, are neither wholly without responsibility for what happens nor entirely without resources to meet the event.

It is only by denying both man's responsibility and his re-sources that the *de casibus* plot of the fall from Fortune's wheel can achieve that sensational and unified ending that is one of the chief characteristics of the genre. Perhaps the narrator is no-where more thoroughly thwarted than in his attempts to bring all the threads of his story together in such a unified ending. In Book 4, in an appeal to the three Fates and to Mars, he reveals his plan:

> This ilke ferthe book me helpeth fyne,
> So that the losse of lyf and love yfeere
> Of Troilus be fully shewed here. [4.26–28]

There are several equations implied here, none of which work out. As we know, the end of the fourth book does not coincide with the end of the work as a whole. Furthermore, Troilus' death does not coincide with the end of the story, and this is true in several senses. It does not decide the political fate of the community, for in that respect Hector's death is the crucial loss. Nor does Troilus' death provide an end, even in a superficial way, for the love story, because he dies at Achilles' hand, not Diomede's. More significantly, Troilus' love does not end with his life.[21] But most telling of all for our present purpose is the disposition of an element of the story that the narrator does not

21. See Chap. 5.

specifically name in his plan for an ending: the judgment of Troilus.

It is only later that we learn that Troilus went "Ther as Mercurye sorted hym to dwelle" (5.1827). This announcement reminds us of judgment while making us aware that this story does not provide a judgment of Troilus' career. Here is the key to the narrator's difficulty in making an ending, for the motive of all those sensational *de casibus* endings is to provide a judgment of the hero's prosperity as evil, or as worthless because impermanent, and that judgment is often sealed by death.[22] But for Chaucer, as for Boethius, no one act or event of a human career, however extraordinary, can be regarded as providing a judgment of all the other acts. Each maintains its own reality and significance in an infinitely intricate pattern. Like Troilus, human beings are all, until the moment of death, still loving and still seeking. Moreover, death itself solves nothing and proves nothing. Death is not an ending but a passage, a passage to that other world where judgment is the prerogative, not of the tragedian, but of the Godhead. Troilus' "double sorwe," then, does not and cannot bring him to a decisive and catastrophic end. Rather it initiates him into those fundamental sorrows that, far from being the special prerogative of tragic heroes, are the common experience of men and women. Troilus passes "Fro wo to wele, and after out of joie" (1.4). The last phrase is teasingly ambiguous; it embraces what Donaldson calls the narrator's simplicity and Chaucer's complexity.[23] The narrator evidently thinks of the phrase, at least retrospectively, as indicating a fall, but Chaucer has carefully withheld that specific designation in favor of a significant negative—"out of joie." This negative signifies the human condition that is neither "wrecchidnesse" nor the perfect happiness human beings desire. But the asymmetry of this phrase

22. For fuller discussion of the relationships of genres, judgments, and endings, see Chap. 7.

23. "The Ending of Chaucer's *Troilus*," p. 28.

in the poetic line conceals and reveals something more: the fact that Troilus' story really has four parts.

Here we have another of those double contradictions. The typical *de casibus* story should have two parts, a rise and a fall. The narrator announces a plot with three parts—"Fro wo to wele, and after out of joie"—unaware of the contradiction, and then eventually tells a story having four parts. The narrator has related only three of these parts at the point where, in his envoy, he pronounces his story a tragedy. During this third stage, his hero is in sorrow and the narrator shares the *de casibus* tendency to seize on what happens last to characterize and judge all that has gone before. In his own digressive way, the narrator is also, at this point, in the process of relating his hero's death (5.1765–1798), which, as we have already seen, he regards as part of the proper ending for a tragic story. Yet unwittingly, with this final "tragic" touch, the narrator seals the *comedy* of Troilus' career, for with characteristic enthusiasm, the narrator provides all that belongs to the death of a noble pagan prince. That includes an ascent to the eighth sphere and a vision of "This wrecched world" and its "blynde lust" (5.1807–1825).[24] As Chaucer read in Macrobius and recounted in his *Parliament of Fowls*, Scipio the Younger was granted such a vision in anticipation of the services he would perform for the commonwealth and as a promise of the eternal reward those services would earn. Troilus too has earned his vision; he has chosen the "comun profyt" and refused to be another Paris. The same choice that contributes to his eventual loss of Criseyde also contributes to the shaping of his life as a comedy.[25]

In retrospect we see that at those two crucial points in the narrative where the narrator discerns tragic falls, once jokingly

24. Some manuscripts place Troilus in the seventh sphere, some in the eighth. For a recent, full review of the controversy, see Steadman, *Disembodied Laughter*, pp. 1–20.

25. Cf. Patricia Kean, *Chaucer and The Making of English Poetry* (London: Routledge & Kegan Paul, 1972), 1, 163; and see Chap. 5.

and once seriously, Chaucer finds the materials of Boethian comedy: the inner enhancement of a person arising from the free commission of good acts. Troilus' career is a comedy in which his will is transformed by love and his intellect by vision. However, if the two "falls" in Troilus' career turn out to be spurious, the two ascents are very real. Our late discovery that there is a second ascent, to the eighth sphere, requires us to reconsider the first, the "wele" of Troilus' love for Criseyde. At the beginning of his story and again at the end, the narrator sees Troilus' life as essentially sorrowful and thus "tragic." In his role as tragedian, he shares the *de casibus* tendency to deprive "prosperite" of all significance and value in its own right and to regard it merely as a prelude to catastrophe. But in narrating the events of Book 3, he is most triumphantly the servant of the servants of love and the clerk of Venus as he evokes the undeniable and ineradicable reality of that "wele." In his analysis of the structure of *Troilus and Criseyde,* Robert Jordan remarks on the peculiarly self-contained nature of Book 3.[26] This structural characteristic is yet another way, I think, in which Chaucer insists that the "wele" cannot be wholly negated by subsequent events. The reader must support the narrator's better judgments even against the narrator's own worse judgments. The Boethian prisoner once believed that sorrow undid and negated all his earlier happiness (1. met. i), but this belief was a symptom of despair and self-pity and, under Philosophy's tutelage, he gave it up.

Thus Troilus' bliss in love is not, as the two-part *de casibus* tragedy would have it, either a bad eminence before a well-deserved fall, or a worthless, because impermanent, "prosperite" before an arbitrary but inescapable "wrecchidnesse." Nor is it, as the narrator's intended three-stage tragedy would have it, a valuable but ultimately sterile experience overwhelmed by the more significant sorrows of Troilus' life. Rather, within Chaucer's four-stage *comedy* of Troilus, Troilus' bliss in love is an anticipa-

26. *Shape of Creation,* pp. 84–86.

tion and an emblem, however fleeting and flawed, of that Love which all human beings seek. Troilus' career, so defined, suggests a vision very different from the *de casibus* vision. It suggests a world governed by a God of Love who is at once man's Creator and his destiny, his beginning and his end. In the pursuit of this end, man is at every moment capable of making his own effective, free choices. His responsibility is correspondingly great, but so is his opportunity to learn. And because the natural goal of a man's choosing and learning and loving is the same as God's goal for man—that is, God Himself, the supreme Good— God's governance is experienced not as an alien tyranny but as the truest freedom. "Subgit unto love" (1.231): the phrase is ultimately paradoxical.[27] It is from this Boethian perspective that Troilus' falling in love can serve as an *exemplum* for other men's "aventures" in "lovynge."

And so the wish that the narrator expresses when he misnames his story of Troilus a tragedy is fulfilled:

> Go, litel book, go, litel myn tragedye,
> Ther god thi makere yit, or that he dye,
> So sende myght to make in som comedye! [5.1786–1788]

Surely here is one of the greatest ironies of the narrator's performance as *de casibus* tragedian. At the very moment of pronouncing his work a "tragedye," he inadvertently reveals one of the most fundamental limitations of his theory simply by reminding us of the existence of comedy.[28] The *de casibus* theory solipsistically remakes the entire universe in its own tragic image and thus eliminates any other kind of career for man; in the Boethian universe, on the other hand, there can be both comedies and

27. Cf. Dante, *Purgatorio*, 16. 79–80, trans. Charles S. Singleton (Princeton: Princeton University Press, 1973), Vol. 2, Pt. 1, 172–173: "You lie subject, in your freedom, to a greater power and to a better nature. . . ."

28. The narrator's remark seems clearly to identify comedy, like tragedy, as a human construct expressing a human vision. It is not for him, as for some critics, a name for the divine vision of things.

tragedies, depending on the nature of man's choices. But as so often happens in this narrative, one moment demonstrates both the narrator's ineptitude and his superior insight and accomplishment. Unlike the Monk, he believes in the possibility of comedy; his own vision is broader than that of his chosen genre. Furthermore, the narrator has, in spite of his own imperfect awareness and articulation of it, actually helped to compose a tragedy—the tragedy of Criseyde—greatly superior in kind to the *de casibus* tragedy of Troilus he thought he was writing. As we have already noted, *de casibus* tragedy, in theory and practice, has room for only one protagonist and tends to draw all other persons and events into the vortex of that one career of power. But Chaucer, working behind and through the narrator, is trying to dramatize a universe within which all human experience, comic and tragic, can be enacted. And because his theme is love, not power, his plot must and can make room for two careers, the hero's and the heroine's.

In this chapter I have examined the *de casibus* vision, at once ineptly handled and superbly transcended by the narrator, as the "contrarie" of Chaucer's Boethian vision. In the next two chapters, I shall examine in detail the two "contraries" which that Chaucerian-Boethian vision itself embraces: the comedy of "this kynges sone" and the tragedy of "this in blak."

5

The Boethian Comedy
of Troilus

Like a typical late medieval tragedian, the narrator of *Troilus and Criseyde* vacillates between the two *de casibus* plots by treating Troilus first humorously as the hero of a tragedy of pride and then solemnly as the hero of a tragedy of fortune. In addition, he vacillates in yet another way by implicitly assigning his hero and heroine to two different plots. As the hero of the narrator's solemn tragedy of fortune, Troilus dwells in a world where man is the fated but innocent victim of Fortune. Seen merely as a manifestation of Fortune's fickleness, Criseyde fits neatly enough into this world. But the story and modern criticism of it embody a second attitude toward Criseyde: she is perceived as an unfaithful woman subject to moral judgment. Indeed the problem of judging Criseyde preoccupies the narrator throughout much of Book 5. Here the heroine is presumed to be a responsible agent dwelling in a world where human beings have significant freedom, while the hero continues to be seen as the helpless pawn of Fortune in a world where all is fate.

The narrator, of course, is unaware of how the inner contradictions of his tragic theory tend to skew the treatment of his characters. Yet since the Boethian universe admits and reconciles fate and freedom, Chaucer, working from behind the narrator, is able to allow all his characters to be both fated and free. Fate prevents Criseyde from fully expressing her "entente," however, and thus contributes heavily to that shaping of her career as a tragedy, which she finally confirms by a deliberate choice. In contrast, fate places Troilus in a position to fulfill his "entente," and he confirms this comic opportunity by several crucial choices. Thus Chaucer directly reverses the underlying pattern of the narrator's *de casibus* tragedy in which Troilus is presumed to be fated and Criseyde is presumed to be free. While both his characters remain both fated and free, Chaucer's tragedy of Criseyde focuses on the burden of being fated at the same time that his comedy of Troilus, as I hope to show in this chapter, focuses on the burden of being free.

In the Chaucerian genres of comedy and tragedy, as in the lives of his characters, fate and freedom intersect. By defining the context within which man exercises his free will, fate provides situations that are weighted toward the tragic or the comic, but the potentiality in the situation must be actualized by human choice. A potential tragedy might be transcended by a truly heroic choice, and a potential comedy might be wasted by a cowardly choice. As an alternative to the *de casibus* term "fall," I am going to use the term "crisis" to refer to these especially significant intersections of fate and freedom in a character's career. The *de casibus* fall, as we have seen, can be only "tragic," but the Chaucerian crisis may be resolved in either a comic or a tragic way. The *de casibus* tragedian emphasizes the outward event, which lies in the realm of fate, while Chaucer emphasizes the inward response, which lies in the realm of freedom. Consequently, a *de casibus* fall imposes a wholly external change on a character, whereas the character's response to a Chaucerian crisis produces an internal change. In Chaucer's terms, a tragic change moves the character toward rigidity and disfigurement, a comic change toward growth and healing. Change conceived as fateful and external may be, as it is for the *de casibus* tragedian, absolute and definitive, a change that fixes the meaning of a life forever. But for Chaucer, each internal change produced by a critical choice—though ineradicably real— is only partial, part of a pattern of choices and changes. Thus while the career of the *de casibus* hero can have only one fall, the careers of Chaucer's characters are marked by multiple crises. Chaucer's characters must bear the terrible burden and the terrible power of being at every moment, even after a comic or tragic crisis, still fated and still free.

The contrast between the narrator's tragedy of Troilus, where the emphasis falls on fate, and Chaucer's comedy of Troilus, with its emphasis on freedom, can perhaps best be perceived by considering the relationship between the first three books and the last two books. In a sense the narrator's tragedy really begins at Book 4 with the turn of Fortune's wheel; since the hero of a tragedy of fortune does not act but is only acted upon in the fall, nothing that he has been or has done can really be of any significance to that experience. His "prosperite" is merely a prelude to catastrophe; its purpose is not so much to represent an intelligible character as it is to prepare the audience to feel the required pathos when Fortune's wheel turns. Because Chaucer's narrator is morally superior to his own tragic theory, however, he has given us much more in the first three books than the usual sentimentality of such a rise-and-fall structure—yet he is unable to articulate the connection between Troilus' experiences before and after the turn of the wheel. The work of integration is Chaucer's. The new importance of the rising action in Chaucer's version is suggested by the fact that Chaucer has greatly expanded this part of the story as he found it in Boccaccio.[1] The "prosperite" of Chaucer's story dramatizes the hero's acquisition of spiritual goods, of a Boethian "estat roial," that cannot be taken away by Fortune.

Troilus' initial commitment to the craft of love opens him up to the possibility of a comic transformation that will lead him toward a new maturity. He actualizes this comic potentiality by

1. In number of lines the rising action is twice as long in Chaucer's *Troilus* as it is in Boccaccio's *Il Filostrato;* as a proportion of the work, it constitutes nearly three-fifths of Chaucer's poem, but only two-fifths of Boccaccio's. See Sanford B. Meech, *Design in Chaucer's Troilus* (Syracuse, N.Y.: Syracuse University Press, 1959), p. 6.

making subsequent commitments to the education love requires. These decisions mark off the stages in the maturation of his love: the courtly phase of his first infatuation; then his serious education in love, first in the mode of aspiration, after his meeting with Criseyde at Deiphoebus' house, and second, in the mode of possession, after the meeting at Pandarus' house. Troilus' responses to the events of Books 4 and 5 spring from the quality of his transformed love, and those responses in turn provide the definitive proofs of the maturity of his love. Neither the crisis of Criseyde's exchange nor the crisis of her infidelity is simply a stroke of Fortune which renders Troilus powerless to react. He responds to the exchange by deliberately rejecting the alternative of running away with Criseyde; having outgrown the role of courtly servant, he is able to avoid the reciprocal role of ravisher. But the knowledge that he cannot protect Criseyde from the suffering that awaits her makes this decision a painful one. Chaucer devotes much of Books 4 and 5 to a detailed dramatization of the burden of being free as he shows Troilus trying to pass the responsibility for his own decision to fate and then to Criseyde herself. The pattern is reversed in his responses to Criseyde's infidelity. Troilus falters in his initial jealous reaction to the fantasy of Criseyde's infidelity, as embodied in his dream of the boar, but he corrects his error, is cured, and applies what he has learned to the crisis of her actual infidelity by loyally reaffirming his love for her. This characteristically Boethian affirmation finally transcends both Criseyde's limitations and death itself. In the last two books, Troilus appears not as a *de casibus* hero experiencing the helplessness and frustration of being fated, but as a Boethian comic hero experiencing the agony and the triumph of being free.

Near the end of his journey up the mount of Purgatory, Dante must pass through a purifying curtain of flame. It is the hope of reunion with Beatrice that gives him the courage to submit to such an ordeal. On the other side, Virgil crowns and mitres

him as king and bishop of himself (*Purgatorio,* Canto 27).
Troilus' experience of transformation through love is very different from Dante's and yet Dante's is not irrelevant. The fire
Chaucer describes as afflicting Troilus is more than lust; it, too,
is refining and creative.

> In hym ne deyned spare *blood roial*
> *The fir of love,* the wherfro god me blesse!
> Ne him forbar in no degree for al
> His vertu or his excellent prowesse,
> But held hym as his thral, lowe in destresse,
> *And brende hym so in sondry wise ay newe,*
> That sexti tyme a day he loste his hewe.
>
> [1.435–441; italics mine]

In a matching passage, the narrator later tells us that love has
purged Troilus of every vice (3.1800–1806). A new opposition
between "blood roial" and pride replaces the initial opposition
between "blood roial" and love, and thus measures the distance
Troilus has come.

This transformation suggests that Troilus' "estat roial" (1.432,
4.1667, 5.1830) is not a designation merely for his hereditary
and political position as Priam's son. It is also the Chaucerian
equivalent of the Boethian inner kingdom, a metaphor for self-
possession, maturity, wholeness. The Chaucerian terms are "resoun," "goode governaunce," and "manhood." Troilus' "estat
roial" as Priam's son is an outward sign of an inward potential
to be realized through love. The members of Criseyde's household say it all, in a way, when they run to see Troilus pass by in
the street. Here, and in a later passage (5.540–553), the "paleys"
belongs to the group of figurative terms signifying the inner
kingdom.

> "A! go we se, caste up the yates wyde;
> For thorugh this strete he moot to paleys ride;
>
> "For other wey is fro the yate noon
> Of Dardanus, ther opyn is the cheyne." [2.615–618]

This first procession before Criseyde's window is not part of a Pandaric plot (as the second is) but it is not mere chance either. Like Dante, Troilus, because he is human, must pass through fire to true Boethian kingship.

The importance of this Boethian concept is suggested by the fact that the resignation of his "estat roial" is one of Troilus' first acts upon falling in love. In a prayer to the God of Love he says:

> "But wheither goddesse or womman, iwis,
> She be, I not, which that ye do me serve;
> But as hire man I wol ay lyve and sterve.
>
> . . .
>
> For myn estat roial here I resigne
> Into hire hond, and with ful humble chere
> Bicome hir man, as to my lady dere."
>
> [1.425–427 and 432–434]

The relevance of these statements to what happens is typically complex, however. At this early stage, Troilus is posturing; he is playing the role of submissive lover as courtly "usages" (2.28) have taught him. All his postures here, like the Canticus Troili, are artificial in the sense that they greatly exaggerate the contents of his real experience to this point. But life will imitate art. In particular, his submission to Criseyde as feudal lady is a "game" that will become "ernest." As a social institution the game is, in part, a flattering piece of male self-indulgence. It pretends to reverse the power relationships of male and female in the political world, but in fact this very reversal constitutes a testimony to the male's dominant position. It is precisely because Troilus' political position as a man and a king's son is so secure that he can afford to indulge in playing the role of servant. Nevertheless, while the game includes much "feyning" of various sorts, it also reflects, though in a distorting mirror, some important truths. Love *will* require Troilus to resign his royal estate in a way he does not yet anticipate and, at the same time, that more profound resignation will eventually lead him back to a royalty that will be morally mature as well as politically responsible.

Specifically, Troilus does not yet know that love, human as well as divine, is ultimately a grace. Up to a point it can and must be earned, but it can never really be deserved. Troilus, however, is temperamentally a Pelagian; in his inexperience of love and life, he tends to believe that his merits will always be sufficient to deserve the good fortune he seeks. This Pelagian conviction, and not the cockiness Troilus displays in the temple, is the significant pride of which he must be cured. His swaggering ended with the sight of Criseyde, but his Pelagianism is shaken only by a complex education in love. His aggrieved questioning of Fortune after he hears the parliament's decision to exchange Criseyde reveals one of the most important ways in which Troilus has been the callow youth:

> "Fortune, allas the while!
> What have *I* don, what have *I* thus agilt?
> How myghtestow for rowthe *me* bygile?
> *Is ther no grace, and shal I thus be spilt?*
> Shal thus Criseyde awey, for that thow wilt?
> Allas, how maistow in thyn herte fynde
> To ben to *me* thus cruel and unkynde?"
>
> [4.260–266; italics mine]

Indeed, although Troilus uses the term "grace" here, the tone of the passage (arising from the insistent use of the personal pronouns and the interrogative mood) serves to define the term perversely as something that *can* be claimed on merit. It is ironically revealing that such arrogant self-assurance can coexist comfortably with the courtly lover's ritualized self-abasement. The truth is that despite his pro forma protests, Troilus does not really think of himself as unworthy of Criseyde's love initially. His first letter to Criseyde is humble only "in his speche," and Troilus actually laughs as he writes of his unworthiness (2.1069–1078). But his laughter turns to abashed silence and then to a

swoon in the two crucial meetings with Criseyde, first at Deiphoebus' house, then at Pandarus'. These two encounters do not
merely serve to bring Troilus to Criseyde's bed; they also bring
about deep changes in Troilus' love as he confronts the reality
of another's personhood.

At both meetings Pandarus concocts fictions that confront the
lovers with important truths. The theme of Troilus' first meeting
with Criseyde is unexpectedly "lordshipe." Pandarus' story that
Criseyde is in need of Troilus' political protection against
Poliphete is truer, in a sense, than the courtly fiction Troilus has
been enacting that he is Criseyde's man. Troilus calls out from
his sick bed: "Who is al there? I se nought, trewely" (3.67).
To his surprise the Criseyde who enters is not the courtly lady
of his fantasy, but the real and politically vulnerable woman.
We never know what "lessoun" (3.83) Troilus would have
recited for Criseyde at this meeting, because he forgets it all when
she approaches him as a supplicant:

> "Sire, comen am I to yow for causes tweye:
> First yow to thonke, and of youre lordshipe eke
> Continuance I wolde yow biseke."

> This Troilus, that herde his lady preye
> Of lordshipe hym, wex neither quyk ne dede,
> Ne myghte o word for shame to it seye,
> Although men sholde smyten of his hede. [3.75–81]

The combination of Criseyde's words with her actual presence
makes Troilus aware of both his actual unworthiness and the
hollowness of his earlier protestations of unworthiness. His first
words to her are "mercy, mercy, swete herte!" (3.98). The re-
straint and brevity of Troilus' speeches here distinguish this
"manly sorwe" (113) from the servility of his earlier posturing.

At the same time Troilus no longer places his faith exclusively
in his own merits but sincerely submits himself to Criseyde's
judgment and correction. The "fyn of his entente" (125), he
says, is that

"Ye wolde frendly somtyme on me see,
And thanne agreen *that I may ben he,*
Withouten braunche of vice in any wise,
In trouthe alwey to don yow my servise."

[3.130–133; italics mine]

Criseyde will echo his sentiment, yet with a telling difference: *"If I be she* that may do yow gladnesse" (180). The difference between these two verbal clauses is suggestive; Troilus' version indicates a sense, new to his Pelagian soul, that love requires aspiration and transformation. Although Troilus' speeches here may sound to the undiscriminating ear like the usual protestations of the courtly lover, we must not forget that they represent a genuine response to Criseyde's presence and not the lesson he had rehearsed. The aspect of Troilus' courtly love that draws Chaucer's criticism is not its passionate sexuality but its passionate fantasizing and thus its denial of the beloved's autonomy. As "game" becomes "ernest," Troilus is already transcending the courtly "usages."[2]

On the night of the consummation, another of Pandarus' fictions confronts the lovers with a truth. Love requires not only transformation, but also forgiveness when one falls short of love's

2. In "Masks of Love in *Troilus and Criseyde,*" *Comparative Literature,* 26 (1974), 14–31, Jeffrey Helterman traces Troilus' progress from love as courtly convention through love as metaphysical ideal to love for Criseyde. The more conventional reading sees Troilus performing as courtly lover throughout, but most of the evidence for Troilus' courtliness is usually drawn from Book 1. See Donald R. Howard, *The Three Temptations: Medieval Man in Search of the World* (Princeton: Princeton University Press, 1966), pp. 77–160, and Charles Muscatine, *Chaucer and the French Tradition* (Berkeley: University of California Press, 1957), pp. 133–137. Where I see a solipsism that can be corrected by human love itself, several critics have seen a pagan or courtly sensuality that can be corrected only by Christian teaching. See Alexander J. Denomy, C. S. B., "The Two Moralities of Chaucer's *Troilus and Criseyde,*" *Transactions of the Royal Society of Canada,* 44 (1950), 35–46, rpt. in *Chau. Crit. II,* pp. 147–159; D. W. Robertson, *A Preface to Chaucer* (Princeton: Princeton University Press, 1962), pp. 476–503; and Howard, *Three Temptations.*

ideal. No one, not even a king's son, has such merits that he has
no need of forgiveness. In Pandarus' little plot, Criseyde finds
herself accused of infidelity and Troilus is accused of jealousy.
If we consider merely this fiction of Criseyde's interest in Horaste,
Troilus is accurate enough when he proclaims, just before he
swoons: "god woot, that of this game, / Whan al is wist, than am
I nat to blame" (3.1084–1085). But if "this game" refers to the
intrigue of arranging the meeting, including Troilus' hiding in
the "stuwe" (601), if it refers to all the "contrefeting" and
"feyning" of the whole courtship, then "whan *al* is wist,"
Troilus is to blame and stands in need of forgiveness. And the
need for forgiveness extends into the future as well as the past.
Criseyde will yet be guilty of infidelity, and Troilus will yet be
guilty of jealousy. The mutual contrition and exchange of forgiveness is thus even more appropriate than either of the lovers
realizes. However, Criseyde asks forgiveness for any wrong she
may have unknowingly done Troilus (1182–1183), while Troilus
characteristically believes himself wholly innocent and only feigns
a confession "for the lasse harm" (1158). Nevertheless, these
confessions and absolutions, complicated and ambiguous as they
are, provide the appropriate and effective prelude to the lovers'
consummation.

In the consummation Troilus discovers that Criseyde "A thou-
sand fold was worth more than he wende" (1540). Because of
his Pelagian temperament, Troilus *can* discover the discrepancy
between his merits and the good he seeks—and thus the need for
grace—by reaching a higher estimate of that good, rather than
by entertaining a lower estimate of his own merits. Like the Black
Knight in *The Book of the Duchess,* he arrives at the most just
estimate of himself and of his beloved when he gives up the
fantasy of a goddess for the reality of a woman. Now he prays
to the God of Love in a new way:

> "Benigne love, thow holy bond of thynges,
> Whoso wol grace, and list the nought honouren,

> Lo, his desir wol fle withouten wynges.
> And noldestow of bounte hem socouren
> That serven best, and most alwey labouren,
> Yit were al lost, that dar I wel seyn, certes,
> But if thi grace passed oure desertes.
>
> . . .
>
> Here may men seen that mercy passeth right;
> Thexperience of this is felt in me,
> That am unworthi to yow, lady bright."
>
> [3.1261–1267; 1282–1284]

After his first sight of Criseyde in the temple, Troilus hoped that "yit myghte he falle in grace, / Or ellis for oon of hire servantes pace" (1.370–371). Only now, after observing the transformations of Troilus' love, do we appreciate the antithesis between the two. In order to obtain grace, Troilus has had to transcend the role of servant and its self-deceiving fantasies.

Moreover, Troilus is absolutely orthodox here in his reconciliation of faith and good works, grace and merits, mercy and justice. Chaucer evidently believed that if the great insights of Christian doctrine were really true, they would be reflected in all the projects of the human spirit. Thus the pagan too would have some "experience" of them in this life, even though, deprived of divine revelation, he would be unaware of how they govern the relation between God and man, as well as the relation between man and man.[3] Nor is Troilus unlike the ordinary Christian in his inability to conform all his thoughts and deeds to these highest insights. As we have already seen in our analysis of his address to Fortune, he later reverts, under stress, to his Pelagianism, but Troilus' experience of grace in love is nonethe-

3. This ignorance, along with the pagan's ignorance of the possibility and actuality of redemption, seems to me to be the important difference between pagan and Christian in Chaucer's poem. Cf. T. P. Dunning, "God and Man in *Troilus and Criseyde*" in *English and Medieval Studies Presented to J. R. R. Tolkien on the Occasion of His Seventieth Birthday*, eds. Norman Davis and Charles L. Wrenn (London: Allen & Unwin, 1962), pp. 164–182.

less real or sincere for his later errors. Indeed the value, the "grace," of the moment lies partly in its rarity in human experience. To such a rare and high moment the "resignation" of his "estat roial," the education of his will by his heart (1.226– 228), has all unforeseen brought this "kynges sone."

Chaucer's "estat roial" provides what the narrator's humorously invoked "fall" does not: a positive concept for illuminating and unifying Troilus' actual experience in love. Troilus grows out of a false royalty founded on Pride and into an authentic royalty founded on Love. Moreover, this Boethian concept provides the link between Troilus' two roles as prince and lover, and between the Trojan and the courtly materials of Chaucer's fiction. In *Troilus and Criseyde* Chaucer continues his exploration of a problem posed in *The Parliament of Fowls:* the relationship between the "comun profyt" and romantic love. The figure of Paris always stands just behind Troilus, representing the chief tragic possibility in his career; through Paris Chaucer suggests the inextricable link between sexual and political mores. The exercise of power disguised in the role of courtly servant merely finds another expression in the role of ravisher, with all its political consequences here.[4] In shedding his false royalty, Troilus at once transcends the immediate role of servant and implicitly rejects the potential role of ravisher. He achieves a Boethian "estat roial" based not on the exercise of power but on a respect for one's own and another's moral worth and autonomy. The deep impact of Troilus' education in love affects, and is revealed in its fullness by, his response to the crisis of Criseyde's exchange. By deliberately rejecting Paris' role, he turns potential tragedy into comedy. Chaucer's readers have not often given Troilus the credit he deserves for this decision, although Alfred David has

4. "Ravish" is Chaucer's word (cf. 1.62; 4.530, 548, 637, 643, 1474; and 5.895). For the fourteenth century the *OED* gives the meaning "to seize and carry off" or more specifically, "to carry away a woman by force sometimes implying subsequent violation." The earliest entry for the narrower meaning, "to commit rape upon a woman," is 1436.

cogently argued that Troilus does not weakly fail to act to prevent Criseyde's exchange; rather he deliberately refuses to act.[5]
There are two reasons, I think, why this crucial aspect of Troilus'
character has not been more widely recognized. In the first place,
instead of the narrator presenting the moment of Troilus' choice
as it happens, he has Troilus describe it after the fact. Second,
having once made that heavy and painful decision, Troilus engages in several maneuvers designed to shrug off responsibility
for it. It is our task as readers to give Troilus credit for his decision and to hold him responsible for it.

Chaucer's dramatization of the choice has several stages.
Troilus initially decides to consult Criseyde rather than to oppose
the exchange in the parliament. "Resoun" triumphs over "love"
that "hym made al prest" not to run away with her, but to
"don hire bide" (4.162–168). Next we witness the bursting
forth, in Troilus' chamber, of the "heped wo" and "woodnesse"
he had repressed in the assembly (225–343). Some time elapses
before Pandarus arrives to comfort Troilus, and apparently
Troilus makes the essential decision during this interval. The
interview with Pandarus provides the evidence. First of all, the
relationship between Troilus and Pandarus exhibited here offers
a sharp contrast with their relationship in Book 1. Troilus'
"chaumbre," like the "paleys," functions as a symbol of his mind
and, significantly, Pandarus finds that for the first time he does
not have immediate access to that chamber; instead he must
wait for a "certeyn knyght" to admit him (4.351–355). Furthermore, Troilus' rejection of Pandarus' first attempt at comfort—
his suggestion that Troilus take another love—reveals Troilus'
new independence of judgment and his ability to see through
Pandarus' arguments (cf. 496–497). Most telling of all, however, is Troilus' interruption of Pandarus' second argument.

5. "The Hero of the *Troilus*," *Speculum*, 37 (1962), 575; and very
recently, Donald W. Rowe, *O Love, O Charite!: Contraries Harmonized
in Chaucer's Troilus* (Carbondale, Ill.: Southern Illinois University Press,
1976), pp. 137–139.

Pandarus asserts that any true man, certainly any Trojan, would ravish his woman (533–539). Paris is the exemplar. Pandarus' defense of such conduct and his implicit definition of manhood serve to bring out the irony, latently present from the beginning, of the practice of courtly love service in a society that has chosen to defend, with all its resources, a ravisher of women. But Pandarus has made only a brief statement of his idea when Troilus breaks in:

> To this answerde hym Troilus ful softe,
> And seyde: "parde, leve brother deere,
> Al this have I my self yit thought ful ofte,
> And more thyng than thow devysest here.
> But whi this thyng is laft, thow shalt wel here;
> And whan thow hast me yeve an audience,
> Therafter maystow telle al thi sentence." [4.540–546]

That is, Troilus has already made an irreversible decision against ravishment; he agrees to hear Pandarus out, but only after he has stated his own position and thereby made clear that his mind cannot be changed. Troilus' vehement reaction to the suggestion that he take another love, a suggestion he calls leechcraft for a fiend (435–438), is the result of confronting that idea for the first time in this interview. In contrast he reacts calmly to the suggestion of ravishment, because he has already carefully considered that option himself and rejected it.

Troilus' rejection rests on loyalty to Troy and to Criseyde herself. The king, the parliament, and the people believe that Criseyde's exchange is "for the townes goode" (553), and Troilus will not oppose the common good for a private good. Moreover, he sees that to choose Criseyde in such circumstances, far from exalting love and the woman, would cheapen their affection and proclaim Criseyde less worthy then she is: "this were hire accusement" (4.556). Finally, he understands that while he might win Criseyde's assent, the action would still remain a rape, in a sense, for it would deeply violate her personality: "Yit drede I most hire herte to perturbe / With violence" (561–562).

The Troilus who was willing to employ the aid of trickery to bring Criseyde to bed now declines to persuade her, even if he could, to an action in conflict with her best instincts.

This last point is crucial. Here, as in Book 1, Pandarus advises Troilus not to draw any conclusion until he has "assayed" the lady (4.639). Yet Troilus is no longer the infatuated lover nor the courtly servant. He has become a true friend, one who, as Criseyde herself later testifies, "best kan ay his lady honour kepe" (5.1077). He knows that he must choose Criseyde's honor though she might weakly and mistakenly reject it. The courtly servant, on the other hand, submits himself not to his lady's honor but to her will, even her whim. Or pretends to submit himself, because such submission not only depends on a position of actual power, but can also constitute a strategy for exercising more power through the exploitation of the other person's weaknesses. So it is that the servant may become the rapist—and eventually the hen-pecked mate; in an exploitative relationship, the exploitation tends to work in both directions. After all, it is not so surprising that Helen may now "leden Paris as hire leste" (2.1449). If Troilus had chosen Paris' role, he would truly have lost his "substaunce" for "accident" (4.1505). The conclusive evidence that Troilus has outgrown the role of servant in his relationship with Criseyde is that in this crisis he does not swing to the opposite pole of playing the ravisher. The "fyn" of his love for Criseyde is not his loss nor her infidelity; it is instead this critical moment of decision in which the honorable and manly qualities of his love are displayed, enabling him to reject Paris' role and to express his profoundest loyalties both to Troy and to Criseyde.

Although Troilus can help to preserve Criseyde's honor, he cannot protect her from the pain and suffering that now await her. In the end he cannot be that "wal / Of steel" (3.479–480) that she would like him to be, and that he would like to be for her. It is the repressed pain, humiliation, and frustration of this circumstance that drives Troilus to try to transfer the respon-

sibility for his decision to fate and to Criseyde herself. He begins
this maneuver at the end of his conversation with Pandarus:

> ". . . it is nat myn entente,
> At shorte wordes, though I deyen sholde,
> To ravysshe hire, but if hire self it wolde." [4.635–637]

Here Troilus clearly, if unconsciously, invites Pandarus to make
the very suggestion that he does make: that Troilus "assay"
Criseyde (639). This plan to consult Criseyde about a ravishment, which is the prompting of "desir," contradicts Troilus'
earlier plan to consult her about love's prompting to keep her
in Troy (cf. 4.162–168 and 572–574).[6] Furthermore, it contradicts his actual behavior while in the throes of desire; then he
understood the requirements of a woman's honor without consulting what might have proved to be the weakness of her will.
Far from indicating that Troilus is changing his mind, however,
this contradiction shows him stumbling under the burden of a
heavy decision he will not unmake.

Awaiting this interview with Criseyde, Troilus meanwhile
visits the temple of Apollo and meditates, in a long passage drawn
from the *Consolation* (5. pr. iii), on the relation of the gods' foreknowledge to man's free will. Like his earlier hymn to Love
and his later pronouncement from the eighth sphere, this speech
shows Troilus projecting his experience on the universe.[7] If he
feels constrained by fate, then there is only fate and no true freedom. By omitting Philosophy's solution to the problem, Chaucer
suggests to the knowledgeable reader the solipsism of Troilus'
reflections. But as with the other speeches, Troilus' theory here
does not provide an entirely accurate description even of his own

6. In "Chaucer's Troilus of Book IV," *PMLA,* 79 (1964), 542–547,
Siegfried Wenzel discusses these two passages and the related passage,
4.1674–1680; Wenzel contrasts reason and desire but does not distinguish
between desire and love.

7. In "Action and Passion in Chaucer's *Troilus,*" *Medium Aevum,* 43
(1974), 26–27, Georgia Crampton accurately observes that "Troilus'
theses . . . always arise from his personal experience,"

experience and practice. Ironically, a man who has just made a crucial decision concludes that he has no freedom, since the decision is too painful, particularly in its consequences for Criseyde, to be fully accepted as his own. Although in his initial argument (956–966) Troilus refers only to his own sorrow, in his prayer to Jove at the end he reveals the real motivation for his philosophizing when he asks the god to "bryng Criseyde and me fro this destresse" (1082). In the temple Troilus is not a *de casibus* hero experiencing the frustration simply of being fated, though he would like to think he is; rather he is a Boethian comic hero experiencing the agony of making a responsible free choice within the terms dictated by fate.[8]

The timing of this speech, coming as it does while Pandarus is making arrangements for the lovers' last meeting, should alert us that Troilus' desire to transfer responsibility will be an important key to the lovers' debate. While Troilus has been meditating, Pandarus has been pleading with Criseyde to hide her own pain lest it produce a fatal sorrow in her lover. As a result when Criseyde meets Troilus, she is intent principally on easing his grief with whatever interpretation of events "short avysement" can suggest (4.936). She cannot tell Troilus this outright, of course, but she does make it clear that all her specific proposals are merely tentative illustrations of the general idea that all is not lost:

> "But, for the love of god, foryeve it me,
> If I speke aught ayeyns youre hertes reste;
> For, trewely, I speke it for the beste,

8. My interpretation has been anticipated, in part, by David, "Hero of the *Troilus*," 575–578 and by Charles Owen, "The Significance of Chaucer's Revisions of *Troilus and Criseyde*," *Modern Philology*, 55 (1957), rpt. in *Chau. Crit. II*, pp. 160–166. But both interpret the speech as itself representing, ironically, the moment of Troilus' choice, while I see it as part of the psychic aftermath of an earlier decision. Consequently, they tend to see his decision as a somewhat negative one, a decision not to oppose fate, whereas I see it as a more positive choice of the common good, and Criseyde's and his own honor.

"Makyng alwey a protestacioun,
That now thise wordes, which that I shal seye,
Nis but to shewen yow my mocioun,
To fynde unto oure help the beste weye;
And taketh it non other wise, I preye.
For in effect what so ye me comaunde,
That wol I don, for that is no demaunde." [4.1286-1295]

Both the lovers seem to lose sight of this important qualification. Criseyde begins to believe the plans and promises she conceived only to comfort Troilus; and Troilus is only too happy to have this chance to make the arguments for running away, the dictates of desire that reason has compelled him to reject. Aware that Criseyde will not consent, he knows he can safely seek relief in this way. What the debate obscures is that both lovers agree on the fundamental question. Criseyde, too, rejects on principle the idea of running away, citing Troy's good, Troilus' honor, the cheapening of their love, and her own honor (1555-1582) as her reasons. What the debate accomplishes for Troilus is to make it appear that he lets Criseyde go for different reasons than are actually the case. The two lovers come to believe that he permits her exchange, not because of his own choice of honor and the common good, but because he places his faith in her assurances that she will return. So Criseyde, who was willing to obey Troilus' will in everything consonant with her honor and his, ends up bound to the fulfillment of impossible conditions. As his own analysis shows (1450-1498), Troilus knows they are impossible even better than Criseyde herself. Ironically, this is the only time that Troilus explicitly and consciously recognizes the difficulties Criseyde will face in the Greek camp.

As Troilus leaves Criseyde the next morning, the narrator describes his grief with a sympathy that passes into wonder:

For mannes hed ymagynen ne kan,
Nentendement considere, ne tonge telle,
The cruel peynes of this woful man,
That passen every torment down in helle. [4.1695-1698][9]

9. The passage seems to echo 1 Corinthians 2.9.

It is this pain that accounts for Troilus' behavior on that last night and, in a similar way, for his behavior in the ten days that follow, because Troilus represses his awareness of Criseyde's suffering and of his helplessness to prevent it; in flight from these realities, he concentrates on the more superficial aspects of his own sufferings. Troilus' last words to Criseyde would seem evidence of a cruel self-absorption beyond forgiveness, if we did not know that they are part of a strategy he has unconsciously chosen to distract himself from the unbearable knowledge of Criseyde's pain:

> And neer he rod, his cause for to make,
> To take hire by the honde al sobrely.
> And, lord! so she gan wepen tendrely!
> And he ful softe and sleighly gan hire seye:
> "Now hold youre day, and do me nat to deye." [5.80–84]

Shortly after Criseyde's departure, Troilus takes to his bed and has a revealing dream

> . . . of the dredfulleste thynges
> That myghte ben: as mete he were allone
> In place horrible, makyng ay his mone,
> Or meten that he was amonges alle
> His enemys, and in hire hondes falle. [5.248–252]

The dream describes Criseyde's plight exactly and calls our attention to his repressed fears for her—yet the waking Troilus sees only his own suffering in it. In his "fantasie," he pities himself and works up his grief again and again so that all men may take pity on his sorrows (260–266). He plans his own funeral in detail and visits the sites of his former life with Criseyde. But his elaborate apostrophe to her deserted, closed house suggests that it is actually the condition of his own inner "paleys" that is now in question (540–553).[10] Moreover, Criseyde is betrayed by the

10. The stagey idolatry, and the possible sensuality, of this passage do not seem to me reliable guides to what Troilus has achieved in love; they are rather, in part, irruptions of aspects of his earlier infatuation, and in

divinization. For Troilus in this mood, she is a saint who does not herself suffer but whose departure is a loss for her shrine and her devotee. The deception and self-deception of his sentiments are revealed by his calculated theatricality:

> Therewith he caste on Pandarus his eye
> With chaunged face, and pitous to biholde;
> And whan he myghte his tyme aright aspie,
> Ay as he rod, to Pandarus he tolde
> His newe sorwe, and ek his joies olde,
> So pitously, and with so dede an hewe,
> That every wight myghte on his sorwe rewe. [5.554–560]

Although some readers have found in Troilus' sufferings, taken at face value, the most moving evidence of his supposed tragedy,[11] even Chaucer's empathic narrator grows tired of his hero's self-pity:

> Who koude telle aright or ful discryve
> His wo, his pleynte, his langour, and his pyne?
> Naught alle the men that han or ben on lyve!
> Thow, redere, maist thi self ful wel devyne
> That swich a wo my wit kan nat defyne.
> On ydel for to write it sholde I swynke,
> Whan that my wit is wery it to thynke. [5.267–273]

The flagging of the narrator's sympathy is more apparent when this stanza is compared with the parallel stanza on Criseyde's

---

part, symptoms of his present distress. But see Robertson, *Preface*, pp. 499–500; and John F. Adams, "Irony in Troilus' Apostrophe to the Vacant House of Criseyde," *Modern Language Quarterly*, 24 (1963), 61–65.

11. E.g., David, "Hero of the *Troilus*," and Meech, *Design*, p. 100. In "Boethius' Influence on Chaucer's *Troilus*," *Modern Philology*, 49 (1951–1952), rpt. in *Chau. Crit. II*, p. 132, Theodore Stroud goes further to suggest that it is by this suffering that Troilus earns his vision from the eighth sphere. But C. S. Lewis suggests in *Allegory of Love* (1936; rpt. New York: Oxford University Press, 1960), pp. 194–196, that here "Chaucer is letting the cat out of the bag," i.e., treating satirically the high passions of heroic suffering.

inexpressible grief, which the narrator fears to "deface" by any description (4.799–805). This apparent callousness in the Troilus whose sensitivity won Criseyde's heart brings us squarely up against Chaucer's willingness to expose his comic hero to the risks of continuing freedom. Having successfully negotiated one of the crises of his career, Troilus must still find a way to live with his decision. His strategy is much like that of all the characters in dealing with the war: he deliberately takes the short view in order to distract himself from the long view that he cannot bear thinking about.[12] Troilus deceives himself into half-believing that Criseyde will be able to return at the end of the ten days. On that assumption, it may be thought that the exchange threatens to have no serious consequences for her. Thus the situation seems to allow Troilus safely to indulge his considerable taste for self-pity and self-dramatization. More importantly, however, this dramatization of his own sufferings is a way of repressing the knowledge of Criseyde's sufferings. As unattractive as Troilus' behavior is, there are extenuating circumstances. On the conscious level, and in the short view, his apparently callous behavior is a reaction not to the prospect of permanent separation and Criseyde's real sufferings, but only to a planned ten-day separation. On the subconscious level, and in the long view, his behavior is, paradoxically, a reaction to the all-too-painful knowledge of Criseyde's plight and the contribution his own honorable decision has made to it.

Troilus' soliloquy in the temple, his treatment of Criseyde on that last night, and his behavior during the ten-day period constitute the psychic aftermath of his critical decision not to oppose or subvert the exchange. Shortly after the passing of the tenth day without Criseyde's return, Troilus enters into what proves to be a psychic preparation for another crisis. He becomes possessed

---

12. Donaldson, in "The Ending of Chaucer's *Troilus*" in *Early English and Norse Studies Presented to Hugh Smith in Honour of His Sixtieth Birthday*, eds. Arthur Brown and Peter Foote (London: Methuen, 1963), p. 33, has described similar behavior in the narrator.

by the "wikked spirit" of jealousy (5.1212–1214) and has the disturbing dream that as he walks in a forest weeping over Criseyde, he sees her lying with and kissing a sleeping "boor with tuskes grete" (1238). He awakens and immediately interprets the dream to mean that Criseyde has taken another lover—but the really significant ironic foreshadowing in this incident concerns Troilus, not Criseyde. Dealing with the fantasy of her infidelity prepares him to deal later with the reality.

It is true that in this fifth book the narrator constantly looks forward to Criseyde's infidelity by specific anticipations and especially by interweaving Diomede's story with Troilus'. As *de casibus* tragedian, the narrator tends to interpret the present events of this interim period wholly in the light of a future event. Yet this appeal to the future is only another version of the *de casibus* belief in Fortune's stroke, a wholly external event that defines man only as fated and not as free. For Boethius and Chaucer, the present does not annihilate the past, and the future does not annihilate the present. Nor do others' actions negate the significance of one's own actions. Troilus' jealousy, like his faith as he stands on the walls of Troy, is a fact about Troilus, not Criseyde. The jealousy is significant primarily as a spiritual condition in Troilus and only secondarily for its ironic relation to Criseyde's eventual infidelity. In particular, we must insist that Troilus' dream is his own work and therefore, above all, self-revelatory.[13] Pandarus administers a proper rebuke when he tells Troilus:

> "How darstow seyn that fals thy lady is
> For any drem, right for thyn owene drede?" [5.1279–1280]

The essential ugliness of jealousy consists in its denial of another's

13. Helen Corsa has stated the principle very effectively in "Dreams in *Troilus and Criseyde*," *American Imago*, 27 (1970), 57. Cf. Beryl Rowland, *Blind Beasts: Chaucer's Animal World* (Kent, Ohio: Kent University Press, 1971), pp. 81–85. It may be revealing of ways that women and men are perceived differently that readers commonly accept Criseyde's dream (2.925–931), but not Troilus', as self-revelatory.

autonomy, its subjection of another to the tyranny of one's own fantasies. The reader who finds in this episode principally an ironic anticipation of Criseyde's infidelity is repeating Troilus' error.[14]

Seen as an episode in Troilus' career, not Criseyde's, Troilus' dream of Criseyde and the boar constitutes something of a crux. The dream does not inspire Troilus' jealousy; rather the jealousy he is already suffering from dictates his interpretation of the dream: that Criseyde has taken a lover. But Chaucer's Troilus, unlike Boccaccio's Troilo, does not immediately identify the boar as Diomede; the identity of the boar is left open to question and, I would argue, to multiple, legitimate interpretations. Indeed, Chaucer signals his different purpose by radically changing the substance of the dream itself. In Boccaccio, the boar rips out Criseyde's heart, an action symbolic of "winning" her heart, while here he is utterly passive. Chaucer transforms the rending of the heart into an exchange of hearts and assigns it to an earlier dream of Criseyde's that represents her falling in love with Troilus (2.925–931). Moreover, Pandarus' countersuggestion that the boar represents not a lover but Calkas is at least plausible, and gives us a very apt emblem of Criseyde's position in the Greek camp, now under her traitorous father's instead of Hector's protection. Calkas is, in fact, the man who instigated Criseyde's exchange, the man who wanted Criseyde for himself and took her away from Troilus.

Nor is the crux that the dream presents satisfactorily solved by Cassandra, Troilus' prophetic sister. The unique authority that modern readers have unquestioningly granted her is entirely undeserved. First of all, she begins her interpretation of Troilus'

14. In her excellent article "Chaucer and the Psychology of Fear: Troilus in Book V," *ELH*, 40 (1973), 307–324, Elizabeth R. Hatcher argues that the dream arises from and gives expression to two understandable fears that Troilus has tried to repress: that Criseyde will not return and that she will love another. Hatcher points out that Criseyde's actual infidelity has none of the lustful and disgusting qualities of the brutal dream.

dream by invoking the very tragic formula that Chaucer is criticizing:

> "Thow most a fewe of olde stories heere,
> To purpos how that Fortune overthrowe
> Hath lordes olde." [5.1459–1461]

And her development of the theory has the old characteristic fault: a ludicrous disproportion between the complexities of the material and the simplicity of the interpretation. From a tangled history in which thirteen persons are named and fifty-nine others referred to (an abridgement of the twelve books of the *Thebaid*), she concludes: "This Diomede is inne, and thow art oute" (1519). Her claim, moreover, that "This Diomede hire herte hath, and she his" (1517) is one that might fit Boccaccio's poem but not Chaucer's, in which, as we have noted, the materials of the original Boccaccian dream have been deliberately transformed and redistributed. In dramatizing Cassandra's character and fate as a prophetess, Chaucer shows that her prophecies are crudely accurate as to the "facts," but that she is rightly never believed for her prophecies are morally repugnant. Here she eliminates all that makes an act human: the intention, the circumstances, the whole process of moral decision, the web of freedom and fate. Cassandra's reference to Troilus' lady, "wher she be" (1516), suggests that in relating his dream Troilus did not identify his beloved. Chaucer's Cassandra, unlike Boccaccio's, knows nothing of the character of Troilus' beloved; she looks only at the act and not at the actor. But if we were always to judge only by the outward event and neglect the inward, even an Alceste might be discredited, as Troilus observes (1527–1529). While Boccaccio's Troilo reacts angrily to a specific attack on his Criseida, Chaucer's Troilus reacts angrily to a *way of thinking*. We can agree with Troilus' judgment of all such prophetesses—and poets and readers:

> "Awey," quod he, "ther Joves yeve the sorwe!
> Thow shalt be fals, paraunter, yit to-morwe!" [1525–1526]

Troilus believes that the boar was shown to him "in figure" (1449), and it seems likely that Chaucer has also presented the reader with a figure whose most compelling significance for Troilus has not been stated explicitly but must be deduced by interpretation. An inconsistency in Cassandra's theory provides an opening clue to yet another dimension of the dream. She says that the boar represents Diomede who is the descendant of Meleager "that made the boor to blede" (1513–1515). Oddly enough, it seems that boars and boar-killers both belong to the same race—as is indeed the case, I would argue, when Troilus and Diomede subsequently meet on the battlefield. Chaucer's point, I think, is that Diomede's "kynde" and Troilus' "kynde" cannot really be separated. When Cassandra promises to reveal "of what kynde / [This boar] comen is" (1462–1463), we must recall the essential identity Chaucer suggests between the Theban and Trojan stories and people. Diomede himself insists on this identity in his very first speech to Criseyde as he leads her out of Troy to the Greek camp (120–147). Troilus' mistake, then, is to assume that the boar must represent someone other than himself! Since Troilus dreams the second dream while he is already possessed by the "wikked spirit" of jealousy, the boar "with tuskes grete" (5.1238; cf. 1454) may be an image of the jealous Troilus who fears that he has been or will be cuckolded.[15] The disturbing sight of Criseyde embracing the beast may express Troilus' repressed sense that his jealousy makes him less worthy of Criseyde's love. The banishment of any sense of unworthiness from his waking life to his dream life would be consistent with Troilus' characteristic inability to recognize his need for forgiveness. In a letter to Criseyde, written immediately after this dream experience, Troilus says quite accurately of his own transformation: "Criseyde shal nat konne knowen me" (1404).

15. As we have seen, Troilus was also mistaken about the identity of the central figure in his earlier dream of being isolated among one's enemies. Cf. 1454 and see 647–658, Troilus' description of the moon's "horns" where the ironic foreshadowing concerns the "horning" of Troilus.

In general, however, Troilus' jealousy seems "excusable" (3.1031) according to the standards Criseyde herself outlined on that first night in Pandarus' house. Although deeply possessed by the wicked spirit, Troilus does try to repress his jealousy with piety (3.1032–1035). The letter just referred to has its virtues as well as its vices. It is chilling to hear the self-involved Troilus— "At wrytyng of this lettre I was on lyve" (5.1369)—tell the helpless Criseyde that his life is in her hands. Yet, to his credit, Troilus does not mention his jealousy or make any charges of infidelity against Criseyde. We feel that the jealousy is an affliction that Troilus suffers as well as a sin that he commits. Knowing his worth, we regret, with Criseyde, that the wicked spirit "Sholde han his refut in so digne a place" (3.1014). Like her, we are "right sory, but nat wroth" (1044); we hate the sin but not the sinner. Most important, of course, is the fact that Troilus finally rejects his own hasty interpretation of his dream. Through Cassandra's cynical interpretation of the dream he sees the ugly injustice of turning his own fears into a charge against Criseyde's virtue.

This temptation to jealousy threatens Troilus with a disfiguring moral change, as his actual physical deterioration (5.1219– 1222) and the boar of his dream signify. Apparently it has this negative potentiality, while Troilus' behavior during the first ten days does not, because the jealousy is conscious. The earlier, superficially callous self-concern, however, is the complex product of unconscious feelings on which Troilus never gains any perspective. On the one hand, Chaucer suggests that much of a person's behavior is motivated by causes he does not understand (though they are intelligible to the objective observer); on the other hand, Chaucer suggests that such behavior cannot radically alter one's moral being. It is only those courses of action to which a person commits himself by an act of the will that can change him. And usually he has an opportunity to confirm or correct the first motions of the will. Troilus becomes so angry with Cassandra, and by extension, with himself, that he forgets

his sorrow "As though al hool hym hadde made a leche"
(5.1537).

Unlike the *de casibus* hero, who is given no chance to respond
to a single fatal fall, Troilus learns something of value from the
crises concerning Criseyde's infidelity that he must confront. The
cure of Troilus' jealousy constitutes an important comic reversal
in his career. The comic career is not without its temptations and
mistakes, but the comic hero at some point corrects his initial
error instead of committing himself to it and its consequences by
further confirmatory acts.

It is true that in this instance Troilus' learning is incomplete,
most conspicuously in his failure to reject seeking revenge against
Diomede. But the idea of competition between men for the possession of a woman is deeply engrained in the Greeks and the
Trojans and in all their Western descendants who have so frequently slaughtered each other over Helen and all she represents.
It is too much, perhaps, to expect Troilus to transcend his culture
completely. At the same time this distortion in his view of
Diomede takes nothing away from Troilus' genuine insight regarding Criseyde's relation to his dream, just as the continuing
Pelagianism of his character does not negate that moment of
grace he experienced on the night of the consummation. Furthermore, what Troilus does learn in his struggle with jealousy
is by no means negligible. He learns to respect the moral autonomy of another person and the moral complexity of human acts.
Such respect also provides the secure foundation for his own
sense of autonomy. The *de casibus* interpretation of this story
assumes that by being unfaithful Criseyde does something to
Troilus and that there is no significant way in which he can
determine the impact of her action. But Chaucer has linked
together two episodes in which Troilus must confront first the
fantasy and then the fact of Criseyde's infidelity precisely in
order to show that Troilus does have a choice. Indeed Criseyde's
actual infidelity becomes the occasion for Troilus' most transcendent act of fidelity.

At some unspecified time after Troilus' triumph over jealousy,

Diomede's coat is captured in battle and Troilus discovers at-
tached to it the brooch he had given Criseyde at their parting.
This brooch provides the first concrete evidence of Criseyde's
interest in Diomede. Although we don't know how much time
has elapsed since Troilus rejected Cassandra's prophecy and was
cured by his anger, we do know that much has happened. Of
greatest importance is the fact that Hector has been killed, and
the narrator invokes the authority of "olde bokes" (1562–1568)
to assure us that Troilus' grief was beyond description. Hector's
death apparently confronts Troilus with his first important sorrow outside the vicissitudes of love and provides both Troilus
and the reader with a catastrophe against which to measure the
supposed tragedy of Troilus' loss of Criseyde. Troilus has also
received a letter from Criseyde that seemed to him a "kalendes
of chaunge" (1634) but it does not cause him to experience any
of the psychological or physical symptoms he suffered when
afflicted by jealousy.

The maturity of Troilus' response to finding the brooch may
be measured by contrasting his variation on the *ubi sunt* theme
here with his earlier outburst on the occasion of the initial
separation:

> "Wher is myn owene lady lief and dere?
> Wher is hire white brest, wher is it, where?
> Wher ben hire armes and hire eyen cleere,
> That yesternyght this tyme with me were?" [5.218–221]

> "O lady bright, Criseyde,
> Where is youre feith, and where is youre biheste?
> Where is youre love, where is youre trouthe?" [5.1674–1676]

Troilus' concern shifts from the physical to the spiritual and
from his own loss to Criseyde's. In the earlier lament his tendency to speak of her as merely an adjunct to his own life and
happiness represents a kind of betrayal; in the later lament, however, he respects her existence as an autonomous person whose
actions are significant primarily as they express and affect her
moral nature. This respect is the profoundest kind of loyalty.

Moreover, Troilus' love does not alter when it alteration finds. Pandarus vows to hate Criseyde evermore (1732–1733), but Troilus cannot find it in his heart to "unloven" her a quarter of a day (1696–1701). Like Criseyde herself earlier, he can distinguish the sinner from the sin. In a way he did not anticipate, Troilus has kept the pledge he made Criseyde on that last night when he concluded a brief protestation of his fidelity with the words: "it shal be founde at preve" (4.1659).

Indeed, this commitment to Criseyde that Troilus never retracts in life is not relinquished even in death. And it is Troilus' triumph over death that places the final seal on his Boethian comic career. The power that *de casibus* tragedy gives to death is commensurate with the power it gives, in life, to Fortune. But Troilus describes the limits of death's power accurately when he says that while death may take the breath out of his body, it cannot take Criseyde out of his soul (4.470–473). It is the soul that loves, and the power that Chaucer grants the soul in death is commensurate with the power he grants it in life, to transcend the limitations of all the objects of our love in this world. Just as the narrator was unable to conclude his story in Book 4, neither is he able to make the loss of life coincide with the loss of love (cf. 4.26–28). In fact, Chaucer suggests the opposite in the narrator's last comment on his hero:

> And thus *bigan* his lovyng of Criseyde,
> As I have told, and in this wise he deyde.
>
> [5.1833–1834; italics mine]

The placement of these lines is also significant: they come at the end of the stanza in which the narrator rehearses the "fyns" of his story; Troilus' "lovyng of Criseyde" stands out as the only element that is recorded as having a beginning but not an ending.[16] In addition, these lines come after the narrator's account of

16. By contrast, in *Il Filostrato,* Part 8, stanza 28, Troilo's "ill-conceived" love for Criseida is said to end and indeed appears first on the list of endings.

Troilus' vision from the eighth sphere. By this strategy Chaucer suggests that Troilus' vision, rightly understood, does not deny or contradict his continuing love for Criseyde.

It is true, of course, that the narcissistic infatuation with which Troilus' love for Criseyde began cannot last, even in this life. Surely we need no revelation from the eighth sphere to tell us that; the subject is more apt for a Pandaric proverb than for an other-worldly vision. The love that Troilus reaffirms late in the story is something very different, though. In this chapter, we have not studied the change in Troilus' love in all the detail with which Chaucer represents it. Still six important stages have been distinguished: the courtly manifestation of Troilus' first infatuation, his submission to being educated in love at Deiphoebus' house, the "newe qualitee" (3.1654) of his love after the meeting and consummation at Pandarus' house, and the three loyal expressions of his love in the decision not to ravish Criseyde, in the rejection of jealousy, and in his continuing love for the unfaithful Criseyde. As Troilus' love for Criseyde moves through each of these stages and responds to each of these crises, it grows and matures. His final commitment to Criseyde is like Boethius' loyalty to the senate. It is a commitment that acknowledges the limitations of the object of one's loyalty. Indeed, all human love, Chaucer seems to suggest, must be able to transcend the experiences of betraying and being betrayed.[17] As the narrator unwittingly but definitively reminds us, love and imperfection are not antithetical; it was "right for love" (5.1842–1844) of the fallen, tainted, limited, imperfect souls of men that Christ died on the cross and rose again.

---

17. In "Chaucerian Irony and the Ending of the *Troilus*," *Chaucer Review*, 1 (1966–1967), 207–216, Anthony E. Farnham has provided an excellent commentary on the narrator's question, "What nedeth feyned loves for to seke?" (5.1848), arguing that Chaucer suggests the necessity of man's attaining celestial love through natural love, which is a "feigned or imperfect imitation of its eternal and perfect counterpart." See also Francis Lee Utley, "Chaucer's Troilus and St. Paul's Charity," in *Chaucer and Middle English Studies in Honour of Rossell Hope Robbins*, ed. Beryl Rowland (London: Allen & Unwin, 1974), pp. 272–287.

The relationship of Troilus' speech from the eighth sphere to his continuing love for Criseyde is admittedly complex, but the commonplaces of the speech come at the end of a very dense experience and they must be interpreted in that perspective. At the least our reading must be subtle enough to distinguish this laughter of the transformed prince from the laughter of the callow young man we first met in Pallas Athena's temple. Troilus rejected love then because of its labor, suffering, uncertainty, and impermanence (1.190–203). If the experienced Troilus were to offer us essentially the same calculation of love's profits, innocence would have turned to cynicism, not wisdom.[18] In addition the careful Chaucerian qualifications in the wording of the speech must be considered. Troilus damns "al oure werk that folweth so / The blynde lust, the which that may nat laste" (1823–1824), but as Kemp Malone has observed, Troilus' love for Criseyde is not explicitly mentioned.[19] Readers must decide whether to interpret Troilus' love as such a "werk," and I have given my reasons for believing that Troilus' transformed love does not come under that definition. Moreover, Alfred David has cautioned against finding in Troilus' speech a total rejection of all manner and degree of goodness in worldly things by pointing to the absolute standard Troilus invokes: "the pleyn felicite / That is in hevene above" (1818–1819).[20] Finally, I doubt that the most careful distinctions about Chaucer's language, important as they are, would bring Troilus' speech fully into harmony with Chaucer's truths, for the speech does not provide a wholly

18. The contrast between the Troilus of the temple and the Troilus of the eighth sphere is wholly Chaucer's, for Boccaccio's Troilo spoke from experience when he initially inveighed against love and women.

19. *Chapters on Chaucer* (Baltimore: Johns Hopkins Press, 1951), p. 136.

20. David, "Hero of the *Troilus*," 580. This particular qualification is especially important, of course, because as Root first pointed out in his edition of *Troilus*, p. 562, the phrase "pleyn felicite" is a Chaucerian addition adopted from Boethius that does not appear in the source for this passage in Boccaccio's *Teseida*.

accurate account of Troilus' own experience or of the Christian vision.

The Troilus who reaffirms his love for Criseyde and the one who then pronounces on the vanity of the world might almost seem two different people, although no more so than the Troilus who deliberately rejects the temptation to ravish Criseyde and the one who then declares that men have no free will. In other words, at critical moments in this story, Troilus' practice is right but his theory is often mistaken. Generally Troilus' speech has been accorded more authority than it deserves. Not only is it one in a series of Troilus' personal and limited visions; since it judges the world, the speech is also one in a series of actual or projected judgments in the poem, all of which are in some sense mistaken: the future judgments of her conduct that Criseyde anticipates, Pandarus' final judgment of Criseyde, the narrator's various judgments of his characters and his story. Moreover, Troilus' final speech is merely one of the narrator's many endings: his proverbial comment on his story (1748–1750), his summary of Troilus' worthy deeds, his analysis of the "fyn" of Troilus' career, his address to "yonge fresshe folkes," his comment on pagan belief and story, his address to Gower and Strode, and finally, his closing prayer. Troilus' speech, like each of these visions, judgments, and endings, contains only part of the truth.

Troilus' speech represents here exactly what its original represents in Cicero's "Dream of Scipio": the highest vision of *pagan* wisdom. Chaucer's readers have generally recognized this fact without seeing, apparently, how it limits and qualifies the authority of Troilus' vision.[21] In Troilus—a hero whose theory is inferior to his practice—Chaucer gives us a precise representation

---

21. An exception is Edmund Reiss who, in "Troilus and the Failure of Understanding," *Modern Language Quarterly*, 29 (1968), 131–144, has convincingly argued that here, as in *The Parliament of Fowls*, Chaucer finds the vision of Scipio wanting in its failure to provide an adequate account of the reality of love in the universe.

of the situation of the pagan who shares all the richness of his humanity with the Christian but is without the aid of Christian revelation to interpret it. In the perspective of that revelation, pagan wisdom is not wrong, but it is seriously incomplete. It sees clearly the imperfection of the world's goods but does not have the Christian knowledge of the Perfect Good. It sets up an irreconcilable opposition between this world and "hevene above" (1819), because it could not know about the circular and unifying movement described by Christ's incarnation, death, resurrection, and ascension (1842–1844). In short, pagan wisdom does not know that the world is redeemable, and in that respect Troilus' speech constitutes one of the last acts of betrayal in the poem, because only the Christian vision *can* be entirely faithful to the world and its goods and their potential for redemption. The Christian should have new reasons, not for hating the world, but for loving it.

In terms of this contrast between pagan and Christian, the *de casibus* vision represents a bastardized version of Christian truth; it is the view of a modern pagan who is philosophically only a nominal Christian. The *de casibus* tragedian would have human beings come to Christ only as the disappointed and embittered lovers of an imperfect world. What both the pagan and *de casibus* visions fail to represent in Troilus' career and in the careers of all heroes and heroines is the final unity of all love: human love must be transformed, "redeemed," but it need not, and cannot, be rejected. But while the narrator has tried to give us "the forme of olde clerkes speche" (1854), Chaucer has given us, sometimes with the narrator's unwitting aid, the substance of Christian truth.[22] If Troilus had been a Christian, he might have

22. Cf. Donaldson, "The Ending of Chaucer's *Troilus*," p. 42, and Peter Dronke, "The Conclusion of *Troilus and Criseyde*," *Medium Aevum*, 32 (1964), 49, n5. Both seem to assume, however, that the phrase provides an essentially adequate description of Chaucer's poem, while I think the word "forme" constitutes a crucial Chaucerian qualification of the adequacy of the phrase. Cf. the phrase "forme of daunger" (2.1243).

made a confession of love in which, like Dante in another comedy, he would have traced the fire of his love for God to its origins in the fire of his love for a woman (*Paradiso*, 26). But although Troilus was deprived of Christian revelation and could not articulate the vision, he might still say with some justice, as he did on the night of the consummation: "Thexperience of this is felt in me."

6

The Boethian Tragedy
of Criseyde

Just as the narrator's expressed wish to write a comedy significantly precedes the account of Troilus' ascent to the eighth
sphere, so his reference to his work as a tragedy follows immediately and significantly on his last reference to Criseyde. The
narrator interrupts his summary of Troilus' heroic career to
speak of Criseyde's guilt, elaborates on one of the implications
of her story by lamenting the frequent betrayals of women, and
then addresses his "litel tragedye." The placement of the generic
characterization, as a digression from a digression from a digression, provides one more humorous example of the narrator's
story-telling idiosyncrasies, but it also allows Chaucer to identify
the tragic strand of his story very precisely.[1] As we would expect,
however, Chaucer's tragedy of Criseyde is something not dreamt
of in the Monk's definition.

We have seen how the conclusion of Troilus' story is elaborated with a complexity that the *de casibus* scheme cannot

1. In *Chaucer and the Consolation of Philosophy of Boethius* (Princeton: Princeton University Press, 1917), p. 129, Bernard L. Jefferson long
ago suggested that the prologue to Book 1 identifies two distinct strands
of the story in much the same way that I am claiming the close of the
poem does:

> Now herkneth with a good entencioun;
> For now wol I gon streyght to my matere,
> In which ye may *the double sorwes* here
> *Of Troilus* in lovynge of Criseyde,
> *And how that she forsook hym or she deyde.*

>   [1.52–56; italics Jefferson's]

contain. It is the beginning of Criseyde's story—with its already intricate pattern of possession and loss, summed up and symbolized by her widowhood—that from the first disqualifies her for the Monk's kind of tragedy. When we first meet her, Criseyde is a daughter deserted and placed in mortal danger by a traitorous father. We know she has been married and widowed but that under Hector's protection she has taken her place as a respected and beloved woman of considerable "estat" (1.130). These have been some of the crises in her life before Troilus sees her in the temple. Even if we knew more about these shadowy early events, how could we plot a simple rise and fall in Criseyde's career? In which event of her life should we see Fortune's decisive stroke? How shall we even judge it happy or unhappy? Neither the narrator nor the characters are ever really sure.[2] The *de casibus* scheme assumes not only that Fortune may render the decisive blow in a person's life, but also that all sufferers and all observers will agree on what that critically unique event is. Chaucer shows that, given the complexities of human lives and the limits of human vision, the possibilities for interpretation are very wide. As Philosophy suggests, Fortune's decisive stroke is only what a person perversely chooses to see as such (2. pr. i.11–14).[3]

That the narrator never considers the possibility of Criseyde's being his tragic figure is evidence both of his deference to his "auctour" and of the sterile simplicity of a generic concept that cannot embrace a life like Criseyde's. Ironically, the *de casibus* portrayal of fate in terms of a single stroke or single turn of the

2. Compare, for example, Criseyde's fear on the night of the consummation that her felicity is at an end (3.813–836), with the lovers' rehearsal, later that same night, of "every wo and feere / That passed was" (1383–1385). From another point of view, of course, the characters' fates are actually being decided on the battlefield and the crucial event is Hector's death.

3. On man's free will in relation to fortune, the stars, and divine foreknowledge, see Augustine, *The City of God*, 5.9–10; Dante, *Purgatorio*, 16; and Jean de Meun, *Le Roman de la Rose*, 17039–17874.

wheel at once grants too much and too little to fate. It grants too much when it interprets that single outer event as a judgment of a whole life from which there is no appeal, but it grants too little when it portrays fate as making only these extraordinary and sensational incursions into human lives. Chaucer's analysis shows rather that fate is a pervasive influence, at work in every moment of a person's existence. In his plotting of Criseyde's complex career, he portrays fate under at least three aspects: the universal human inheritance of original sin; the individual's psychological endowment or constitution; and the force of circumstances—that is, essentially, the impingement of other persons' free choices. To be fated is, simply, to be human: to have a history, a psyche, and a community. Moreover, Chaucer's approach has the complementary virtue of recognizing the full force of fate without thereby denying the simultaneous reality of freedom. Fate appears not as a sudden and overwhelming intervention that stuns a person into submission but as a process within which and against which a person may contend. Fate does not follow the free act to punish or defeat it; rather freedom is exercised within a situation defined by the various coordinates of fate. As Chaucer shows in his *Nun's Priest's Tale,* the cock Chauntecleer can still exercise freedom in the very jaws of the fox.[4]

Yet it is easier to find an image to represent Chauntecleer's freedom within the world of animal fable than it is to find a corresponding image representative of Criseyde's freedom within the fully human milieu of *Troilus and Criseyde.* In a sense fate lends itself more congenially to dramatization than freedom for, in the realm of fate, we observe the action of causality, and we may construct an exposition of the relations of causes and effects. But a free choice is an "effect" for which there can be no adequate cause. Augustine discusses this aspect of freedom in

4. Cf. Paul Ruggiers, "Notes towards a Theory of Tragedy in Chaucer," *Chaucer Review,* 8 (1973), 96–97.

his attempt to explain how the fallen angels could initially have turned away from God:

If one seeks for the efficient cause of their evil will, none is to be found. For, what can make the will bad when it is the will itself which makes an action bad? Thus an evil will is the efficient cause of a bad action, but there is no efficient cause of an evil will. . . . Since the "effect" is, in fact, a deficiency, the cause should be called "deficient." The fault of an evil will begins when one falls from Supreme Being to some being which is less than absolute. Trying to discover causes of such deficiencies—causes which, as I have said, are not efficient but deficient—is like trying to see darkness or hear silence.[5]

That turning of the will, then, that is the essence of every free act dwells in mystery and poses a problem to the poet who would represent it.

Paul Ricoeur's analysis of Adam's sin as portrayed in Genesis 3 provides a suggestive solution to this representational problem. The account of the Fall by the so-called "Yahwist" editor of Genesis has a twofold rhythm, Ricoeur points out. The sin is portrayed as both caesura and transition, as act and motivation, as taking place in an instant and taking place during a lapse of time. The first kind of presentation emphasizes the origin of the act in the actor himself and is the more difficult to dramatize. The second shifts the emphasis to external causes—the serpent, the woman—and is easier to dramatize. Ricoeur says further: "About the instant, as a caesura, one can only say what it ends and what it begins. On the one hand, it brings to an end a time of innocence; on the other, it begins a time of malediction."[6]

5. *The City of God*, 12.6–7, trans. Gerald G. Walsh, S. J., et al. (New York: Doubleday, 1958), pp. 250–254. Or as Sartre puts it, between every act and its "explanation" there exists a nothingness, a nothingness that Sartre cannot describe "since it *is not*." See *Being and Nothingness*, trans. Hazel E. Barnes (New York: Washington Square Press, 1958), p. 71.

6. *The Symbolism of Evil*, trans. Emerson Buchanan (Boston: Beacon Press, 1969), pp. 243–244.

That is, an act, insofar as it partakes of freedom and not of fate, cannot be directly represented, but it can be indirectly represented through the *change* that it works: and suddenly they knew they were naked. I shall argue that Chaucer offers a similar, double account of Criseyde's infidelity. His poem presents a lengthy and complex exposition of the *causes* that constitute the element of fate in her act, but it also presents the "chaungynge of Criseyde" as the *effect* that testifies to the element of freedom in that act.

Criseyde's tragedy, like Troilus' comedy, is the product of both fate and freedom. Fated by original sin, like all human beings, to betray, and endowed with a basic temperament especially fearful of change and loss, Criseyde is divested, by virtue of other peoples' choices, of all her worldly securities. Thus in her career, the three influences of fate converge in an extraordinary way to make the expression of her "entente" all but impossible except by a heroically transcendent act. But, although her options are extremely restricted, Criseyde does still have a choice. Indeed, only by recognizing her continuing freedom can we give her credit for rejecting a worse form of infidelity in her refusal to be another Helen, and also for trying to preserve an essential form of fidelity to Troilus, even in the midst of infidelity. The compromise of her integrity that she finally chooses, however, changes her in a disfiguring way—for our acts have transforming power as well as, and even in spite of, our intentions. Since for Chaucer change is by definition self-imposed, the betrayer must be the tragic figure, not the betrayed, and Boccaccio's story is turned inside-out. Yet the tragic change Criseyde undergoes is not, like the reversal in *de casibus* tragedy, total and final, anymore than the comic changes Troilus undergoes are total or final. Rather we leave her still trying, in straitened circumstances and with diminished inner resources, to preserve what integrity she can amid the deepening ambivalences of her widowhood, its losses, loyalties, and needs.

For Chaucer the paradox of man's being both fated and free is expressed fundamentally by his identity as the child of Adam. In *Troilus and Criseyde* Chaucer has written the true Adamic tragedy the Monk was unable to write. Chaucer's "olde storie" is an analogue of *the* old story and Chaucer dramatizes this relationship by augmenting his Trojan story with the extra depth and dimension of the Theban story.[7] The number of allusions Chaucer makes to Theban characters and stories is significant: Oedipus, Niobe, Athamantas, Capaneus, Alcmena. The two besieged cities have a common supernatural enemy, Juno (5.599–602), and through Cassandra Chaucer discusses in detail their common human enemy, the Greeks (5.1464–1512). The single most important connection between Thebes and Troy is Diomede, whose father Tideus was one of the seven against Thebes. Diomede's title, "sone of Tideus" (5.88, 1764; cf. 1514) is as significant in its way as Troilus' title, "this kynges sone." The first suggests the respect in which man is bound to the past, and like Diomede, has been disinherited of a kingdom (5.932–938). The latter suggests man's capacity for growth and his claims to a new inheritance and a new kingdom. It is surely ironic, and significant, that Criseyde's tragedy should directly involve her with the character Chaucer uses most specifically to dramatize the connection between his story and the first Fall. But Diomede's blood descent is only symbolic of all the characters' spiritual descent from Thebes, and by extension, from Adam. Chaucer invents for Criseyde's mother the name "Argyve," a name she shares with the wife of Polyneices of Thebes, and he also invents for Criseyde a niece named Antigone. Cassandra might have traced for all the characters a genealogy similar to Diomede's: "And so [she] descendeth down fro gestes olde / To Diomede" (5.1511–1512). The genealogy is complete only when it reaches

7. As Robert Jordan puts it in *Chaucer and the Shape of Creation* (Cambridge, Mass.: Harvard University Press, 1967), p. 109, "Chaucer's art is not theology. It is an analogue of theology in the sense that in the God-centered Middle Ages all serious meditations upon the human condition are analogues of one another, ending in God."

Chaucer's audience, reading the story of Troy and inevitably apprehending only partially its significance for them, as they observe Criseyde and her ladies, similarly limited in vision, reading the story of Thebes in their "paved parlour" (2.81–108).[8]

One consequence of the Fall for Chaucer is that all human beings are fated to be traitors. In the *de casibus* world where power is the ultimate reality, pride, a misjudgment of one's power, is the cardinal sin; in the contrasting world of Chaucerian comedy and tragedy, where love is the ultimate reality, infidelity is the cardinal sin. When the narrator says of Criseyde that he will tell us "how that she forsook [Troilus] or she deyde" (1.56), he is not describing a career unique to Criseyde but one common to all the characters in his story and to all human beings. The narrators and the characters remind us constantly of other traitors: Tereus, Amphiorax, Oedipus, Nysus' daughter, Wade, Tantalus, Athamantus. Whatever role a person takes, then, thousands have played it before her. Being part of a plot necessarily reveals one to be part of the old plot of Adam's fall. Nevertheless, being part of a plot also reveals characters to be free as well as fated. The forms of treachery, from the blatant to the subtle, from the malicious to the unthinking, are manifold, and an appeal to fate alone cannot explain how each character finds her role.

Criseyde's acceptance of Diomede reveals her to be both a human being fated to betray and a human being free to choose this act of betrayal and not another. In fact Criseyde's final infidelity cannot be rightly understood in isolation from her rejection of an even graver form of betrayal, for on that last night with Troilus, Criseyde chooses not to be another Helen. That such a transformation would be the result of her running away

8. The story of Troy ought to have had special significance for Chaucer's audience because of the popular legend perpetuated, for example, by Geoffrey of Monmouth and by the *Gawain*-poet, that England was founded by Brutus, a descendant of Aeneas.

with Troilus is ironically suggested by the question Pandarus had earlier put to Troilus:

> "Thenk how that Paris hath, that is thi brother,
> A love; and whi shaltow nat have another?" [4.608–609]

Although Chaucer's use of the Theban material suggests that people seldom learn from history, Troilus' claim that "Ther nys nat oon kan war by other be" (1.203), turns out to be an exaggeration. The story of Paris and Helen is one old story Troilus and Criseyde understand well, and in their circumstances it is the story they most need to comprehend. As we have already seen, they agree on the principles involved; Troilus is counting on Criseyde to reject any plan to run away, and the reasons she gives against it are very much like the reasons Troilus gave Pandarus earlier. Both refer to Troilus' duty to Troy, and he expresses concern for her honor (4.556–574) as she does for his (4.1555–1582). This last point is especially important. While each of the lovers is aware of how he or she would be changed by such an act, each is concerned primarily with the change that would be wrought in the other. One of the most terrible aspects of becoming a Paris is that in the process one contributes to the making of a Helen, and of becoming a Helen, that one contributes to the making of a Paris.

This theme receives more emphasis in Criseyde's interview with Troilus than it did in Troilus' interview with Pandarus, since at the end of the lovers' meeting, Criseyde tells Troilus what qualities in him evoked her love (4.1667–1680). (This speech is separated from her rejection of the plan to run away by two other brief exchanges, but as readers we should supply the connection.) It is important to note that in reinterpreting Boccaccio, Chaucer has transferred this speech from Troilus to Criseyde. I believe Chaucer considered it essential to his characterization of Criseyde because it suggests a crucial difference between the act of infidelity she rejects here and the one she finally commits. The qualities Criseyde describes as evoking her love are the same ones that prevent Troilus from reenacting Paris' role. This juxtaposition suggests, then, how direct and grave would be the betrayal of Troilus and of their love if Criseyde should consent to the ravishment, for there can be no greater betrayal of love than the lovers' mutual collusion in debasing it and each other. By contrast Criseyde's acceptance of Diomede does not change the nature of her love for Troilus nor contribute directly to any change in Troilus himself. Troilus' feeling that in making a decision *for herself*, Criseyde has done something *to him* is a natural and perhaps universal form of solipsism, but it is not an entirely trustworthy interpretation.

Only recently, as we have seen, has Troilus been given credit for his rejection of Paris' role; Criseyde, so far as I can determine, has never been credited with rejecting Helen's. One of the ironies in the poem (and in the history of its reception by readers) is that a woman who virtuously rejects one notorious kind of infidelity should find herself condemned as much or more for committing another. Criseyde herself is all too accurate in anticipating that her name will be equally stained by either course of action (4.1576–1582 and 5.1058–1063). But Chaucer has included these undiscriminating judgments in his poem—just as he has juxtaposed Helen and Criseyde—precisely so that we may make finer judgments. Unfortunately Criseyde, of all the characters, has so far been given the least benefit of the truth that "ther is diversite requered / Bytwixen thynges like" (3.405–406). Criseyde's infidelity, seen against the background of all the characters' infidelities stretching back through time to Thebes and eventually to Adam, reminds us of the fate that makes all persons inevitably traitors. Yet her rejection of one act of betrayal and her eventual choice of another brings us back to her freedom. The consequences of this freedom are that Criseyde must, on the one hand, be given credit for her fidelity and, on the other, be held responsible for her infidelity. As my argument unfolds in this chapter, it is important to remember that Criseyde's tragedy, undeniably real though it is, is a different and a lesser tragedy than it might have been.

Chaucer explores the paradox of freedom and fate, not only in our common human inheritance of original sin, but also in the related mystery of individual character. The long-standing controversy over Criseyde's characterization and the motivation for her infidelity is more than the product of critics' confusion; it is a response to a genuine Chaucerian dilemma in the poem itself.[9] Chaucer is exploring the relation between fate and freedom partly through the relation between character and action. Specifically, he is considering how far a person's acts are determined by her character, and this question is an important aspect of Criseyde's tragedy. The crucial texts are the narrator's formal portraits of Diomede, Criseyde, and Troilus (5.799–840), and Chaucer's own alternative character analyses imbedded in the Boethian speech he assigns to Criseyde on the night of the consummation (3.813–840). Chaucer's analyses produce more understanding of the springs of action in the hero and heroine than do the narrator's, and yet Chaucer's analyses must ultimately be acknowledged to have the same fundamental limitations as the narrator's: no description of traits of character can give a wholly adequate account of a person or her actions.

The narrator's portraits are mosaics of more or less stereotyped epithets, apparently selected somewhat at random. One epithet proved fatally tempting to an earlier generation of Chaucer's readers: the narrator's description of Criseyde as "slydynge of corage" (5.825).[10] Actually, however, this phrase does not receive

9. See Sanford B. Meech, *Design in Chaucer's Troilus* (Syracuse, N.Y.: Syracuse University Press, 1959), pp. 118–121 and 395–397, for a survey of the older scholarship, and more recently, Hans Käsmann, " 'I wolde excuse hire yit for routhe.' *Chaucers Einstellung zu Criseyde*," in *Chaucer und seine Zeit: Symposium für Walter F. Schirmer*, ed. Arno Esch (Tübingen: Max Neimeyer, 1968), pp. 97–122.

10. The phrase has been variously interpreted: "fatally impressionable and yielding" [George Lyman Kittredge, *Chaucer and His Poetry* (1915; rpt. Cambridge, Mass.: Harvard University Press, 1970), p. 135]; "the inability to make a deliberate choice" [Root, xxxii]; dominated by fear [C. S. Lewis, *The Allegory of Love* (1936; rpt. New York: Oxford University Press, 1960), pp. 185–189]; and more recently, mastered by her own "pite" [Peter Elbow, "Two Boethian Speeches in *Troilus and Criseyde* and Chaucerian Irony" in *Literary Criticism and Historical Under-*

any more emphasis in the portrait than any of Criseyde's other traits, and it seems unlikely that Chaucer has hidden a major key to Criseyde's character and action in a single phrase. Instead, as so often happens in Chaucer's works, his readers' response points to the very place where Chaucer's tactics and his narrator's diverge. Insofar as readers have looked for tragic flaws or other specific traits to explain the actions of Troilus and Criseyde, they have remained at the level of the narrator's art and have not reached the level of Chaucer's art. Precisely because the narrator's portraits are not founded on a unifying *concept* of character, and consequently do not provide a rounded sense of the individuals described, each of the isolated traits mentioned in the portraits offers itself temptingly as a possible key. It is this conceptual deficiency that Chaucer remedies with his own alternative character analyses.

Distinguishing the fruit from the chaff in Chaucer's work is never a simple procedure, and Chaucer's presentation of the two fundamental types of human personality identified by Boethius (2. pr. iv.150–166) is one of the neglected fruits in Criseyde's speech on the night of the consummation:

> "O brotel wele! O worldly joie unstable!
> With what wight so thow be, or how thow pleye,
> Either he woot that thow, joie, art muable,
> Or woot it nought, it mot ben oon of tweye.
> Now if he woot it nought, how may he seye
> That he hath verray joie and selynesse,
> That is of ignoraunce ay in derknesse?
>
> "Now if he woot that joie is transitorie,
> As every joie of worldly thyng mot flee,
> Than every tyme he that hath in memorie,
> The drede of lesyng maketh hym that he
> May in no parfit selynesse be;
> And if to lese his joie he sette a myte,
> Than semeth it that joie is worth ful lite." [3.820–833]

standing: Selected Papers from the English Institute, comp. Phillip Damon (New York: Columbia University Press, 1967), pp. 85–107].

Criseyde's monologue exposes one of the critical intersections at
which Chaucer joins Boccaccio's fable with Boethius' philosophy.
In the Trojan prince, Chaucer dramatizes the personality that
instinctively trusts the world and its joys, and in the Trojan
widow a contrastingly distrustful personality. Instead of drawing
characters dominated by single qualities or flaws, Chaucer gives
us characters shaped by basic temperaments or dispositions, both
psychological and philosophical, that are the bases for their
distinctive virtues and vices.[11]

While the narrator finds a single entrance and the simple
phrase "This Troilus" (1.183) sufficient to introduce his inexperienced hero, Criseyde and the complexity of her widowhood require three complicated entrances. Kneeling before Hector
a widow and traitor's daughter, she is the image of political
vulnerability; standing in the temple, she is a "bright . . . sterre"
of womanly beauty contradicted, but also accentuated, by widow's
weeds (1.175); and in her own home she leads a limited but
secure life of sober responsibilities: "a widewes lif" (2.114). In
addition, there is a certain mystery about her past that is never
dispelled. On her first entrance, the narrator admits he doesn't

11. The obvious insufficiency of the theory of the tragic flaw has led
many critics to desert the field of psychological interpretation almost entirely and thus to neglect this aspect of Chaucer's characterizations.
Charles Muscatine's preference for symbolical rather than psychological
interpretation in *Chaucer and the French Tradition* (Berkeley: University
of California Press, 1957), pp. 131–133 and 162–165, has been followed
by Robert Payne who, in *The Key of Remembrance: A Study of Chaucer's Poetics* (New Haven: Yale University Press, 1963), pp. 180–183,
finds Chaucer's art "typical" rather than "naturalistic"; by Jordan who,
in *Shape of Creation*, pp. 98–100, finds it "illustrative" rather than
"representational"; and by Donald W. Rowe who, in *O Love, O Charite!:
Contraries Harmonized in Chaucer's Troilus* (Carbondale, Ill.: Southern
Illinois University Press, 1976), pp. 57–91, finds Chaucer's art both
"sacramental" and psychological. The importance of psychology in Chaucer's art has been defended by Donald R. Howard, *The Three Temptations: Medieval Man in Search of the World* (Princeton: Princeton University Press, 1966), p. 134, and more recently by Dieter Mehl, "The
Audience of Chaucer's *Troilus and Criseyde*" in *Chaucer and Middle
English Studies in Honour of Rossell Hope Robbins*, ed. Beryl Rowland
(London: Allen & Unwin, 1974), pp. 177–178. See Chap. 7.

know whether she has any children, and much later, in his formal portrait, he pleads ignorance of her age. Nevertheless, these details give the impression that Criseyde is deeply rooted in the world, in contrast to Troilus who seems almost untouched by it. Moreover, Troilus' title, "this kynges sone," suggests his privileged position in the world, while Criseyde's title, "this in blak" (1.309; cf. 2.534), suggests her persistent deprivation and vulnerability. Troilus is conscious of his own power in a world he expects to be responsive to his wishes. He is a devotee of a Fortune that he believes distributes favors on the basis of merit, and he is convinced of his own merits. Troilus is self-centered, constantly aspiring, oriented toward the future. But Criseyde is other-directed, intensely fearful of loss, and deeply enmeshed in the present. She feels powerless in a world she cannot control but can only sometimes propitiate. She even attributes man's conception of the gods to his search for means of allaying his own fears (4.1408). It is Troilus who is "celestial" (1.979, 983), Criseyde who is earthly. Troilus swoons at the prospect of not attaining a goal he has sought (3.1086–1092); Criseyde faints at the thought of losing a good she has possessed (4.1149–1155). It is appropriate that we leave Troilus in the eighth sphere and Criseyde in the Greek camp. Ironically, Chaucer shows that the person who trusts most in the world may be the one most inspired to transcend it, while the person who most distrusts the world may yet be the one who feels most deeply the pain of its transience and who is most unable to rise above it. When Pandarus exhorts Criseyde to cast off her "widwes habit" (2.222), he has little understanding of how profoundly, in both senses of the phrase, it is hers.

When we consider the depth and breadth of this primal endowment of temperament, we see that Chaucer's characters are much more deeply affected by fate than the "fateful" working of any single trait or group of traits could make them. But just as Chaucer's characters are more profoundly fated than has generally been recognized, they are also more truly free. Moreover, in representing the freedom of Troilus and Criseyde,

Chaucer's character analyses are not superior to the narrator's. The placement of the narrator's portraits near the end of the work is Chaucer's way of exposing the inadequacy of *all* attempts to take account of a person or his acts by tabulating his qualities or describing his character, a method that can only record predispositions and the effects of past actions on the person. It can neither predict nor explain those turnings of the will that may yet occur. Although we might have accepted the narrator's portraits without question if they had come at the beginning of the work, near the end we can hardly be satisfied with these static pasteboard figures as representations of the dynamic characters we have been observing. Indeed, these figures seem already to be fading back into the past, into that shadowy world "bokes us declare" (5.799; cf. 816 and 834) from which they have so brilliantly, if briefly, emerged. These ineffectual portraits warn us that the fundamental error in attempts to explain Criseyde's acts wholly by an appeal to her character is the assumption that in the relation between character and act, all is fate.

The perennial attractiveness of this error may be itself an evidence of, and a frightened flight from, the reality of freedom. The belief in the fatedness of character locates the origin of acts in a "something" rather than in the motions of the will. Character is accepted as innate, fixed, predictable, but the motions of the will are not so construed and therein lies their threat. Readers of Criseyde's story may prefer to hope that that "something" productive of tragic acts does not lie within them. By emphasizing "flaws" in Criseyde, they can insulate themselves from the threatening implications of their own freedom—though at the price of insuring that they will learn nothing for their own lives from Criseyde's experience. Or, if more sympathetic to Criseyde, readers can appeal to that fateful donnée of her character, for which she is not fully responsible, instead of requiring her to take responsibility for a choice. Whether or not readers give Criseyde the benefit of this fateful interpretation of character, either way they can take the "benefit" of fleeing freedom for themselves.

Criseyde herself sets a better example for our imitation, however. Although hemmed in by several fateful influences and circumstances, she cites no excuses for her own ultimate choice. Putting aside for the moment Criseyde's last letter, we find that Criseyde excuses herself only three times: when she appeals to Hector for protection after her father's desertion (1.112); when she initially declines Pandarus' invitation to dinner because of inclement weather (3.561); and when she defends herself against the false charge of infidelity with Horaste (3.810). In all these cases she is innocent of any wrongdoing. Troilus, on the other hand, regularly excuses himself when he is indeed blameworthy. The most obvious, though admittedly complicated, case is his refusal to take any responsibility for his and Pandarus' deception of Criseyde on the night of the consummation (3.1084–1085). In Criseyde's case, of course, the crucial instance is the infidelity itself. In the soliloquy in which she admits to betraying Troilus, Criseyde makes no appeal to any excuse whatsoever, neither to the weaknesses of human nature, to weaknesses of her own character, nor to the force of circumstances: the three forms of fate dramatized in the poem. Indeed she rejects all these excuses when she refuses to plead that she is not the first unfaithful woman (5.1067–1068). Chaucer's readers must confront the reality of Criseyde's freedom as honestly as Criseyde herself does.

In Chaucer's story, character plays a great role, just as original sin does. It sets limits; it cannot be escaped; it is one of the prisons. Moreover, as we shall see, when circumstances powerfully evoke Criseyde's characteristic distrust of the world and her sensitivity to its transience, the weight of fate in her act of infidelity is multiplied many times. But ultimately, the proximate and efficient cause of an action is that free choice which dwells in mystery. The Boethian dispositions of Chaucer's characters do not predetermine them to commit any specific acts. It is the whole person, fated and free, who acts. Arthur Mizener's formula for Criseyde's tragedy, that there is a contrast between what she is and what she does, becomes powerfully precise only when we consider the terrible contingency implied by man's freedom.[12] Just as isolated qualities of character can never constitute the totally adequate cause of an action, neither can they furnish a guarantee of protection from the commission of any act, even the most tragic.

Perhaps it is some sense of this latter truth, as enacted in the self-debasement of the admirable Criseyde, that moves readers to seek the sufficient cause of Criseyde's infidelity in her character—to flee the terror of freedom for the comfort of fate. It is surely ironic that readers commonly seek an explanation only for Criseyde's action when the acts of the other characters stand no less in need of explanation. Pandarus' service to Troilus provides an especially interesting case, for Pandarus himself emphasizes its uniqueness in his experience, its ambiguity, and the change it has worked in him:

> "For the have I bigonne a gamen pleye
> Which that I nevere don shal eft for other,
> Although he were a thousand fold my brother.
>
> "That is to seye, for the am I bicomen,
> Bitwixen game and ernest, swich a meene
> As maken wommen unto men to comen." [3.250–255]

That readers do not generally require a causal explanation of this act, or of many others in the story, is evidence, among other things, of a common intuitive acceptance of the reality of freedom. Only when there is a striking discrepancy between what

12. "Character and Action in the Case of Criseyde," *PMLA*, 54 (1939), rpt. in *Chaucer: Modern Essays in Criticism,* ed. Edward Wagenknecht (Oxford: Oxford University Press, 1959), p. 363. Roger Sharrock has discussed the "irruption" of Diomede into Criseyde's life as part of the "horror of the contingent" in her career, but I think Chaucer's more fundamental concern is to portray the existential contingency of all human acts. See "Second Thoughts: C. S. Lewis on Chaucer's *Troilus,*" *Essays in Criticism,* 8 (1958), rpt. as *"Troilus and Criseyde:* Poem of Contingency" in *Chaucer's Mind and Art,* ed. Arthur C. Cawley (1969; rpt. New York: Barnes & Noble, 1970), pp. 148–149.

a person is and what a person does do we confront the terror of contingency, including the contingency of our own acts; then we may be tempted to seek refuge in "an attitude of excuse."[13] Thus, although readers sometimes choose deterministic solutions to the problem of Criseyde's infidelity, their very concern with the problem is an indirect evidence of the power of Chaucer's dramatization, even in the midst of Criseyde's heavily fated career, of the mystery of human freedom.

In Chaucer's poem this freedom is limited still further, however, by a third factor that I have called force of circumstances and that arises essentially from the existence of a multiplicity of freely willing individuals. A person's freedom could be absolute only if hers were the only will in the universe. As it is, every person's exercise of freedom impinges on and limits that of every other person. The exchange of Criseyde for the captured Trojan warriors Antenor and Thoas—her treatment, in effect, as a prisoner of war—is largely the result of others' choices. The Greeks meet in a "consistorie" (4.64–133) and accede to Calkas' request for the exchange of his daughter; the Trojans hold a parliament (4.141–217) in which they reject Hector's argument against selling women and accept the Greek terms. Things might have been otherwise but for the free choices of many individuals. Even the war itself Chaucer presents ultimately as the complex effect of free acts. To characterize the war exclusively as a product of fate is to prevent effective analysis of those political realities that are an important part of Chaucer's concern in this intensely political poem.[14] Thus Chaucer suggests

13. Sartre's phrase, *Being and Nothingness*, p. 78.
14. Walter Clyde Curry has been the foremost spokesman for the view that "destinal forces . . . produce the city's downfall." See "Destiny in *Troilus and Criseyde*," *Chaucer and the Mediaeval Sciences*, 2d ed. (1960), rpt. in *Chau. Crit. II*, pp. 34–70. But in his article "The Trojan Scene in Chaucer's *Troilus*," *ELH*, 29 (1962), 263–275, John P. McCall has argued, correctly I believe, that the fall of Troy must be ascribed partly to foolish pride and criminal lust: to the city's determination to defend the crime of Paris and Helen.

that what the individual experiences as fortune or fate is partly the result of being trapped in somebody else's plot. Calkas, Pandarus, and Troilus generate plots that trap Criseyde; Paris and Helen generate a plot in which all the Greeks and Trojans are eventually trapped. Even at the root of that universal human fate—the Fall—we find freedom in Adam's sin and consequently the origination of the first and fundamental plot in human history. Our wills are free to choose only within a context that has been created and is constantly being reshaped by other wills.

Yet while the influence of character on Criseyde's infidelity has sometimes been over-stressed by critics, the effect of circumstances has been curiously slighted.[15] Readers who assume that the story is Troilus' tragedy inevitably become involved to some degree in Troilus' own solipsism and thus neglect Criseyde's losses and pains. Looking out at the towers of Troy from her exile in the Greek camp, Criseyde might well ask of some of her readers the same question she addressed to Troilus: " 'O Troilus, what dostow now?' she seyde; / 'Lord! wheyther thow yit thenke upon Criseyde!' " (5.734–735). Moreover, the new circumstances into which Criseyde is so violently cast have a direct relation to her ability to love. Criseyde's ability to love and her manner of loving are always qualified by her fears, and by her success or failure in securing assurances against those fears.[16] Chaucer reveals the sources of her fear in his two-part analysis of her reaction to the news of Troilus' love: Pandarus' announcement and arguments awaken fears of love as a political decision, and Troilus' appearance at her window awakens fears of love as a personal decision. The latter Chaucer presents as the common human sensitivity to the risks of intimacy and to the possibilities of "mystrust," "nice strif," and "tresoun" (2.778–798). One of the chief func-

15. Robert apRoberts, in "Criseyde's Infidelity and the Moral of the *Troilus*," *Speculum*, 44 (1969), 389–393, has placed valuable new emphasis on the force of circumstances in Criseyde's career.

16. C. S. Lewis' discussion of Criseyde's fearfulness, in *Allegory*, pp. 185–190, remains a brilliant analysis in spite of its philosophical limitations as an "explanation" of Criseyde's infidelity.

tions of any "usage" in love (cf. 2.28), courtly or otherwise, is
to provide a stylization of roles and behavior that neutralizes
and resolves such fears and thus makes way for love. But Criseyde's political fears are specific to her position in Troy and have
an ambiguous relationship to the role assigned to her by the
courtly usage.

In the world of love, Criseyde is the sovereign lady, holding
the power of life and death over her vassal-lover; but in Trojan
society she suffers under all the disabilities of being a woman,
the king's subject, Calkas' daughter, and her husband's widow.
She reminds us of this contradiction in roles even as she assumes
her ladyship over Troilus in the interview at Deiphoebus' house:

> "A kynges sone although ye be, ywys,
> Ye shal no more han sovereignete
> Of me in love, than right in that cas is." [3.170–172][17]

Obviously Criseyde takes some courage, as well as some frank
satisfaction, from the position of power that love's usage grants
her, yet there is a deep conflict between her two roles not present
in Troilus' case. It is precisely because Troilus' position as a
man and as a king's son is so secure that he can afford to indulge
in playing the role of servant in love. Criseyde's two roles, however, cannot reinforce each other in this way. Other supports are
needed to enable a woman of her fearful nature and social
vulnerability to play the role that usage requires of her if she is
to fall in love. These supports include being in Troy; being
in her own home, surrounded by her ladies; the Trojans' relative success in the war during this time; Pandarus' counsel and
his approval of the love between Troilus and Criseyde. Especially
critical is Hector's powerful presence as the "holder up of Troye"
(2.644), as Criseyde's special protector, and as the worthiest

17. In *The French Tradition,* pp. 159–160, Muscatine notes this contradiction but interprets it not as a social phenomenon but as part of
Chaucer's dramatization of Criseyde's symbolical ambivalence or
instability.

Trojan, a kind of moral sponsor and guarantor for Troilus, who is "Ector the secounde" (2.158; cf. 739–740 and 5.1803–1804). Such considerations are foreign to the artificial world of love's usage and in some respects actually antithetical to its codes. Nevertheless, only their silent presence and operation make it possible for the fearful Criseyde to give herself as fully in love to Troilus as she does.

When Criseyde is exchanged for the Trojan prisoners of war, all of these circumstances of her life are exchanged too. The tide of war turns against the Trojans, and it is Hector himself who has planned and led the unsuccessful battle. This time Hector's championship of Criseyde, in the parliament, is ineffective. She must leave her own city for an enemy camp of Greek soldiers, she must give up her home for a tent, she is without friends or counselors. Most significant of all, Calkas replaces Hector as her protector and symbol of manliness. Her recognition of Calkas' power over her, the sorrow of it for her, and her characteristic way of dealing with oppression, are summed up in her response to his welcome:

> She seyde ek, she was fayn with hym to mete,
> And stood forth muwet, milde, and mansuete. [5.193–194]

The appeal of Diomede must be seen against the background of these new circumstances. On the night of the fateful tenth day, Chaucer describes Criseyde lying "Inwith hire fadres faire brighte tente" (5.1022) as she considers Diomede's words. It seems certain that Criseyde does not finally accept Diomede until after Hector's death, the end of all her hopes for Troy and for herself.

In his punning reiteration of the phrase "the chaungynge of Criseyde" (e.g., 4.146, 158, 231, 553, 665, 878), Chaucer emphasizes the powerful link between these new circumstances and Criseyde's infidelity and subsequent change. In other circumstances Criseyde might have been faithful. She might have been another Penelope if, like Penelope, she had enjoyed the assurance of dwelling in her own city, in her own home, with her own friends. She might even have been another Alceste, because Criseyde consistently puts another's pain before her own. Witness her concern for Troilus' possession by jealousy, rather than with the wrong done to her by the charge of infidelity with Horaste. Similarly her attempts to assuage Troilus' grief on their last night together, although she is the one being sent to the enemy camp, attest to her compassion. Her weeping over Diomede's wounds is yet another instance. True, she cannot defy death and fortune for an abstract principle—as Troilus would by suicide—but if her death might directly purchase a loved one's good, her pity might overcome her great fear. Her attitudes are clearly expressed in the soliloquy addressed to Troilus during her first private grief over the impending exchange:

> "But how shul ye don in this sorwful cas,
> How shal youre tendre herte this sustene?
> But, herte myn, foryete this sorwe and tene,
> And me also; for, sothly for to seye,
> So ye wel fare, I recche nat to deye." [4.794–798]

The converse of these possibilities is also true; that is, that in other circumstances even Penelope and Alceste might have lost their "name of trouthe in love" (5.1055). Such an awareness should soften the judgment of Criseyde that otherwise might seem implied by the invocation of these heroines' names. Criseyde is not a different and lesser kind of woman than they; she is a woman whose virtues are very like theirs and who found herself in entirely different circumstances.

This is not to say, however, that Penelope and Alceste do not deserve their good names. We know that circumstance alone could not be responsible for Alceste's choosing death or for Penelope's choosing fidelity against great odds for twenty years; when the career is comic, we readily recognize the operation of free will and admire it. And there is free will, too, in Criseyde's tragedy, despite the weight of circumstance that, in justice to her, we must recognize. Significantly, Criseyde herself provides us with the explicit recognition of this fact. On her tenth day in the Greek camp, when Diomede predicts the fall of Troy and offers his love, Criseyde responds, in part:

> "Herafter, whan ye wonnen han the town,
> Paraunter thanne so it happen may,
> That whan I se that nevere yit I say,
> Than wol I werke that I nevere wroughte." [5.990–993]

Criseyde finds it incredible that Troy should fall, but her own plight is one she could never have foreseen. Who would have predicted that the Trojans, fighting to defend their homes, would voluntarily surrender one of their own women? Still more extraordinary, though, is the way the three expressions of fate in human affairs have come together to weave an imprisoning net for Criseyde: the human fatedness to betray, Criseyde's own characteristic disposition so fearful of change and loss, and the radical "exchaunge" of all her worldly securities. Nonetheless, as Criseyde herself anticipates in this passage, even in the most unexpected and constricting circumstances, the individual will may yet make a response.

Criseyde's plight and her response are analogous to those of Dante's Piccarda and Constance (*Paradiso*, Cantos 3, 4, and 5).[18] Both were taken from a cloistered life vowed to Christ and required to marry; as a consequence of their unfulfilled religious vows, their glory in heaven is diminished. Drawing on an Aristotelian distinction, Beatrice explains to a perplexed Dante that the two women cannot plead the excuse of violence because the practical will, if not the absolute will, consented to the evil in order to avoid a worse evil. By such partial consent the women fell short of the heroic alternative of complete resistance, as exemplified by St. Lawrence and Mucius. In making her decision to remain in the Greek camp Criseyde, like Piccarda

18. C. S. Lewis' very different estimate of Criseyde's infidelity is reflected in his suggestion, *Allegory*, p. 184, that it might be compared in some sense with the crimes of Dante's Brutus and Iscariot.

and Constance, fails to choose the heroic alternative; rather, as she did when she first admitted Troilus to friendship (2.464–473), she chooses what seems to her the lesser of two evils. It would require a special heroism, especially for one of her temperament, to confront the violence that would threaten her in an attempted escape from the Greek camp (cf. 5.701–707) and in the doomed Trojan city itself. No just evaluation of Criseyde's infidelity can overlook the reality of the potential violence she faced nor the magnitude of the heroism a different choice would have required. Perhaps Chaucer is subtly reminding us of these facts when he represents Troilus as considering but finally rejecting a plan to go to the camp in disguise (5.1576–1582)— Criseyde is unable to traverse the distance between the camp and the city, but so is Troilus. On the other hand, with Dante, we cannot deny the possibility of a different choice nor can we ignore the fact of Criseyde's free rejection of this choice. Indeed, we may agree with Criseyde's decision, for her death could not in any way purchase Troilus' good. Her situation is not Alceste's.

While Criseyde's decision to remain in the Greek camp does not lead inevitably to her acceptance of Diomede, there is a close link between the two decisions: the first contributes to but does not require, the second. Criseyde's situation is not Penelope's either, although at first she herself conceives of it as such—that is, as involving only Troilus' absence (4.783).[19] Instead, the total exchange of all Criseyde's securities, and especially the reemergence of Calkas as her protector, acts upon Criseyde's own fearful and dependent nature creating an almost irresistible need for another male sponsor in the enemy's camp, despite the fact that this need conflicts with Criseyde's "entente" to remain faithful to Troilus. Ironically, Criseyde unknowingly anticipated

19. This passage and the narrator's earlier references to absences of Troilus' (3.488) and to times when the lovers could not meet (3.509–510) suggest that Criseyde's love was one that could pass the test of mere absence.

this dilemma when she declared that she would go to the camp as Troilus' widow (4.778–784), since such a status suggests vulnerability and dependency at the same time that it expresses her devotion to a "husband" who still lives and commands her loyalty. In her soliloquy, Criseyde makes a desperate attempt to reconcile her need and her "entente": "To Diomede algate I wol be trewe" (5.1071). Her solution is a poignantly ironic version of the admissible remedy Beatrice describes for an unfulfilled vow (*Paradiso* 5). A vow has two aspects, Beatrice explains: the making of the compact, which constitutes essentially a sacrifice of the will, and the specific subject matter of the vow. Although one cannot be released from the vow itself, new matter, worth half again as much, may be substituted for the original matter. In Criseyde's case, the irony arises from the fact that in a question of fidelity in love—at least as this is commonly understood—to change the matter, the person, is the most serious violation of the vow. Moreover, it is unlikely that any of Chaucer's readers would judge Diomede to be half again as worthy as Troilus. So this, too, is part of Criseyde's tragedy: that Diomede should be the choice that chance and fate put in her way.

Still Diomede is not the despicable and villainous Greek some readers would have him be. Certainly in his attitude toward women and personal relationships he emerges as a shallow and limited man; and yet there is truth in the narrator's portrait of a courageous and chivalrous man whose traditional virtues are doubtless valued by his peers. As we have seen, we might isolate many moments in Troilus' courtship of Criseyde when he would not appear to best advantage. Most importantly, Diomede's wish to "conquer" Criseyde (5.792–794) only makes explicit the cultural ethic that underlies both the war and Troilus' desire to take revenge on Diomede. What Diomede lacks is Troilus' potential for growth and that capacity for deep response that enables Troilus on the night of the consummation sufficiently to quiet Criseyde's fears that she "Opned hire herte, and tolde al hire entente" (3.1239). The difficulty of imagining such a high and moving moment between Diomede and Criseyde provides ironic support for the narrator's unwillingness to say that Criseyde gave herself wholly to Diomede: "Men seyn, I not, that she yaf hym hire herte" (5.1050).

Chaucer keeps alive the possibility that Criseyde, like Dante's Constance, preserved her heart's veil although, under pressure, she surrendered the outward veil. As Beatrice explains, although the practical will consents to an evil, the absolute will may yet resist. On the night of the consummation, Criseyde gave Troilus a brooch "In which a ruby set was lik an herte" (3.1357), signifying her own self-surrender. The brooch she later gives to Diomede is not this brooch, but another one that Troilus, in a self-dramatizing gesture, gave her on her departure from Troy as a reminder of him and his sorrow (5.1660–1663). The evidence that Troilus takes as conclusive proof of Criseyde's infidelity may in fact be a silent indication of her inward fidelity. That is, this second brooch, which is not said to contain a ruby, reminds us of the first brooch and its heartlike ruby, a jewel that Criseyde gave once and has not withdrawn or given to another.[20] Like the ruby, Criseyde's heart may yet be Troilus'.[21] Indeed, even the narrator's sources seem to allow for some qualification of the judgment that Criseyde betrayed Troilus:

> For how Criseyde Troilus forsook,
> Or at the leeste how that she was unkynde,

20. Of course, Criseyde's giving of anything of Troilus' to Diomede is distasteful, as both the narrator's remarks (5.1040) and Troilus' (1688–1691) suggest. It may be, though, that Criseyde has, however unconsciously, negative feelings toward a token through which Troilus dramatized his suffering at the time of her greatest distress.

21. The narrator's statement that "bothe Troilus and Troie town / Shal knotteles thorughout hire herte slide; / For she wol take a purpos for tabyde" (5.768–770) might seem to flatly contradict my argument. But I think that the last line here and particularly the illogical "for" are Chaucer's indications that the narrator, in his fatalistic and almost despairing reaction to the pain of his story, is mistakenly coalescing into one what are really two separate decisions. Criseyde's decision to remain in the Greek camp does not constitute proof that she withdraws her heart wholly from Troilus.

Moot hennesforth ben matere of my book,
As writen folk thorugh which it is in mynde. [4.15–18]

For whatever reasons, it is a qualification that modern readers have generally not cared to pursue.

The final Chaucerian irony is that from this point of view Criseyde's relationship with Diomede both mitigates and aggravates her tragedy. By her own choice she may keep her heart's veil and thus preserve fidelity even in the midst of infidelity. At the same time, she must endure the sorrow of being joined to the lover fate has provided, one to whom, though she should wish it, she can never hope to open her heart and reveal her "entente."

Imprisoned by this threefold fate—the human inheritance of original sin, the primal endowment of character, and the impingement of other people's choices—Criseyde is forever prevented from fully expressing her "entente." Yet in her prison, as in Boethius', freedom remains, and she may, indeed she must, still make choices although her options are now severely restricted and unfulfilling. To deny her freedom, limited though it is, would be to diminish her dignity as a person and to rob her of the credit she deserves for preserving fidelity in the midst of infidelity. By making a false divorce between freedom and fate, admitting the one only to exclude the other, the *de casibus* tragedian evades the dramatic problem that an adequate representation of this complex reality involves. Chaucer's more profound apprehension of fate and freedom as simultaneous phenomena, however, confronts the problem squarely.

Thus far, in my analysis of the burden of being fated, I have been examining principally those dimensions of Chaucer's presentation that correspond to what Paul Ricoeur calls transition, motivation, and process in time. But a full appreciation of Criseyde's freedom also requires consideration of those dimensions of Chaucer's presentation that correspond to caesura, act, and instantaneousness. For Chaucer, as for Ricoeur and Augustine, that instant in which the will moves is wrapped in mystery, and he does not attempt to represent it directly. Rather he approaches it as closely as he can by representing its immediate aftermath, in which we see, again in Ricoeur's terms, what that exercise of freedom ends and what it begins: the *change* that it works. Like Troilus' decision not to oppose the exchange, Criseyde's decision to accept Diomede is not explicitly represented; her dramatic soliloquy (5.1058–1085) is the evidence that the decision has been made. And like Troilus' behavior in the interview with Pandarus (4.351–658), Criseyde's subsequent behavior dramatizes the change in her that her own critical choice has brought about.

The view fashionable for some time now that Chaucer's characters are static must be put out of court simply on the evidence of words (for instance, "chaunge," "exchaunge," "transmuwen," "disfigure," "bicomen," "newe") and images (for example, the unleaving tree, the molting bird, the waxing and waning moon, the turning wheel) that document Chaucer's fascination with the phenomenon of change. If, as some critics have argued, Chaucer's concept of character does not include a concept of change,[22] it is odd that his hero's does: "Allas, I nevere wolde han wend or this, / That ye, Criseyde, koude han chaunged so" (5.1682–1683). Even when the possibility of change in Chaucer's characters has been recognized, however, the tendency has been to look for changes that precede and "explain" action—the type of change that Troilus' lament no doubt assumes. But Chaucer gives us changes that succeed and reveal action. Change understood as explanatory of acts functions as a cause in the realm of fate, while for Chaucer change is primarily an effect in the realm of freedom, and only secondarily and consequently a cause. Chaucer insists, therefore, not that human beings must change in

22. See Arthur Mizener, "Character and Action." His argument is echoed in J. S. P. Tatlock's "The People in Chaucer's *Troilus*," *PMLA,* 46 (1941), rpt. in *Chaucer: Modern Essays,* pp. 328–347, and adapted by Muscatine in *The French Tradition,* pp. 133 and 162–165.

order to act, but that when they act they are changed. As all the characters demonstrate, people are capable at any moment of surprisingly beautiful deeds and surprisingly ugly ones. Troilus does not need to change in order to fall in love, but he is changed by the experience of loving; likewise Criseyde need not change to be unfaithful, but her infidelity changes her.[23]

Moreover, Chaucer is faithful to Boethian psychology when he focuses, not on changes that are assumed to produce action, but on changes that flow from action. As we have already seen,[24] Boethius presents a concept of change first poetically in his re-working of the Circe legend (4. met. iii) and then analytically in Philosophy's description of the unhappiness of evil men (4. pr. iv. 17–33). As Philosophy explains, sinners are afflicted by three "unselynesses": the will to do evil, the power to do evil, and the actual performance of the deed. Each of these dimensions of a choice affects the person. Boethius offers here a subtle analysis of the reflexive nature of acts, of their profound effect always and primarily on the actor herself. Dante, too, especially in his *Inferno,* would have reinforced for Chaucer this Boethian teaching that every act affects, remakes, the person. Each act originates in freedom, but through the change that it works in the actor, it contributes to the making of her fate.[25]

For Criseyde, Chaucer marks the turning point very clearly. The Criseyde we have known leaves the stage with a very moving soliloquy and with an appropriate exit line: "But al shal passe; and thus take I my leve" (5.1085). Of course, the line does not have precisely this resonance for Criseyde herself. Rather, in

23. Cf. Augustine, *The City of God,* 12.9: ". . . [the rebel angels] changed themselves into bad angels by defection from good will. The only thing that 'made' their will bad was that they fell away from a will which was good" (Walsh, p. 256).
24. Cf. Chap. 2, "Tragedy and Comedy in a Boethian Universe."
25. In "The Problem of Free Will in Chaucer's Narratives," *Philological Quarterly,* 46 (1967), 441, Charles Owen argues that "the characters bear the responsibility for their choices and show this responsibility in the quality of their development."

response to some awareness that her act will change her, she seems to express here a desperate wish that it should not, that her sorrow and the moral effects of her infidelity should be as transitory as her joy. The narrator reports this soliloquy, in which Criseyde acknowledges her decision to accept Diomede, out of chronological sequence—immediately after his accounts of Diomede's visits to Criseyde on her tenth and eleventh days in the Greek camp. But this moment of self-communion must actually have taken place more than two months later—after Criseyde's first letter to Troilus and before the writing of her second.[26] The narrator's behavior reflects his emotional response to Diomede's interviews with Criseyde, but Chaucer's tactic suggests that just as the narration of Criseyde's choice has been lifted out of chronological sequence, out of time so to speak, so the choice itself exists in an important sense outside the chain of fateful causes and effects. Here is Ricoeur's caesura, the representation of an act under the aspect of its significant freedom. The change in Criseyde that is forecast in this soliloquy and that her own free choice imposes on her is represented dramatically in her second letter to Troilus.

Criseyde's first letter is written two months after her departure (cf. 5.1348). The narrator has earlier told us that "or fully monthes two" (766–767) Criseyde had already decided that she could not return to Troy. Apparently she has not yet decided to accept Diomede, however; the two decisions are distinct although both the narrator and Troilus tend to confuse them. In this first letter, more telling than her promises to return, which she cannot mean, are the extraordinary "festes" she makes Troilus and her oath that "she loveth hym best" (1429–1430). These seem to reflect both a desperate hope that she can con-

26. Cf. Benjamin R. Bessent's valuable article "The Puzzling Chronology of Chaucer's *Troilus*," *Studia Neophilologica*, 41 (1969), 99–111. But Bessent inexplicably concludes his discussion at the point where Troilus writes his first letter to Criseyde in the Greek camp, thus leaving untouched the important chronological relationships of Criseyde's soliloquy, her two letters, Troilus' conversation with Cassandra, Hector's death, and Troilus' finding of the brooch on Diomede's coat.

tinue to love Troilus loyally even though she cannot return, and a troubled awareness that her love is changing. The assertion that she loves Troilus best suggests that perhaps she no longer loves Troilus alone. Because of the narrator's fatalistic attitude (for example, 1432–1435) and because of the framing accounts of Troilus' jealousy (1212–1421 and 1436–1540), it is difficult to bring this first letter into focus. But, once these distractions are put aside, the letter reveals a Criseyde still trying, with great poignancy, to be honest with herself.

The character of this first letter becomes clearer when contrasted with the second letter (1590–1631). By this time Criseyde has apparently decided to accept Diomede, a decision that inspires feelings of guilt as the decision to remain in the Greek camp, quite properly, did not. The style of the letter is, as Troilus says, "straunge" (1632). Opening with rhetorical flourishes, it spins an often contradictory tissue of excuses, such as Criseyde's allusions to some unspecified danger, to "wikked speche" (1610) about Troilus and herself, and to some supposed disloyalty of Troilus'. Ironically, some truth could be found in all these charges, but Criseyde's use of them here is patently dishonest. The last is the worst and most incriminating excuse, for she thereby impugns another's virtue in an effort to cast off the responsibility for her own action. Her letter ends with the most bathetic excuse of all: "Ne nevere yit ne koude I wel endite" (1628). Although the substance of the two letters is much the same, Chaucer chose to present the second in full, while giving only a summary of the first.[27] The reason for this, I think, is that the significance of the second letter is almost wholly in its disingenuous style—in the signs that style betrays of Criseyde's surrendering the task of being honest either with herself or with others.

The Criseyde we knew in Troy could be shrewd and coy with Pandarus and yet refreshingly frank with herself. Troilus never

27. The text of this second letter is Chaucer's own; Boccaccio provided only a very brief summary here.

has a moment of candor comparable to Criseyde's reflection on her own beauty, for example:

"Al wolde I that no man wiste of this thought,
I am oon the faireste, out of drede,
And goodlieste, whoso taketh hede,
And so men seyn, in al the town of Troie." [2.745–748]

That same sort of candor is still evident in the soliloquy in which she acknowledges her acceptance of Diomede, and the act of betrayal itself is carried out with the most startlingly clear-eyed vision. Nevertheless, Troilus correctly characterizes her second letter as a "kalendes of chaunge" (5.1634). In the enemy camp, with Hector dead, Criseyde will have one characteristic way of dealing with difficulties: "I shal with dissimulynge amende" (1613). We have already seen her dissimulating, understandably, with Calkas (5.193–194), and speaking "straungely" to Diomede (5.955), yet in this second letter to Troilus, she is no longer able to be honest either with the man she once most trusted or with herself. Significantly, it is in this letter, and not in her soliloquy, that she retreats from the complexity of her own choice into the desperate and self-justifying simplification "Then-tente is al" (5.1630). But the truth is tragic: our acts change us whatever their intent; the outward show has its reality, too, as well as the heart's truth.

The transformation that Chaucer presents as the consequence and dramatic evidence of Criseyde's tragic choice is not equivalent, however, to that sensational fall into total ruin that the *de casibus* scheme requires. Rather, with her choices severely restricted by forces beyond her control, Criseyde commits an act unworthy of her that cannot be undone, and whose real though limited consequences cannot be escaped. This is the tragedy many men, and women, and not just "tragic heroes," know intimately. But traces of the *de casibus* conception of a "fall" can still be observed in critical interpretations. The despicable character, and the extraordinary power over Criseyde, that some readers attribute to Diomede are motivated by the need to find

an outside force that can impose on Criseyde that absolute metamorphosis the *de casibus* idea requires.[28] Certainly, Troilus'
"kynde noriture" (4.768) has been a factor in Criseyde's life and
Diomede's influence will be too, but Criseyde did not derive her
virtues from Troilus and she will not contract her vices from
Diomede. Indeed, Chaucer specifically rejects the idea that
either a single act of one's own or the influence of another person
can amount to fate and thus leave one effectively without a free
will, because he incorporates into his poem predictions of a more
complex sort in the persons of Calkas and Helen. These two
characters, being notorious traitors, could certainly have been
expected to experience sensational and final falls, and yet they
do not receive such treatment at Chaucer's hands. Although
neither portrait is simple, the chief effect of Calkas' portrait is to
remind us of fate, and that of Helen's to remind us of freedom.

The consequences of Calkas' treachery for his community are
apparently less tragic than Helen's; and yet his is the more
malicious act of betrayal and his act is more directly expressive
of, and in turn more formative of, his character than Helen's is
of hers. At the beginning of Book 4, where the theme of change
is insistently stressed, Calkas addresses the Greek noblemen:

> "lo, lordes myn, *ich was*
> *Troian,* as it is knowen, out of drede;
> And if that yow remembre, *I am Calkas,*
> That alderfirst yaf comfort to youre nede."
>
> [4.71–74; italics mine]

28. C. S. Lewis, in *Allegory*, p. 189, has offered the most extreme
portrait of Diomede as the degraded and degrading lover, finding the
"further descent" of "such a woman" "from being Diomede's mistress to
being a common prostitute, and finally a leprous beggar, as in Henryson,
not improbable." Roger Sharrock, in "Poem of Contingency," pp. 148–
149, criticizes Lewis for failing to appreciate Criseyde's representative
humanity, but significantly, he does not question but rather commends
Lewis' portrait of Diomede. Charles Owen, in "The Problem of Free
Will," pp. 444–447, sees Criseyde's letters and the gift of the brooch as
evidences of the coarsening of her attitude under Diomede's influence and
he argues that "Chaucer's unwillingness to show Criseyde's fall in greater
detail . . . verges on the sentimental."

Calkas sheds and dons allegiances like a man changing clothes, but he is consistent in consulting his own self-interest first— "calkulynge" as Chaucer punningly describes him (1.71). As a result we feel very little discrepancy between what he is and what he does, precisely because what he has done has increasingly made him what he is. Calkas is the character who has been most transformed by his own unworthy acts, and in this sense he is the most fated character in the poem, despite the fact that, ironically, he will apparently escape the doom of Troy. Although Chaucer withholds judgment, and we must too, Calkas is the character who reminds us most of the damned in Dante's hell. Even in his desire to save his daughter from the doomed city, he cannot repress that calculation which now seems almost instinctive. He speaks of Criseyde as if she were part of his treasure and goods (4.82–93), and he cannot resist driving a good bargain for his new patrons by demanding the warrior Toas, as well as Criseyde, in exchange for Antenor. Nevertheless even Calkas is not totally fated by his past actions. Criseyde makes the mistake of thinking so when she supposes that by appealing to her father's "coveytise" she can convince him to let her return to doomed Troy (4.1366–1414), but her father turns out to have some uncalculating human feelings. For Chaucer, every human life, even Calkas', is an unending enactment of the mystery of freedom and fate.

Helen, too, although she is a notorious traitor, fails to undergo the metamorphosis the *de casibus* theory requires, remaining instead a complex personality. In Chaucer's version of the Trojan story, Helen is not solely or even chiefly responsible for the war any more than Criseyde is responsible for Troilus' trying to kill Diomede. But Helen's infidelity does have tragic implications and consequences for the common good of the Greeks and Trojans, and for this reason, among others, her infidelity is of a graver nature than Criseyde's. And yet Helen appears in Chaucer's poem principally as an attractive woman who can be appealed to in any good cause. Ravished herself (1.62), she offers to protect Criseyde against harassment (2.1604–1610); herself a prize men die for, she receives a man's appeal from sentence of execution (2.1692–1701). Furthermore, one of the poem's few direct comments on Helen refutes some critics' expectation that the woman who yields to an inferior lover must sink to his level. On the contrary, there is an ironic but convincing logic in Deiphoebus' observation that Helen may now "leden Paris as hire leste" (2.1449). Thus, where we would least expect it, in the characterization of one of the prototypes of the unfaithful woman, Chaucer dramatizes the continuing operation of free will and gives us, in all the admitted ironies of Helen's portrait, not a moral but a mystery. The reader who tries to find in Helen's or Criseyde's infidelity a sufficient and simple prediction of either woman's future is trying to flee the anxiety freedom provokes by forging an iron link between the past and the future. Neither her own single act of infidelity, nor the fantastical influence some readers attribute to Diomede, can wholly unmake the admirable Criseyde we have known.[29]

Indeed, at the end of the work, Criseyde is still preeminently the widow. That complex widowhood the exposition of which required three entrances at the beginning of the work has become increasingly ambivalent and complicated here. Others still regard her, of course, as her deceased husband's widow. Inwardly Criseyde regards herself as Troilus' widow (4.778–784). Even her statement to Diomede that her deceased husband has been her only love (5.974–978) may be motivated in part by loyalty to the secret love between Troilus and herself. At the same time, this status of widowhood—whether inwardly as

---

29. Cf. Augustine, *The City of God*, 12.1: "Certainly, no blemish in a thing ought to be blamed unless we are praising the thing as a whole, for the whole point of blaming the blemish is that it mars the perfection of something we would like to see praised" (Walsh, p. 246). And 12.3: "Thus, good things without defects can sometimes be found; absolutely bad things, never—for even those natures that were vitiated at the outset by an evil will are only evil in so far as they are defective, while they are good in so far as they are natural" (Walsh, p. 248).

Troilus' "widow," or outwardly as her husband's—exposes her to the very compromise of her integrity that she finally chooses, because within each frame of reference, Criseyde's claimed status is both a truth and an untruth. Spiritually, she is indeed Troilus' widow and not her husband's, for it is with Troilus that "love, al come it late,'/ Of alle joie hadde opned hire the yate" (3.468–469). Legally, however, she may still be her husband's widow and not Troilus', since this trifling with the truth began much earlier when she and Troilus "pleyinge entrechaungeden hire rynges" (3.1354). Although, as Henry Ansgar Kelly suggests, the lovers may be regarded as having entered into a clandestine but legally binding marriage, the status of their relationship with respect to marriage remains ambiguous to the end.[30]

Given this ambivalent position, one partially imposed upon her and partly chosen by her, Criseyde's whole way of life must now be permeated by dissimulation. Her position dramatizes the spectrum of meanings implied by that rich Middle English word "trouthe." Criseyde has compromised her "troth," her "fidelity," and the "truth" and, as a result, her "integrity" is stretched almost to the breaking point by the consequent tensions and ambivalences. Yet I think it would be a rash reader who would say that her integrity has been utterly forfeited. Not only has she been impelled toward this compromise in part by forces and events beyond her control, but to a significant degree, the very ambivalence of her position arises from her attempts to preserve fidelity in the midst of infidelity. Troilus' renowned "trouthe" never has to meet such a challenge, and Chaucer's readers may well hope that in a similarly complex situation, they would be able to rescue as much integrity as Criseyde does. When Criseyde asks "What is Criseyde worth from Troilus?" (4.766), she implies that once parted from her lover, she becomes worthless. For Chaucer's readers Criseyde's rhetorical question should be a

30. *Love and Marriage in the Age of Chaucer* (Ithaca, New York: Cornell University Press, 1975), pp. 225–242.

genuine one and the answers complex. Whatever the details of those answers, though, I am convinced that they must affirm Criseyde's worth in her own right, apart from Troilus, and that they must value the woman we leave in tragic unfulfillment as much as the "hevenyssh perfit creature" (1.104) who led the hero to grace.

7

Conclusion: "Thende is every tales strengthe"

The task of verifying the narrator's claim that *Troilus and Criseyde* is a tragedy is a demanding and exacting one. It requires us to reject one concept of tragedy and to evolve another, while simultaneously trying to come to terms with two complex protagonists. Throughout our reading there is a continual need to question, qualify, correct, and sometimes reject the narrator's interpretation of his "tragedye." Consequently, we may be tempted to end where too many readers end or even begin—enjoying a certain smug sense of superiority to the narrator. But the narrator's problems with the disposition and interpretation of his "matere" are always profound and representative, never shallow and merely personal; to be unsympathetic to his problems is to reveal an ignorance deeper than his. We should not be too confident that the discovery of Chaucer's Boethian genres puts us in a radically different position with respect to the "matere" of *Troilus and Criseyde* than the one the narrator occupies. It is instructive to recall the relationship of the narrator's character portraits (5.799–840) to Chaucer's alternative character analyses (3.813–833).[1] Although Chaucer substitutes for the narrator's compilation of traits a deeper psychology of character, still Chaucer's approach remains subject to the same ultimate limitation as the narrator's: it cannot fully dispel the mystery of how character is related to act. Similarly, Chaucer's Boethian genres permit a more faithful representation of human experience as it

1. See Chap. 6.

is shaped by freedom and fate than does *de casibus* tragedy, and yet Chaucer's genres cannot, any more than the narrator's "tragedye," unfold the whole truth of the hero's and the heroine's experience.

De casibus tragedy, as we have seen, typically regards a single event as capable of determining and revealing the meaning of the protagonist's career. Once this mistaken premise is accepted, it becomes possible to arrive at clear, though nonetheless spurious, certainties about the judgment of the characters and about the moral of the story. Chaucer's Boethian genres, by contrast, depict multiple crises in the lives of the two protagonists and do not claim to decide which, if any, is the crucial experience. Judgment does not fall on the person but only on his or her separate acts with all their tangled web of motives, circumstances, and consequences. Because of this more faithful depiction of human action, Chaucer's work, in Robert Payne's phrase, *is* moral but does not *have* a moral.[2] The interpretation of Chaucer's poem as Troilus' Boethian comedy and Criseyde's Boethian tragedy does not merely offer a different set of judgments about the protagonists than a *de casibus* tragedy would imply; it provides judgments of a different kind.

The difference is both epistemological and moral. As I have suggested before and hope to demonstrate more fully here, *de casibus* tragedy implicitly lays claim to the complete and perfect knowledge appropriate to a god. In this claim, it seemed to Chaucer, I believe, not so much unique among literary genres as representative: no longer merely a foil for his alternative genres, but a paradigm for all those kinds of art that assume a false authority. Indeed the pretension to omniscience is a common habit of readers as well as a frequent pose of artists, and a work of art may invite or seem to invite this sort of response in a number of ways. It is interesting that several critics have attributed such omniscience to Chaucer, his narrator, and his readers

2. *The Key of Remembrance: A Study of Chaucer's Poetics* (New Haven: Yale University Press, 1963), p. 231.

while attending to aspects of the work other than its "tragical" character.

Morton Bloomfield has formulated an influential version of Chaucer's and the reader's supposed omniscience by emphasizing our common, prior knowledge of the story's end:

Chaucer sits above his creation and foresees, even as God foresees, the doom of his own creatures. . . . We cannot leap the barriers which life imposes on us, but in the companionship of an historian we can imitate God *in parvo*. As God with His complete knowledge of future contingents sees the world laid out before Him all in the twinkling of an eye, so, in the case of history, with a guide, we share in small measure a similar experience.[3]

I would argue, though, that the prior knowledge we share with the narrator would better qualify us to be Calkases or Cassandras than to be gods. We know that Troilus will experience a great happiness in love that will be followed by a great sorrow, and we know that Criseyde will eventually, in some way, betray him. We are not aware beforehand, nor is there any way we could be, of those things that only the depiction of the characters in action can reveal: Troilus' education by love and his final loyalty both to Troy and to Criseyde; Criseyde's noble rejection of Helen's role and the interplay of fate and freedom reflected in her ultimate infidelity. These intricate outcomes arising from the characters' responses to events constitute the true ends of the story and not that end, conceived as outward event only, to which, as Bloomfield states (p. 204), the narrator continually refers us. We do not know these outcomes "in the twinkling of an eye," but we gain awareness of them through the usual slow and faltering processes of human reasoning. Our knowledge is earned, not conferred.

Another reading suggests that while Chaucer's narrator and his readers do not begin with godlike knowledge, they achieve

3. "Distance and Predestination in *Troilus and Criseyde*," *PMLA*, 74 (1959), rpt. in *Chau. Crit. II*, p. 205.

something very like it at the end of the poem. The narrator's recollection of Christ's incarnation (5.1842–1848) and his prayer to the Trinity (1863–1869), Robert Jordan argues, produce "an ending whose power is that of revelation."[4] This "ultimate shift of perspective brings the poem, the poet, and ourselves into communion with the divine order of creation" (p. 107). Apparently, according to Jordan, the reader's vision of things becomes one with God's: "The distinctions between past and present, life and death, man's fictions and his truths, dissolve in the eternal simultaneity of divine vision. Within this perspective the affairs of humanity—including loving and writing about lovers—can be contemplated only with cool, assured laughter." Would it not be more accurate to say, however, that at the close of the poem we are reminded of the existence of a divine vision but do not share it? In fact the close can be thought of as enforcing the point that we have not achieved and, in this life at least, cannot achieve godlike omniscience. The knowledge of the characters that we have earned with such difficulty is imperfect and incomplete at every stage and remains so to the end.

Against the view that the reader begins with godlike knowledge, I must let stand my attempt to elucidate in Chapters 5 and 6 Troilus' comedy and Criseyde's tragedy. But in this final chapter I would like to deal more fully with the alternate view that the reader ends with godlike knowledge by considering in detail two aspects of the narrator's story telling: his continual exposure of the story as a human artifact of limited authority, and his difficulty in achieving a unified and definitive close. The two are related. Since, as Boethius teaches, man's true end is in God, every humanly constructed ending must be a deficient image of that ultimate goal. The wholly predictable, perfectly unified, and absolutely definitive close of *de casibus* tragedy confirms for the tragedian and his audience their shared illusion of godlike knowledge. By contrast, in Chaucer's work a multiplicity of un-

4. *Chaucer and the Shape of Creation* (Cambridge, Mass.: Harvard University Press, 1967), p. 106.

anticipated endings, characterized by varying degrees of closure, confirms that human fallibility the narrator has all along dramatized through his exposure of the artifice of the story. In *Troilus and Criseyde* Chaucer seems to have solved the problem he could not solve in *The House of Fame:* how to provide an ending for a work that, in Sheila Delany's words, "as a literary statement about the unreliability of literary statements . . . tends to render itself superfluous."[5] Perhaps in *Troilus and Criseyde* Chaucer has come to realize that an understanding of human fallibility is valuable and positive knowledge. Fallibility itself is not just the absence of godlike vision but an essential part of the definition of man's creatureliness; it is part of the bond that draws men to each other and one of the inspirations for man's worship of that Trinity "uncircumscript, [which] al maist circumscrive" (5.1865). The discussion that follows is an attempt to illustrate in some detail the grounds for another of Robert Payne's cogent formulations:

In *Troilus and Criseyde* . . . the narrator's role as developer of our consciousness of limitation in the processes of poetry does not produce a circular and self-defeating irony. It is a way of validating the moral generalizations which the poem serves by including the poet and ourselves and the poem within the humanity which they are to measure.[6]

In the midst of describing his hero's activities after the lovers' first meeting at Deiphoebus' house, the narrator pauses to defend his treatment of the "matere":

> But now, paraunter, som man wayten wolde
> That every word, or look, or sonde, or cheere
> Of Troilus that I rehersen sholde,
> In al this while unto his lady deere.
> I trowe it were a long thyng for to here,

5. *Chaucer's House of Fame: The Poetics of Skeptical Fideism* (Chicago: University of Chicago Press, 1972), p. 108.
6. *The Key of Remembrance,* p. 220.

Or of what wight that stant in swich disjoynte,
His wordes alle, or every look, to poynte.

For sothe, I have nat herd it don or this,
In story non, ne no man here I wene;
And though I wolde, I koude nat, ywys;
For ther was som epistel hem bitwene,
That wolde, as seyth myn auctour, wel contene
An hondred vers, of which hym liste nat write;
How sholde I thanne a lyne of it endite? [3.491–504]

As the narrator correctly notes, the practice of excluding material, even vast amounts that could be construed as being highly relevant, is not peculiar to him but is characteristic of all narratives. Indeed on several other occasions the narrator tells us that his "auctour" has failed to provide some important information about the heroine: whether Criseyde had any children (1.132–133); if she knew about Troilus' initial infatuation (1.492–497); whether she believed Pandarus' claim that Troilus was out of town on the evening of the dinner party (3.575–578); why she didn't ask Troilus to rise from his knees when he first entered her chamber (3.967–970); what was inscribed on the rings she and Troilus exchanged on the night of the consummation (3.1354–1355); how old she was (5.826); and finally, how much time elapsed before she accepted Diomede (5.1086–1092). The narrator's own exclusions of material are considerable, too. To define his "matere" properly, he must exclude "other thing collateral," however significant in itself (1.260–266; cf. 1.141–147 and 5.1751–1771). Furthermore, even in relevant matters, his purpose is to strive for the "grete effect" (3.505),[7] and so he does not report every detail but only the representative ones. The narrator's formula for his brief treatment of Troilus' speech of gratitude to Pandarus actually applies to many situations in the story: "This is a word for al" (3.1660). It would appear that

7. Cf. 2.1219–1220, 1564–1567, 1595–1596; 3.1576–1587, 1674–1680, 1814–1817; 4.141–147.

many of the deficiencies the narrator finds in his source reflect similar decisions by his "auctour" in the course of attempting to define *his* "matere" and its proper "effect."

These two factors taken together, one's source's and one's own lapses and deliberate omissions, would almost seem to suggest a law of artistic diminution: that the more often a story is told, the more its truth, or at least its truth-to-fact, shrinks. But the narrator has still weightier reasons for silence on other occasions. First, he claims that his "wit" is incapable of describing the joy of Troilus and Criseyde's first night together although this time his "auctour" has told all (3.1310–1316; 1401–1414). He apparently feels that even empathy and authority together cannot wholly compensate for lack of experience, and he appeals to the experienced reader to correct his effort and supply its deficiencies. Second, on the occasion of Criseyde's private grief over the exchange, he expresses doubt that his language, "my litel tonge," can adequately express "Hire heigh compleynte" (4.799–805). Finally, in his comment on the "felicite" of Troilus and Criseyde's second night together, he suggests that some kinds of experience are beyond the powers of expression of any artist or language: "This joie may nat writen be with inke" (3.1688–1694). In these last instances, the narrator paradoxically reminds us of those very forces that can infuse an old story with new life: the powers of imagination of both the artist and his readers. Yet, taken all together, these comments on the narrator's and his "auctour's" behavior powerfully remind us of the radical selectivity and of the expressive limitations of all stories.

The narrator's treatment of characters offers us an even more startling sense of a brightly lit foreground standing against a dim and deeply mysterious background.[8] Many of the Trojan char-

8. For other treatments of this characteristic of the poem, see Charles A. Owen, Jr.'s discussion of the impenetrability of the story in "Mimetic Form in the Central Love Scene of *Troilus and Criseyde*," *Modern Philology*, 67 (1969), 125–132; and E. T. Donaldson, "Chaucer and the Elusion of Clarity" in *Essays and Studies in Honour of Beatrice White*, ed. T. S. Dorsch (New York: Humanities Press, 1972), pp. 23–44.

acters with famous names appear in strangely unfamiliar roles. For instance, the infamous Helen appears as a gracious lady of considerable political power who can be appealed to in any good cause—from the protection of a woman against a lawsuit to the pardoning of a man condemned to death. The hero Aeneas appears as a scheming prosecutor of lawsuits against an admired but vulnerable woman, and as a friend of Antenor, the prospective traitor. Deiphoebus, whom Chaucer's sources reported to have fought with his brother Helenus for Helen after Paris' death, appears as a man especially loyal and devoted to his family and friends.[9] Indeed, Troilus loves Deiphoebus the best of all his brothers, even preferring him to Hector, the Trojan who enjoyed first place in story and legend. The treatment of minor characters is no less tantalizing. Was there ever a story strewn with more important characters who remain almost totally shrouded in anonymity: Criseyde's mother Argive, whose name is first revealed in Book 4 (762); Criseyde's husband, who goes unnamed; and Pandarus' love, also unnamed. In the course of trying to tell the story of Troilus' double sorrow, then, the narrator leaves many other stories untold and opens up depths of mystery in old stories his audience probably thought they knew well. His management of his material suggests the general principle that a character is revealed only in those ways, and to such a degree, that a particular plot requires. Every individual story and every tradition of story telling make a severe selection of "facts" from a character's "history." As a consequence, tradition may preserve ignorance as well as knowledge. The tears of Niobe the queen, but only her tears, "yit in marble ben yseene" (1.700).

It would take many books to tell the full truth about any single character, assuming this were possible. The point emerges with particular clarity in *Troilus and Criseyde* because the work draws its materials from several powerful traditions of story

9. See Edward Kelly, "Myth as Paradigm in *Troilus and Criseyde*," *Papers in Language and Literature,* 7 (1971), 28–30.

telling: *de casibus* tragedy and the romance of courtly love, as already noted, and also the epic of heroic deeds. Each tradition tends to require of an audience total allegiance to its particular values; thus each claims to be rendering the significant truth and exposing the essential worthiness or unworthiness of its characters. The narrator is aware that the heroic background for his story of love and tragedy might in another book command the audience's central interest, so he never claims to be telling the whole truth about his hero. Significantly, it is Troilus whom he seems to know most about and whom he thinks he best understands; and yet the narrator also knows that Troilus has almost another life in other books:

> And if I hadde ytaken for to write
> The armes of this ilke worthi man,
> Than wolde ich of his batailles endite.
> But for that I to writen first bigan
> Of his love, I have seyd as I kan,—
> His worthi dedes, whoso list hem heere,
> Rede Dares, he kan telle hem alle ifeere. [5.1765–1771]

What is true for Troilus is true for all the characters; in other stories, we would no doubt hear of their other worthy, and unworthy, deeds.

Or rather this would be true if all the characters were as privileged as Troilus. In Criseyde's case, however, other stories present the same limited facet of her life: "Ye may hire gilt in other bokes se" (5.1776). We must be dissatisfied with this situation, if only because the narrator himself has made us aware of the rich complexity of Criseyde's experience. He tells us early that he does not know whether Criseyde has any children, but it is very late when he tells us that he does not know her age (5.826). Here is Chaucer's reminder that our real ignorance of Criseyde is still great. We know almost nothing, for example, of the stately life Criseyde is said to lead as a woman with three nieces and a considerable household; a woman involved in lawsuits with powerful figures like Aeneas, Poliphete and Antenor;

a woman admired and befriended by members of the royal family like Deiphoebus; and a woman whose complex affairs require the frequent and detailed counsel of her uncle Pandarus. We learn relatively little about the nature of her relationship with a father who deserted her while she slept, another detail of which the narrator belatedly informs us (4.90–93). Likewise, we learn nothing about the marriage in which she apparently did not experience the depths of love (cf. 3.468–469): was she aware of any deprivation in that marriage, or did she simply not yet know what love could be? What was it like for her to be threatened with death at the hands of a mob, to be exchanged as a prisoner of war, to live in permanent exile among her enemies? Of these facets of Criseyde's life we hear tantalizingly little. Moreover, it is extremely difficult to imagine the genre that would be able to deal adequately with the variety of Criseyde's experience.

In the extraordinary narrowness of its vision, then, *de casibus* tragedy differs in degree but not in kind from other genres. Chaucer's point is that all constructs, including his own Boethian genres, are inadequate for the description of any human life, real or imagined, male or female. In part, Criseyde's case simply allows him to make this point with special force; but this is so because Criseyde as a female character does suffer special disabilities. Our judgment of Troilus' performance in love is tempered by the knowledge that he does have another story. Our estimation of Criseyde's performance, on the other hand, is likely to be inappropriately absolutist because of the built-in assumption that she has no other story and thus, by implication, no other significant experience. The courtly man always has an escape clause. When the narrator refers us to Dares for an account of Troilus' "worthi dedes," he is, in effect, reflecting a cultural agreement that the judgment of a man which really counts—that is, his judgment by other men—lies in a different sphere from love. But the courtly woman, although she is depicted as the godlike judge of her lover, is herself the real subject of love's judgment, since she has no other sphere of accomplishment to which she can escape and in which she can demand recognition and judgment. Outside of hagiography, the narrator's traditions provide only one important frame of reference for the portrayal and judgment of women: their fidelity to men. When the narrator asks his women readers not to blame him for Criseyde's "gilt," but rather those "other bokes" (5.1772–1776), he is more accurate than he knows.

Although the narrator is not able wholly to transcend these cultural and literary limitations on the portrayal of women, he does, to his great credit, give Criseyde a greatly expanded role in the love story itself, a role not anticipated in his initial decision to confine his "matere" to his hero's "aventures." Indeed, it is principally the emergence of the heroine, traditionally a supporting player in a man's story, into a fuller personhood of her own that exposes and challenges in Chaucer's poem those acts of inclusion, exclusion, and shaping that are connatural to all works of art. The narrator intended to conclude his story in four books, and he could have done so if the story had remained Troilus' alone. Instead the narrator discovers that Criseyde's career, as well as his hero's, has become inescapably compelling. Almost simultaneously with the announcement of his plan to conclude, the narrator first considers the possibility that the old books might lie about Criseyde (4.15–21). Perhaps we are to understand that the narrator's inability to carry out his plan confirms the suspicion of old books. In other words, the narrator begins to understand that the books have lied at least in the sense of not giving equal attention to heroine and hero. In any case it is his attempt to give equal attention to Criseyde that unexpectedly lengthens his story, and the fifth book exists, to an important degree, because of her.[10]

10. Cf. John P. McCall, "Five-Book Structure in Chaucer's *Troilus,*" *Modern Language Quarterly,* 23 (1962), 297–308; and the discussion of the wheel of fortune structure of the poem in Russell A. Peck's "Numerology and Chaucer's *Troilus and Criseyde,*" *Mosaic,* 4 (1972), 13–16.

In that last book, which is presided over by women in a special way,[11] the narrator begins to weigh the evidence concerning Criseyde with great care. He assures us, on the strength of the authorities, that Criseyde's intention to return to Troy (4.1415–1421) and her deep sorrow on leaving Troy (5.19–21) were utterly sincere, and that she suffered a great deal when she "falsed Troilus" (5.1051–1053). Also he conscientiously reports the negative evidence: that Criseyde gave Diomede various gifts and wept over his wounds (5.1037–1050), and that later she gave him Troilus' brooch (5.1653–1666). But he is careful to point out the gaps in the evidence: we don't know how long it was before Criseyde actually accepted Diomede (5.1086–1092). Eventually the narrator is able to make a subtle distinction between fact and interpretation so that, although he cannot challenge any of his authorities' facts, he still withholds his concurrence from the conclusion that Criseyde gave Diomede her heart (5.1050). Finally, having made every conscientious effort not to condemn Criseyde "Forther than the storye wol devyse" (5.1094), he is willing to oppose simple human compassion to the authorities and "excuse hire yit for routhe" (5.1099). In other words, the narrator goes as far as one can toward correcting the tradition without the aid of two further insights: first, that the tradition is weighted not just against Criseyde but against all women; and second, that all stories, being human constructs, must ultimately betray all men and women, all human experience.

When the narrator struggles, then, not to condemn Criseyde "Forther than the storye wol devyse," he adopts an inappropriate standard; the story itself, as he has received it from his "auctour" and from their shared traditions, turns out to be in need

11. Troilus, who was first introduced as Priam's son (1.2), is suddenly referred to as "the sone of Ecuba the queene" (5.12). The book opens with a brief address to the Parcae (5.3), to whom Jove has committed the execution of Troilus' fate, and closes with a reference to the Christian version of this hierarchy: the narrator's appeal to Christ's love for His mother, an acknowledgement of Mary's role as mediatrix.

of that very correction for which the narrator repeatedly appeals to his readers (3.1310–1337 and 5.1856–1859). Too often, however, readers have not corrected the narrator's work but undone it. Just as many have tried to read the work as that sort of "tragedye" even the narrator to a degree transcends, many have also reinforced the authority of that story tradition which the narrator has helped, however confusedly, to call into question. Again we must linger over the case of Criseyde, because her treatment by many modern critics exhibits those very attitudes toward the authority of the work of art that Chaucer was so concerned to challenge. Too frequently critics assume that the narrator's story represents or claims to represent the whole of Criseyde's significant experience, that it provides a basis for judging the person rather than some of her acts, and that such a judgment can be definitive. It is then all too possible to assimilate or reduce the character to the single act of hers highlighted by the story. When these critical assumptions are joined to the *de casibus* definition of Criseyde as a worldly good and to the still powerful tendency to judge women primarily in terms of their fidelity to men, the result is the interpretation of Criseyde as a symbol of the world's mutability—the most popular interpretation for more than twenty years now and one to which vast amounts of learning have been devoted.

In Charles Muscatine's influential version of this interpretation, Criseyde represents "the many-sided complexity of the earthly fact whose mixture of qualities provides to each beholder the abstraction that he takes for the thing itself. . . . She is as the world is and goes as the world goes."[12] The complexity of Chaucer's representation of her is not psychologically meaningful, Muscatine claims; rather "Criseyde's ambiguity is as the world's": "Read it one way and you make Troilus' ennobling discovery, and also, his error; read it another and you do Pandarus' zestful business, and get his returns. But either way,

12. *Chaucer and the French Tradition* (Berkeley: University of California Press, 1957), pp. 153–154.

the world will pass" (pp. 164–165). Where a *de casibus* tragedy would represent Criseyde as a possession to be gained and inevitably lost by men, Muscatine sees her additionally as an enigma to be interpreted and as a test or crisis to be engaged, for good or ill. Both the generic vision and the critical theory consider Criseyde only from the point of view of the male characters, a grave error that Chaucer incorporates into the poem itself and criticizes there in manifold ways.

The three chief male characters all begin by taking positions that discount, in some measure, Criseyde's autonomy. In unthinking deference to his old books and to the *de casibus* idea of tragedy, the narrator initially assumes that the story is his hero's and that Criseyde is essentially an aspect of Troilus' experience. Acting partly out of an allegiance to an ideal of friendship, Pandarus subordinates Criseyde's interests to Troilus' in a rather extreme degree. Troilus himself, exhibiting a solipsism that is both a personal characteristic and a cultural feature of courtly love, at first regards Criseyde as material for his imagination to work on. Chaucer stresses the theme even more emphatically in Books 4 and 5. The Trojan parliament and people act out the grossest violation of Criseyde's personhood in the poem when they "exchange" her for Antenor: she is reduced to a commodity, an asset in war, a pawn. Ironically, the people closest to Criseyde seem to offer her the least comfort in this crisis. During their visit, the Trojan women speak more sympathetically about some of the meanings of this experience for Criseyde than Pandarus does in the visit he devotes to pleading with Criseyde to comfort Troilus. Even Diomede's first courting speech, stereotyped and self-serving as it is, registers Criseyde's presence in a way that the self-pitying Troilus' departing speech to her, moments before, does not. Finally, Calkas discovers, surprisingly, that Criseyde is worth more to him than any other "treasure" he has left behind in Troy. Because Diomede and Calkas are clearly Troilus' and Pandarus' moral inferiors, their awareness of Criseyde's individuality, though limited, highlights the more powerfully what is wanting here in lover and uncle. Thus, in a great variety of ways, Chaucer invites us to correct the tendency to see Criseyde as something that is observed, interpreted, manipulated, used, experienced, worshipped, possessed, lost, exchanged, coveted, or conquered by others.

The interpretation of Criseyde as a symbol of the mutable world is frequently accompanied by disclaimers of hostile judgment and by expressions of sympathy. Muscatine urges us to see in Criseyde's infidelity "a weakness that is not so much personal and narrowly reprehensible as pathetic, universally human in its mixture with so much that is good" (p. 155). But Muscatine's sympathy, unlike the narrator's "routhe," though similar to Troilus' early idealization of Criseyde as a goddess, exacts a high price: Criseyde's autonomy. If Criseyde is limited to *representing* the instability and ambiguity of the world, then she does not herself *experience* it, and thus her sufferings are once again discounted. Of course, Criseyde is part of Chaucer's depiction of mutability as are all the characters and incidents in the poem; but her infidelities do not make her a symbol any more than Troilus and Pandarus become symbols by virtue of their many infidelities.[13] Moreover, the symbolic approach requires, a priori, that Criseyde be unquestionably and typically unfaithful, thereby precluding any investigation of her possible fidelities. But the woman who clearly rejects Helen's example and who

---

13. In *O Love, O Charite!: Contraries Harmonized in Chaucer's Troilus* (Carbondale, Ill.: Southern Illinois University Press, 1976), Donald W. Rowe treats both Troilus and Criseyde as symbols of a perfect Good of which they are both distorted images, and indicates that all the persons, places, things, and acts of the poem are to be seen as symbols (p. 69 ff.). In the development of Rowe's argument, however, Troilus retains personality while Criseyde loses it. Troilus represents "the human spirit giving expression to the joy and sorrow of life in this world" (p. 78) while Criseyde represents sublunar nature (p. 82), "primordial chaos" and "body awaiting the unifying form of soul" (p. 83), "a 'worldly vanitee'" (p. 83), the world or the way of the world (p. 85), and fortune (pp. 136 ff.). The attention Rowe gives to Criseyde's psychology subserves this symbolical interpretation; as he says, "her psychological character is indeed the key to her symbolic import" (p. 83).

may have preserved her heart's veil for Troilus cannot serve the critics' purposes. Muscatine's interpretation is sophisticated and elegantly stated, but in important ways it merely refurbishes those errors that were already ancient when Chaucer's narrator struggled with them so heroically. I am inclined to believe that Chaucer had the glossers as well as the writers of books in mind when he made his narrator warn women against men who would betray them "with hire grete wit and subtilite" (5.1779–1785).

It is unfortunate that instead of looking more deeply into the possibility that the old books lie, many critics have laughed at the "joke" of the narrator's closing expression of concern for women betrayed.[14] Much significance is thereby lost, for through the narrator's remark Chaucer once again calls attention not only to the special disabilities of women, but also to the larger fact that works of art inevitably betray reality. Books do lie; if only because their representations are necessarily incomplete, they must distort, they must be fallible. The narrator's "auctour" is not likely to be more immune to this charge than, say, Homer who, as Chaucer observes in the *House of Fame* (1475–1480), was sometimes charged with lying.[15] The narrator himself, by the very act of story telling, becomes involved in the lie. This is the

14. E.g., Kemp Malone, *Chapters on Chaucer* (Baltimore: Johns Hopkins Press, 1951), p. 132; E. T. Donaldson, "The Ending of Chaucer's *Troilus*" in *Early English and Norse Studies: Presented to Hugh Smith in Honour of His Sixtieth Birthday,* eds. Arthur Brown and Peter Foote (London: Methuen, 1963), p. 38; Jordan, *Shape of Creation,* pp. 101–103; Ida Gordon, *The Double Sorrow of Troilus: A Study of Ambiguities in Troilus and Criseyde* (Oxford: Clarendon, 1970), pp. 87–88; John Steadman, *Disembodied Laughter: Troilus and the Apotheosis Tradition* (Berkeley: University of California Press, 1972), p. 146.

15. For important statements on Chaucer's distrust of fictions, see Jordan, *Shape of Creation,* esp. pp. 6–9, and Delany, *Poetics of Skeptical Fideism,* esp. pp. 48–57 and 87–112. See also Morton W. Bloomfield, "Authenticating Realism and the Realism of Chaucer," *Thought,* 39 (1964), 335–358. Bloomfield defines "authenticating realism" as a set of narrative strategies designed to establish an air of plausibility and to avoid the accusation of lying, and remarks: "all authenticating devices not only authenticate but also call attention to the need for authentication and hence to the inauthenticity of the work of art" (p. 340).

germ of the irony when in one breath he both warns women against men and urges them to trust him: "Beth war of men, and herkneth what I seye" (5.1785). Nor can Chaucer himself be wholly exempt from this involvement in untruth. One of the responses to his poem that Chaucer would have enjoyed most, I think, is Henryson's question: "Quha wait gif all that Chauceir wrait was trew?"[16]

To all of the betrayals represented in the poem, then, we may justifiably add the infidelity of the story itself.[17] The story unavoidably betrays reality in the very process of shaping and ordering it by acts of inclusion and exclusion. Those acts are both cultural, reflecting commonly shared values, and personal, reflecting the preferences of individual artists. Important judgments have already been built into the narrator's "matere" before he even takes up his pen, and a long line of "auctours" has already added and subtracted, highlighted and suppressed, clarified and obscured elements of the story. The narrator receives the story in all good faith as a given and yet inevitably molds it anew in his own fashion. Thus the story is a much more unstable entity than we probably assumed it to be. Certainly it has become a very different thing from the rigidly structured, entirely self-assured construction that *de casibus* tragedy at first appears to be. But does not chaos threaten? How are we to interpret, to judge, if the "matere" itself is not wholly trustworthy?

Let us admit the chaos, or seeming chaos, first. Once we recognize that even the story's central emphasis on the waxing and waning of the love affair may distort the *reported* experience of the characters, we are immediately faced with baffling uncertainties. We begin to wonder how to take account of acts that appear on the periphery of that affair. Is it possible, for example, that Criseyde's plan to appeal to her father's covetousness, which

16. Line 64, *The Testament of Cresseid* in *Robert Henryson: Poems,* ed. Charles Elliott (Oxford: Clarendon, 1963).

17. For a different discussion of the "fidelity" of the story, see John Lawlor, *Chaucer* (New York: Harper and Row, 1969), pp. 64–69.

constitutes a deliberate exploitation of another's weakness, is a graver offense than her disloyalty to Troilus, which avoids precisely that pitfall? How horrendous is Troilus' passionate slaughter of the Greeks, not in patriotic defense of his homeland and people, but as a displacement of erotic energy and a form of wooing? Does Pandarus' devoted friendship for Troilus balance out his various betrayals of Criseyde? Since the narrator wonders aloud whether Criseyde has children, are we not invited to speculate how motherhood would affect our final estimate of her career?[18]

In Book 5 we witness the breakdown of the work's pretensions to judgment and the massive intrusion of just such uncertainties. We are presented with a whole series of bad judgments that are symptomatic of this breakdown: the anticipated misinterpretations of Criseyde's career by the writers and readers of books (5.1058–1063); Pandarus' declaration of hatred for Criseyde (1732–1733); Troilus' pagan rejection of the world (1814–1825); the narrator's continuing misinterpretation of Criseyde's "gilt" despite his partial redemption of her reputation, his continuing misapprehension of his story as his hero's tragedy, and his final, confused rejection of "feyned" love (1835–1848). More instructive than these misjudgments that *are* made, however, is the judgment that is *not* made. As Troilus leaves the eighth sphere, he is conducted "Ther as Mercurye sorted hym to dwelle" (1827), certainly a strikingly vague fate for the hero of a traditional story. Of the final divine judgment rendered on his hero's life, and by implication on the lives of all his characters

18. The narrator's interests in his characters are wider than those the conventions of *de casibus* tragedy and courtly romance usually allow, and help to define the new conventions of Chaucer's Boethian genres. Thus the reader's concern with Criseyde's possible motherhood does not reflect that sentimental, nonliterary interest in character that L. C. Knights has warned against but illustrates Knights' own principle that the reader should be guided by generic conventions. See his classic article "How Many Children Had Lady MacBeth?" (1933), rpt. in *Explorations* (1947; rpt. New York: New York University Press, 1964), pp. 15–54.

including Criseyde, the narrator can tell us nothing. The narrator's "auctour," his muses, his theories, his bits of commonplace wisdom, even his great and admirable sympathy as the servant of the servants of love and clerk of Venus—all are inadequate to the task of rendering a last judgment.

It should be clear that the narrator's failure in this respect is not a sign of special ineptness on his part. Rather Chaucer's profound analysis of "storie" reveals that such last judgments, when they do occur in other works, are really illusions, deceptions based on an inappropriate attribution of authority to the material and to the artist. It follows, then, that Chaucer's own achieved comedy and tragedy must ultimately be subject to the same limitations as the narrator's attempted tragedy: they cannot provide definitive judgments of the characters or their careers. Given the amount of time and effort we have devoted to elucidating Chaucer's comedy and tragedy, this may seem a disappointing conclusion indeed. But all is not chaos. The very nature of Chaucer's Boethian genres helps to define the kind of authority Chaucer grants to "storie" and the kind he denies it. The Boethian genres self-consciously focus only on certain critical choices and acts. The portrayal of these is intended to represent in miniature the whole reality of man's existence, fated and free, in a mutable world. Thus, while it does not confer on the audience that sense of omniscience that an illusory, last judgment of the characters would, still such a portrayal teaches men all they need to know if they would apply the wisdom of "olde bokes" to the examination and conduct of their lives. A correct interpretation of Troilus' and Criseyde's choices in love is a secure and illuminating achievement, the more so when it relies on no illusions of omniscience in the artist or the audience.

We have experienced something of the difficulty of arriving at judgments of a very few of the hero's and heroine's acts, and the poem hints at other important acts, each of which might prove equally complex. Having once recognized this multiplicity, we encounter the further problem of determining which acts count most. For the Christian, only God is finally competent to judge that almost infinitely intricate pattern of choices and acts that is a person's life. No human person, artistic construct, or social institution can really keep the promise Criseyde made to Troilus at Deiphoebus' house: to "Chericen yow right after ye deserve" (3.175). That is why, for the Christian, the Last Judgment is not only something to be feared but also something to be hoped for. Then shall men witness the final proof of the truth that Christ "nyl falsen no wight" (5.1845).

But the Last Judgment is not here yet. In the meantime, how does an artist convinced of the limited validity and persistent fallibility of even the most careful human judgments bring a work of art to an end? Although what has proved to be the enigma of Chaucer's epilogue is usually approached as if it arises from a problem in the nature of love, I believe that it arises chiefly from what Chaucer saw as a problem in the nature of art.[19] Making an ending presents a substantial problem both

19. See J. S. P. Tatlock, "The Epilog of Chaucer's *Troilus*," *Modern Philology*, 18 (1921), 625–659; Walter Clyde Curry, "Destiny in *Troilus and Criseyde*," *Chaucer and the Mediaeval Sciences*, 2d ed. (1960), rpt. in *Chau. Crit. II*, pp. 66–69; S. Nagarajan, "The Conclusion to Chaucer's *Troilus and Criseyde*," *Essays in Criticism*, 13 (1955), 174–177; Donaldson, "The Ending of Chaucer's *Troilus*"; Alan T. Gaylord, "Chaucer's Tender Trap: The *Troilus* and the 'Yonge, Fresshe Folkes,'" *English Miscellany*, 15 (1964), 29–36; Peter Dronke, "The Conclusion of *Troilus and Criseyde*," *Medium Aevum*, 33 (1964), 47–52; Patricia M. Kean, "Chaucer's Dealings with a Stanza of *Il Filostrato* and the Epilogue of *Troilus and Criseyde*," *Medium Aevum*, 33 (1964), 36–46, and *Chaucer and The Making of English Poetry* (London: Routledge & Kegan Paul, 1972), 1, 148–178; Anthony E. Farnham, "Chaucerian Irony and the Ending of the *Troilus*," *Chaucer Review*, 1 (1966–1967), 207–216; Murray F. Markland, "*Troilus and Criseyde*: The Inviolability of the Ending," *Modern Language Quarterly*, 31 (1970), 147–159; and Steadman, *Disembodied Laughter*, esp. pp. 112–168. I use the familiar term "epilogue" for convenience's sake and refer to lines 1748–1869. But as Steadman, p. 150, has observed, there is little agreement about where the epilogue begins, and both the use of the term and the identification of its contents are acts of interpretation.

for the narrator, who is not fully aware of how his story-telling behavior has challenged certain conventional literary assumptions, and for Chaucer, who is.

It is not surprising that as a *de casibus* tragedian the narrator believes "thende is every tales strengthe" (2.260). In some versions *de casibus* tragedy focuses exclusively on the end of the hero's career and in all works in this genre, the meaning of the hero's career is revealed authoritatively in its end. The narrator's belief also voices a more general expectation of a literary work, though—the expectation that the work's ending will not only conclude an action but do so in a way that answers all questions and resolves all issues with great definitiveness. Perhaps one of the clearest aspects of the narrator's closing performance is simply his determination to achieve such closure as evidenced particularly by his chanting of the phrase "swich fyn" (5.1828–1834). The preference of modern readers for this stanza as offering the essential conclusion of the work may provide further evidence of a powerful and widely felt need for endings. Although it is not at all clear what the narrator means by Troilus' end or "fyn," and although readers do not always pause to interpret it, the very concept of a "fyn," perhaps the mere word itself, is enough to draw many readers wholeheartedly into the spirit of this stanza.[20]

Chaucer seems to have perceived a connection between the requirement readers make of literature and what Boethius identifies as man's philosophical search for an ending (1. pr. vii.37–53). The true end of man that Philosophy reveals is synonymous with the good, perfect happiness, unity. It is synonymous, in other words, with that godhead which is also man's beginning. Because man's end is also his beginning, it is part of his nature always to be seeking that end, of which he retains a shadowy image. The demand for definitive endings in literature can be

20. See Barbara Herrnstein Smith's discussion of "closural allusions" in *Poetic Closure: A Study of How Poems End* (Chicago: University of Chicago Press, 1968), pp. 172–182.

seen as a displacement of this teleological longing. The construction of a wholly satisfying ending, however, would require precisely that perfect knowledge, that perfect judgment which, as we have just seen, Chaucer denies to the work of art and to the artist. To attempt such an ending in defiance of one's human nature would be to create a specious image that would threaten to deflect man from his true end. Chaucer's artistic problem, then, was to construct an ending that would both satisfy some of man's teleological longings and, by revealing its own human origins, simultaneously point man toward his true end.

Chaucer's solution was to construct a set of multiple endings that are in varying degrees open and closed. The story of Troilus and Criseyde's love has an integrity of its own and, through the critical decisions that Troilus and Criseyde make, an appropriate close. This is the aspect of the work that was analyzed in detail in Chapters 5 and 6. It is true, as the narrator himself tells us, that we do not learn about "every word, or look, or sonde, or cheere" of the love affair, and it is true that we do not know how our judgment of that love might be affected by more knowledge of the larger pattern of the lovers' lives. Yet we feel confident that we have the essential information about that love and that we can arrive at a basically reliable judgment about it. We have also noted, however, especially in this chapter, many ways in which the story reminds us that the hero and heroine are not lovers only: Troilus is a royal personage and a warrior; Criseyde is the mistress of a large household and perhaps a mother; both are Trojans. Chaucer does not allow the story of their love to coincide patly with their entire careers *as projected in his poem*. Rather those fuller careers arrive at no conclusion; they remain to the last open, undefined, indeterminate. This aspect of the narrative is worth pausing over, for a hazy consciousness of this openness affects the narrator as he attempts to bring his work to a close.

We notice what seems at first a strangely inconclusive quality in many aspects of the story in which we would ordinarily expect conclusiveness. It has been observed that Criseyde's career has no ending.[21] Certainly we learn very little about her new life among the Greeks, and Pandarus' expressed wish that she may soon be delivered from the world (1742–1743) makes us aware that her story, tragic though it is, does not carry us through to her death. Criseyde's soliloquy does provide her with a formal, and powerful, leave-taking but, since the soliloquy is reported out of chronological order, its conclusive quality is greatly diluted. In the order of the narrator's account, the last thing we hear about Criseyde concerns her bestowal of the brooch upon Diomede, an action that has a significant impact on Troilus but that is presumably a very minor episode in the pattern of Criseyde's experience. The type of treatment Criseyde receives within the narration is not unique to her, however. The last meeting between Pandarus and Troilus is strikingly anticlimactic. The reduction of Pandarus to impotent silence provides a neatly ironic contrast to the earlier brilliance of his rhetorical performances, but it does not serve to complete the story of a man who is not only Troilus' friend and Criseyde's uncle but also an unsuccessful lover and a king's counselor. Most surprising of all, Troilus, the alleged hero of the tragedy, is not even granted within the boundaries of the love story the sort of formal and thematically apt last speech assigned to Criseyde. The last speech of his earthly career (1674–1722), though it contains some important matter, is a rambling affair that ends on an ambiguous note. Troilus does not appear to advantage when, displaying one of his less attractive attributes, he once again emphasizes that his sufferings have been undeserved (1720–1722).

The narrator is understandably most sensitive to the inconclusive quality of his hero's career. Thus he interweaves with other parts of his closing exercises repeated attempts to terminate Troilus' career more definitively and in a way that is linked to the love story. After epitomizing one theme of his work in an

21. Muscatine, *The French Tradition*, p. 164.

appropriate bit of proverbial wisdom (1748–1750), he reverts to Troilus' circumstances, describing how Troilus hopes to kill Diomede in battle. Unfortunately, the facts do not support the narrator's effort at making an ending here, for Troilus' plan is frustrated when neither warrior is able to kill the other. Thus the problem reasserts itself moments later, and at a most revealing juncture. The narrator concludes the envoy to his book by expressing a wish: "And red wherso thow be, or elles songe, / That thow be understonde, god I biseche" (1797–1798). That anxiety to be understood leads the narrator to make another attempt at concluding his hero's story, this time by introducing the "foolproof" topic of his death. Of course, Troilus' death at the hands of Achilles, rather than Diomede, has no connection with the narrator's story of love. Moreover, the power of the death as a potential ending is then undercut in several ways: by the vision with which Troilus is rewarded after his death, by his own laughter at those who weep over his death, and by his exit to his final dwelling place, escorted by Mercury. This last detail is itself so indefinite that it undercuts not only the significance of the death but also what first appeared to be the conclusiveness of the vision as an additional, alternative ending. Finally, in describing Troilus' exit, the narrator does not at last achieve the close he sought; rather he merely, and inadvertently, places his hero beyond the reach of his art. Now he must, simply, *stop;* he *can* go no further. Thus the "swich fyn" stanza that immediately follows does not climactically elaborate an achieved ending but merely confirms what it is the narrator has been so anxiously seeking—a definitive "fyn" or end for his hero.

Yet the search for Troilus' "fyn" is only one of the narrator's closing projects; he is also looking for the definitive commentary to interpret the love story. His forays into definitive interpretation tend to end in anticlimax, however.[22] After five exclamations on Troilus' "fyn," the quiet summary of his career—"And

22. I am indebted to Markland's suggestion in "The Inviolability of the Ending," pp. 156–157, that stanzas 262 and 265 end anticlimactically.

thus bigan his lovyng of Criseyde, / As I have told, and in this wise he deyde" (1833–1834)—seems curiously out of place and may serve only to make us uneasily aware that there is no clear connection between Troilus' love and his death. The rhetorical question, "What nedeth feyned loves for to seke?" with which the narrator attempts to round off his address to "yonge fresshe folkes" backfires when, for some readers at least, it turns into a genuine question (1835–1848). Similarly, an all-out attack on paganism aborts itself when the stanza ends with the surprising suggestion that we may well go on reading the poetry of this despised culture (1849–1855). The tendency of these individual endings to sputter out and the competition between these multiple endings may represent not only the narrator's imperfect under-standing of his own story but also Chaucer's belief that it is im-possible or unprofitable to draw large morals from the fraction of human experience any work of art can represent. Or to put it another way, while it may be appropriate for man to attempt synthesizing visions, none are likely to be more accurate than the narrator's. Because of the limitations of human knowledge, the interpretation of the story's largest meanings cannot be settled and closed once and for all; it is one of the aspects of the work that must always remain open-ended.

Finally, the narrator is also striving to conclude appropriately his own performance as storyteller. Several sections of the epilogue deal with the narrator's activity and with the entity that is his book. He clarifies his topic—Troilus' love not his "armes" (1765–1771)—defends his representation of Criseyde's infidelity (1772–1785), and expresses his hopes for his "litel book" (1786–1798). Later, after being diverted to the problems of concluding Troilus' career and of interpreting the love story, he returns to the task of concluding his own performance by petitioning Gower and Strode for correction (1856–1859) and by addressing a prayer for protection and mercy to the Trinity (1860–1869). In a sense, these last two gestures give an open-ended quality to his performance since they suggest, first, that the human work of attempting to bring the story into conformity with truth, passed to other hands, will continue and continue indefinitely; and second, that yet another, and possibly different, divine perspective on the truth of the material is always to be assumed. But there are also ways in which these last gestures provide traditional gratifications of closure. Not only are they conventional endings for medieval works,[23] but also they precisely mark the end of the narrator's work by confessing that he has done his best and that his best is undoubtedly imperfect. Drawing on what the work has taught us about the nature of "storie," we know that this is in fact the *only* appropriate way to end the performance of a human artist. Finally, the whole of the epilogue, understood as a dramatization of the narrator's effort to conclude his own performance, satisfies our need for closure in a general way, because it fits and completes our experience with the narrator throughout the work by approaching the making of an ending as an *issue,* and it treats that issue with what John Steadman calls "copiousness."[24]

Thus the "matere" of *Troilus and Criseyde* has four distinct endings: the conclusion of the love story proper, the conclusion of Troilus' and Criseyde's mortal and immortal careers, the commentary or (supposedly) definitive interpretation of the material, and the conclusion of the narrator's action of story telling. Ordinarily, we expect at least some of these aspects of a story to coincide so as to provide a single, unified ending. We expect the thematic and temporal principles of a work to coincide in such a way that we are convinced we know everything of significance we need to know about the characters' existence in time. We also expect the artist's telling, his shaping of the material, to convince us that it reveals the innate and necessary meaning of that material and not just one possible meaning. These convictions are built, however, on certain customary

23. See Olive Sayce, "Chaucer's 'Retractions': The Conclusion of the *Canterbury Tales* and Its Place in Literary Traditions," *Medium Aevum,* 40 (1971), 230–248.
24. *Disembodied Laughter,* p. 149.

illusions about the authority of the work and of the artist, and Chaucer chooses to expose and examine those illusions. Although the love story has an integrity of its own, Chaucer makes us aware of other areas of experience for the characters prior to, simultaneous with, and subsequent to their love. This splitting apart of the thematic and temporal principles of the narrative helps to mark off clearly the limited area of the characters' experience that the work of art is competent to judge. As a result the stories of Troilus and Criseyde are both closed and open; their love story is relatively complete, but their full stories as persons living both fated and free in a mutable world has hardly been begun. Similarly, it is possible for the narrator to bring his action of story telling to an end, but it is not possible for him to provide an absolutely definitive interpretation of the material, because a commentary that would presume to state the "fyn" of human experience would require precisely that totality of knowledge that the work of art does not, and cannot, represent. The corollary to the expressive limitations of the work of art is the fallibility of the human artist who, whatever his pretenses, cannot, anymore than Philosophy, expound his "matere" as if he were a god.

From one point of view, the epilogue can be seen as a long litany of the limitations of the artist and his work of art. Each work can treat only a limited aspect of its subject matter (1765–1771); the traditions it relies on may be inaccurate (1772–1783); the artist, whatever his good intentions, may be unable to rise entirely above these limits (1783–1785); each genre has its own perspective and may have to sacrifice insights that would be made available by another generic perspective (1786–1788); the greatest artists and their works can be only themselves and must rest content with that and not "envie" other accomplishments (1789–1792); language is an uncertain instrument of communication and methods of preserving texts even less sure (1793–1796); audiences vary in their degrees of understanding (1797–1798). Moreover, even granted the most favorable conditions, one person cannot bring to the task the insight that the collective wisdom of men might provide; every artist requires a Gower and a Strode (1856–1859). Finally, whatever heights of truth the work of the human artist may attain, it always remains imperfect and incomplete from the perspective of divine knowledge and wisdom (1860–1869). Like human love, it always remains a "feyned" thing.

Indeed, Chaucer's management of the narrative of *Troilus and Criseyde,* and especially of its ending, amounts to a new definition of how poetry feigns, of how it is related to extraliterary reality and to an ultimate Truth. As Barbara Herrnstein Smith suggests, works of literature may be thought of as "enclosures . . . separated as if by an implicit frame from a background of relative disorder or randomness, and integral or complete."[25] Ordinarily, the more emphatic the devices of enclosure in general, and of closure in particular, the more clearly the work marks a boundary between art and reality, and the more clearly it identifies itself as an artifice. The same devices that enclose also operate to create a "sense of truth," however. In a highly organized structure, one element predicts or predetermines another, the latter fulfills the former, and the whole utterance seems self-validating (pp. 154–157). Thus the danger arises, as I see it, in a work that does not preserve in its structure a reminder of the primary act of enclosure that a limited, contrived truth may come to be mistaken for a larger, existential truth. The boundary between art and reality that has been so clearly marked comes to be assumed and then can be in some respects ignored.

Obviously, the fault lies as much in the habits and motivations of readers as it does in the structures of works of art, and Chaucer modifies the latter precisely in order to challenge the former. In *Troilus and Criseyde* the action of the love story and the action of the narrator's story telling achieve a close, but the total careers of the characters as represented in the fiction itself

25. *Poetic Closure,* p. 2.

and the definitive interpretations of those careers remain open. On the one hand, the achievement of closure in the first two respects marks the boundary between art and reality, for the love story can then be seen as an artificial structure created by the selecting and shaping activities inherent in the narrator's telling. On the other hand the failure to achieve closure in the latter two respects tends to break down the boundary between art and reality, for the characters are thereby granted a complexity and an indeterminateness that is like our own. One consequence of this elaborate set of Chaucerian endings is that we are inhibited from reposing an inappropriate faith in the story as an account of our reality, while at the same time we are not allowed to dismiss the characters as mere pasteboard figures whose experiences do not in their implications touch our own lives. A second consequence is that we are required to exercise our powers of insight and judgment more strenuously than usual, although we are simultaneously confronted with the limitations and fallibility of those powers. Having done their utmost, Chaucer's artist and Chaucer's audience are invited to contemplate, like Philosophy, the hydra-headed nature of reality, and to stand, like the prisoner, in the dignity of their own responsibility and in the sight of a more perfect Judge. Through its own structure Chaucer's work of art provides the Platonic antidote to the dangers of poetry—knowledge of what such things really are— and thereby invites and assists the audience to answer Philosophy's question: "What thyng is a man?" Surely this was a major reason for Chaucer's profound interest in genres and in the very nature of literary artifacts: he believed that as we define our art, so we define ourselves.

Index

252   Index

Designed by R. E. Rosenbaum.
Composed by York Composition Company, Inc.,
in 11 point linotype Baskerville, 2 points leaded,
with display lines in monotype Baskerville.
Printed letterpress from type by York Composition Co.
on Warren's Number 66 text, 50 pound basis.
Bound by John H. Dekker & Sons, Inc.
in Joanna book cloth
and stamped in All Purpose foil.

Library of Congress Cataloging in Publication Data
(For library cataloging purposes only)

McAlpine, Monica E   1940–
    The genre of Troilus and Criseyde.
    Includes bibliographical references and index.
    1. Chaucer, Geoffrey, d. 1400.   Troilus and Criseyde.   I.   Title.
PR1896.M3   821'.1   77–12511
ISBN 0-8014-0962-4